Infallibility, Integrity and Obedience

Infallibility, Integrity and Obedience

The Papacy and the Roman Catholic Church, 1848-2023

John M. Rist

James Clarke & Co.

JAMES CLARKE & CO.

P.O. Box 60
Cambridge
CB1 2NT
United Kingdom

www.jamesclarke.co
publishing@jamesclarke.co

Paperback ISBN: 978 0 227 17939 0
PDF ISBN: 978 0 227 17938 3
ePub ISBN: 978 0 227 17940 6

British Library Cataloguing in Publication Data
A record is available from the British Library

First published by James Clarke & Co., 2023

Contents

Contents

Author's Preface

Who would not know that the holy canonical Scriptures both of the Old and the New Testament have a priority over all subsequent writings of bishops such that there cannot be any doubt or dispute at all as to whether whatever is written there is true or right; but that the writings of bishops after the settlement of the canon may be refuted both by the perhaps wiser words of anyone more experienced in the matter and by the weightier authority and more scholarly prudence of other bishops, and also by councils, if something in them perhaps has deviated from the truth; and that even councils held in particular regions or provinces must without quibbling give way to the authority of plenary councils of the Christian world; *and that even the earlier plenary councils are often corrected by later ones, if as a result of practical experience something that was closed is opened, something that was hidden becomes known.*

Augustine, *De baptismo contra Donatistas 3.2*

The Pope is to be judged by no one, save in the case where he deviates in a question of faith.

Humbert of Silva Candida (eleventh century)

Since my reasons for writing the following tract are partly personal, it is incumbent on me to explain what otherwise might seem the composition of a Vanity. When I was received into the Roman Catholic Church in 1980, I never expected to find paradise on earth: I knew enough history not to make that mistake. I did, however, find the moral teaching of the Church, especially on abortion and other 'pro-life' issues, compelling and challenging. I had always opposed abortion even when I was a non-Christian, seeing it as an offence against justice – and I realized that the Catholic Church was chief among the remaining bulwarks against it. I also recognized that the Church's stance on abortion – reaffirmed at the Second Vatican Council (*Gaudium et Spes* 51) – is part of a larger account of morality whereby its commands and prohibitions depend on the recognition of a set of objective standards – perhaps like Platonic Forms of the virtues, though I long hesitated to pursue that line of thought since it implied that such Forms must be numbered among the attributes of some divinity. Eventually I overcame my hesitations and joined up.

Now, more than 40 plus years on, I have come to recognize that the Church's hold on these moral standards, though 'officially' dependent on Scripture and Tradition (however related), is rapidly weakening, not only under the assault of contemporary secularism, consequentialism, even nihilism, but because of serious unresolved problems in the understanding and governance of the Church itself: in particular problems related to attitudes to the pope, the papacy and papal infallibility, as indeed to unclarity about the concept of 'infallibility' more generally. The present book is an attempt to show – in part – how and why these attitudes have developed: to argue, that is, that especially since the First Vatican Council, Catholic teaching (not, of course, Catholic truth) – and not only in morals – has come to be seen as too dependent on the will and authority of the Roman bishop.[1] I would argue that this is an aberration which points to a new version of voluntarism in moral theory, with the risk that doctrinal error in moral teaching will entail new varieties of Arianism – that is, an implicit denial of the divinity of Christ – with too often in practice the reduction of morality to mere obedience.

Not that I should be misinterpreted as denying infallibility as intelligibly interpreted; thus Catholic teaching of the Resurrection of Christ, for example, must be held by the Church to be infallible if her teaching is to be even worth considering. But such 'dogmas', which the Church insists are to be believed as part of the *depositum fidei*, must be distinguished from moral claims and other 'non-dogmatic' doctrines which are to be 'held' as teaching of the theoretically inerrant 'ordinary magisterium', though some of them, as the historical record shows, have

---

1. Some signs that the implications of this are at last becoming clearer can be found: cf. P. Kwasniewski, *The Road from Hyperpapalism to Catholicism: Rethinking the Papacy in a Time of Ecclesial Disintegration* (Waterloo, ON: Arouca Press 2022); J.P. Joy, *Disputed Questions on Papal Infallibility* (Lincoln, NE: Os Justi Press, 2022). Elsewhere Kwasniewski warns of the 'Spirit of Vatican I'.

been drastically revised – and unfortunately Church apologists have frequently denied that such 'revisions' have occurred. In strict Catholic-speak to deny dogma makes you a heretic, while to deny non-dogmatic teachings is to promote falsehood.

That said, my primary concern in the present study is with what has sometimes been called 'creeping infallibility' and especially with the presumably *unintended* effects of the version of papal infallibility *defined* – historically that is the key word – at Vatican I. I shall argue that that definition has brought to light over time various dangerous incoherences in the concept of infallibility itself as often interpreted: in particular that, whatever the reasons for the present version of papal infallibility being originally judged 'opportune', it has revealed itself as encouraging both confusion about 'definitive' teaching – which is to say about the relation between 'dogma' and 'doctrine' – and an unwarranted respect for imme-diate utterances of the Supreme Pontiff even if these might appear contrary to both Scripture and Tradition intelligently understood.

That in its turn has encouraged an excessively autocratic – at times even domineering – attitude at the top and a self-deluding servility easily identifiable as plain bad faith among the 'lower ranks'. The purpose of the present study, therefore, is less to evaluate theological trends since Vatican I – though my view of some of them can hardly be concealed – but to scrutinize the effects they have had on Catholic believers, clergy and lay alike. What follows is written in the hope that as others come to see the seriousness of the problem, some proper solution, however apparently drastic, may eventually be found. On a worst case scenario the book may serve as some sort of historical record of a catastrophe.

George Weigel has improved my chapter on John Paul II and I hope will pardon me for not accepting all of his challenging comments. On the book as a whole, I have received much helpful comment from two friends whose peace will be safeguarded if they remain anonymous in these 'interesting times' – and as usual Anna Rist has checked the text meticulously for clarity, quality-English and discretion. As also in the past, and in homage to Plato and to the reality of things, I have at times had recourse to satire to temper earnestness.

Chapter 1

Toward the *Syllabus of Errors*

We never make mistakes.

Alexander Solzhenitsyn

You need to watch your back in this city.

Anytus in Plato's *Meno*

The present book is not a monograph on the wider history of the recent papacy, let alone on the ordinary and universal magisterium of the Catholic Church, though the understanding – or lack of it – of the latter will receive scrutiny when it relates to the authority and influence of the papacy itself. Rather, it is a study – claiming to be based in accurate accounts of the relevant historical events – of actions and their social, moral and spiritual effects: in particular the effects of the Decrees of Vatican I promulgated on 18 July 1870, which defined the dogma of papal infallibility, thus establishing that solemn (*ex cathedra*) dogmatic definitions of the pope are (as it was put) 'irreformable of themselves without any consent of the whole Church'.

That determination would seem to maintain that in certain well-defined respects the Catholic Church was revealing herself as a spiritual autocracy where the writ of the pope must run whatever the wider Church might wish (and however 'Church' might be understood). That accepted, the actual *proclamation* of 'papal infallibility' – rather than the assumption of it among at least some of the Catholic 'sheep' – could not but produce (and was intended to produce) a relationship between pope and Church (and an understanding of that relationship) very different from that which had pertained hitherto. As we shall see, the effects of the change could be good, less than good or outright bad, thus suggesting that papal infallibility, indeed infallibility itself, requires further and more careful consideration: not least for the effect it has and has had on the mentality and indeed the integrity of adherents.

Prescinding for now from questions of the Church's ordinary and universal magisterium, it is clear that the problem of excessive papal power and the corresponding risk of subservience, with morality in Western Christendom being reduced to obedience, lurked beneath the surface long before the times of Pius IX. Yet in earlier days even the great Leo I, speaking through his legates at the Council of Chalcedon, though applauded for his 'Tome' by the Eastern bishops ('Peter has spoken through Leo'), had failed to win support on an important jurisdictional issue. For Chalcedon confirmed the decision of the Council of Constant-inople (381) that Constantinople, imperial capital and upstart patriarchate, should outrank the apostolic sees of Alexandria and Antioch. And Leo accepted defeat.[1] Nor indeed was his eventually definitive 'Tome' accepted without debate: though authoritative, it had to be approved.[2]

But that was before 1054, and scholars are now usually agreed that the problem of increasing papal power (not least over the deposition of kings and emperors and already moving in the direction of reducing Catholic behaviour to obedience to the pope[3]) became serious after the Great Schism of that year which finally separated Western and Eastern Christi-anity. Rome remained the only patriarchate in the West: untrammelled now by Constantinople, Alexandria, Antioch and Jerusalem whose patriarchs had always resisted Roman claims to absolute jurisdiction and who would prefer to continue on their own less centralized way.

The 'Great Schism', however, allowed Pope Gregory VII to begin the long process of increasing papal power, and to maintain that it should be recognized both inside and outside this his own 'patriarchate', a development – and not only of jurisdiction – widely welcomed in the West.[4] Thus Catherine of Siena, now declared Doctor of the Church,

---

1. For an introduction to the see of Rome as a patriarchate see Y. Congar, *Eglise et papauté* (Paris, Cerf, 1994), pp. 11-30.
2. This was pointed out at Vatican I by Bishop Hefele, distinguished conciliar historian, to the expressed annoyance of many of the assembled bishops who thus showed themselves unwilling to listen to reason and ultimately to truth (see J.W. O'Malley, *Vatican 1: The Council and the Making of the Ultramontane Church* (Cambridge, MA: Belknap Press of Harvard University, 2019), p. 201.
3. Cf. Congar, *Eglise et papauté* 100.
4. For a helpful summary of the process of papal expansion see J.M.R. Tillard, *The Bishop of Rome* (English translation by John de Satgé, London: SPCK,

noted in her letter 207 that 'even if the pope were a devil incarnate, rather than a kind father, we must nevertheless still obey him – not because of his person, but for the sake of God, since Christ wants us to obey His vicar'. This view, though perhaps intended as a counterfactual, is both revealing and disturbing.

That accepted, it is still reasonable to believe – not least from the historical fact of strong hostility to the decisions of Vatican I during the Council itself – that the development of a different ecclesial climate and an enhanced papal absolutism dependent on papal infallibility as now defined is an important historical event: an absolutism, that is, which (with possible variants, as we shall see) points to the near-inevitability of a faulty and confused understanding of infallibility past and present. In and after Vatican II this would affect not only ecclesiastical jurisdiction but the nature and solidity of the most basic revealed and scriptural elements of the 'rule of faith'. Indeed, from the very start, one effect of Vatican I was that many thought no further Church Councils necessary. As a writer in the *Dictionnaire de Théologie Catholique* (3/1) put it in 1903, the primacy of the Roman Pontiff is all we need.

Any account of the nature and effects of papal power as reinforced at Vatican I needs to be fleshed out in detail, for while the phrase *ex cathedra* might seem both to establish and severely to limit the newly determined papal authority, it lacks precision. Its effects on the wider community of Catholic believers – as can be seen with hindsight, or so I shall argue – have been such as to change – perhaps better, to 'develop' – the attitude of both popes and their flocks not only to papal power but to their understanding of religious truth itself, and to a degree hardly imaginable to any except to the most extreme (if not most cynical) infallibilists in 1870.

As has turned out, only one later papal pronouncement (that of the Assumption in 1950) has been recognized as strictly meeting the *ex cathedra* requirement, though the Immaculate Conception had already been pronounced to be such (that without the support of any proclaimed definition of papal infallibility and with only limited consultation of

---

1983), pp. 50-60. See also Y. Congar, 'The Historical Development of Authority in the Church: Points for Christian Reflection', in J.M. Todd (ed.), *Problems of Authority* (London: Darton, Longman & Todd, 1962), pp. 119-55. For an introduction to Pius IX see R. Aubert, *Le pontificat de Pie IX* (Paris: Bloud & Gay, 1952) and C. Butler, *The Vatican Council 1869-1870* (London: Longmans, Green & Co., 1930). For more authoritative accounts see G. Martina, *Pio IX*, 3 vols (Rome: Gregoriana, 1974-90) and K. Schatz, *Vaticanum I*, 3 vols (Paderborn: Schöningh, 1992-94).

bishops) by Pius IX's own Bull *Ineffabilis Deus* of 8 December 1854: whether prophetically, as some came to see it, or, as others thought at the time, as a trial balloon.[5] An earlier encyclical (*Ubi primum*, 1849) had requested episcopal comment on the proposed new dogma and to that request about 600 replies were received, only two calling the proposal indefensible, while 24 considered it 'inopportune' (word whose ambiguity will require further comment), while a fair number of those approached failed to reply, thereby probably indicating, if not indolence, a certain degree of easily disregarded opposition.

That 'consultation' – the results of which in significant respects foreshadow the behaviour of bishops when confronted with the possibility of defining infallibility itself – being satisfactorily completed without further debate, work on the text of the encyclical was undertaken by a commission of theologians already established under the chairmanship of the Jesuit Carlo Passaglia.[6] After further limited consultations, significantly among others with a second influential Jesuit, Giovanni Perrone (1794-1876), who had already published extensively on the subject, Pius, defying precedent, proclaimed the Bull, on a fundamental matter of Catholic dogma, entirely on his own authority, Conciliar backing being neither received nor even sought, with Pius, it seems, displaying his soon-to-be vindicated authority, seeing his action as throwing down a gauntlet to all the errors of the 'modern world'. The ground for *ex cathedra* pronouncements being thus conveniently prepared, authorization could follow – and it is to be noted that ultramontanists and their successors (being usually less than ecumenically minded)

---

5. In a letter to Henry Oxenham (1874) Ignaz von Döllinger claimed that Pius's handling of the Immaculate Conception was a 'calculated precursor to the actions of 1870'. He made similar comments to others, including to the Anglican cleric, Alfred Plummer. For wider unease in Germany, see G. Müller, 'Die Immaculata Conceptio im Urteil der mitteleuropäischen Bischöfe', *KD* 14 (1968), pp. 46-70. I owe these references to T. A. Howard, *The Pope and the Professor: Pius IX, Ignaz von Döllinger, and the Quandary of the Modern Age* (Oxford: Oxford University Press, 2017), p. 245.

6. Passaglia, it is to be noticed, later 'broke ranks' with the majority of the Society and with the Vatican when on the morrow of the near-unification of Italy in 1860 he urged Pius to accept the loss of the Papal States and was promptly excommunicated. This intriguing demonstration of Pius's deeply held belief that the spiritual authority of popes is necessarily backed by political power would form a paradigm case of the link between throne and altar in a confessional state. Cf. O. Chadwick, *A History of the Popes, 1830-1914* (Oxford: Oxford University Press, 1998), pp. 152-53.

have always seen the further development of Marian dogma as a corollary of their ecclesial claims, while Mary herself, by her appearances at Lourdes in 1858, might seem to have vindicated Pius's actions.

*   *   *

Disputes not only about growing papal power but even about the possibility of papal infallibility had arisen briefly in the Middle Ages,[7] and they underlay (or were later claimed to underlie) the Counter-Reformation ecclesiology of (among others) Cardinals Bellarmine and Baronius. As yet the matter was left vague, for despite vigorous Roman objections in the seventeenth and eighteenth centuries to 'Gallican' moves to limit papal power and papal authority, there was as yet no immediate call to *define* infallibility. After 1789, however, the growing ultramontane party determined to settle the matter once and for all, the extreme anti-Catholicism of the times seeming to demand infallibility as a way of shoring up the threatened bastions of the wider Church.

In order, therefore, to evaluate the intellectual state of the Church and of those of its members who pondered such matters after 1850 (comparatively few were laymen, for the 'sense of the faithful' was still officially identified with the attitudes, and attitudes to one another, of the pope and the bishops, though a further few of these laymen would

---

7. The first medieval dispute leading to claims about specifically *papal* inerrancy – as distinct from the inerrancy of the Roman See or of the wider Church – concerned the making of final decisions on the canonization of saints. This was a comparatively minor juridical development, with only indirect implications for papal infallibility in matters of faith and morals. Later, the 'Spiritual' Franciscans called for a wider definition of papal inerrancy: not viewed as increasing papal power but – ironically – as diminishing its practical implications, and for the very specific reason that Pope Nicholas III, especially in his Bull *Exiit* of 1279, had agreed with the Franciscans that their way of life represented the perfection taught by Christ to his apostles. This thesis met with considerable resistance, to subvert which, and fearing that a later pope might cancel Nicholas's pro-Franciscan stance – as indeed turned out to be the case with John XXII – the 'Spirituals' followed the lead of Peter John Olivi, then William of Ockham, in arguing that no pope could revoke the teachings of his predecessors on faith and morals but was bound by them since they had been taught infallibly, and popes, though infallible, were constrained by the decrees of their infallible predecessors. For details see B. Tierney, *Origins of Papal Infallibility, 1150-1350* (Leiden: Brill 1972); D. S. Prudlo, *Certain Sainthood: Canonization and the Origins of Papal Infallibility in the Medieval Church* (Ithaca, NY: Cornell University Press, 2015).

turn out very influential, not least in the press), we need to look further both at the reasons for Ultramontanism's growing strength even before 1789 – not only in Rome and in France, but also in Catholic Germany where it was designated 'Roman Theology' – and at the immediate threats its supporters set themselves to defuse. For it should be recognized that before the Council, and even at times within it, Pius and his majority faction, in seeing the principal threat to his authority coming from France in its Gallican aspect, were seriously mistaken. French concerns about papal authority receded more readily, as it turned out, than those from the German-speaking and German-influenced world, and we shall need to look at this development in more detail.

Surprisingly perhaps, a good place to start is with Jansenism, which found its theological origins in Bishop Jansen's *Augustinus*, published posthumously in 1640. In 1653, five propositions drawn from it – though the source was not identified – were condemned by the Bull *Cum Occasione* of Innocent X. The Jansenists accepted the condemnation (while denying that *Augustinus* contained such heresies) but persisted in holding that what they took to be Augustine's views on grace had been improperly disregarded in the Church. Hence Jansenism soon developed (not least at the abbey of Port-Royal and more widely in France) into what amounted to a new version of Conciliarism whereby it was believed that those learned in the Christianity of the early Christian centuries should – in some sort of Conciliar, or perhaps preferably nation-based structure – be promoted as a counterbalancing theological authority to the overweening claims of popes who, it was implied, were seeking to overturn the wisdom of the Fathers of the Church, especially of Augustine.

Since the Concordat of Bologna (1516), the kings of France had been able largely to control the appointment to bishoprics in their territories; that might have been convenient for the Jansenists inasmuch as it weakened papal authority, but by 1660 it was clear that Louis XIV had lost patience with Jansenism and, backed now by the pope and his loyal Jesuits, had determined to wipe out the new movement which seemed a threat not only to ecclesiastical but also to civil autocracy.[8] Certainly on the ecclesiastical side it was not by chance that Antoine Arnauld, in the

---

8. For a helpful introduction to the various mutations of Jansenism and its relationship to debate about the authority of the Roman Pontiff, see G. Simmonds, 'Jansenism versus Papal Absolutism', in J. Corkery and T. Worcester (eds), *The Papacy since 1500: From Italian Prince to Universal Pastor* (Cambridge: Cambridge University Press, 2010), pp. 90-106.

preface to his essay on frequent communion (1644) – which he strongly opposed as 'laxist' – had already referred to Peter *and* Paul as the 'two heads' of the Church, echoing the very early witness of 'pope' Clement of Rome that the Church of Rome owed its special prestige to the fact that both Peter, the founder of the Church of the Jews, and Paul, the founder of the Church of the Gentiles, were buried in the city. 'If you go to the Vatican or to the Ostian Way', a priest wrote in about AD 150, 'you will find their memorials'. Already in the seventeenth century some wondered in France whether 'Peter' had usurped too much authority in latter-day Rome.

In the Jansenist versus Jesuit warfare which continued in France for decades, one side accused the other of moral laxism (an interesting claim in light of the boast of a recent Jesuit historian that one of the most characteristic marks of the Society has been its 'adaptability'), while the other won official support for damning the Jansenists as double-predestination Calvinist wolves in Catholic clothing.[9] For a time in the eighteenth century the pope could rely on the king (plus the Jesuits) for the emasculating of the Jansenists, but the Jesuits too fell out of royal favour – and who could tell whether state power would always be willing to prop up papal autocracy? Port-Royal was destroyed by royal command in 1711, but Clement XI's bull *Unigenitus* (aimed in 1713 at Pasquier Quesnel in particular and Jansenists more generally) only sparked a new (and royal) phase of 'Gallicanism' and closet conciliarism which built on the 'Four Gallican Articles' of the French clergy of 1682.

Of these 'Articles', in no small part inspired by Jacques-Bénigne Bossuet, the fourth was held in Rome to be exceptionally obnoxious; in it we read that 'In questions of faith the leading role is that of the Supreme Pontiff, and his decrees apply to all churches in general and to each of them in particular. But his judgment is not unreformable unless it accords with the consensus of the church.' In 1691 all the Articles were declared null and void by Pope Alexander VIII in *Inter Multiplices*. As

---

9. For 'adaptability' see T. Worcester, 'Jesuits Today', in T. Worcester (ed.), *The Cambridge Companion to the Jesuits* (Cambridge: Cambridge University Press, 2008), p. 319. In the present study attention will be paid to such 'adaptability', especially to regnant power and culture, whether ecclesiastical or civil. As we shall see, with few exceptions (Passaglia being one, the 'school' of Fourvière being another, plus Arrupe and his neo-Marxist or liberal followers in more recent times), the Jesuits prefer to cling closely (as they were founded to do) to papal theology of whatever colour. In our own day most of them have been delighted to return to the papal fold, Pope Francis having revealed himself as 'liberal'.

for the Jesuits, however, their papalism came to a (temporary) end when in 1773 Pope Clement XIV, yielding to French royal pressure, suppressed the whole Society. They had already been suppressed in Portugal (1759), France (1764) and Spain (1767).

'Gallican' worries for the pope and the 'Roman theologians' could not but be enhanced by their legitimate fears of the French Enlightenment: both for its immediately political effects as espoused by the revolutionaries of 1789 and by Napoleon (as on the fate of Church political power, lands and property) and for its intellectual pretentions, especially claims about the sovereignty of reason and conscience. 'Enlightenment' seemed a fearful challenge, both in the form of 'modern' post-Cartesian philosophy, represented especially by the French *philosophes*, then by Kant and Hegel, and later in a new 'historicism'. This, already apparent in the eighteenth century and first developed in the study of classical antiquity, moved both into biblical criticism and, importantly for the ultramontanes, into the history of the Church itself and the construction of its theological practices and dogmas.

The most important founding texts of the resulting post-Revolution Ultramontanism were pope-to-be (as Gregory XVI) Bartolomeo Cappellari's *Triumph of the Holy See and the Church against the Attacks of the Innovators* (1799), and above all Joseph de Maistre's *Du Pape* (1819). (A more politically 'liberal' version of Ultramontanism was to come later, in France from Felicité de Lammenais and in Germany from Joseph Görres.) De Maistre argued that civil peace depended on the 'throne', that the 'throne' is only legitimized by the 'altar', that the power of the 'altar' is guaranteed only by papal infallibility, and that popes can only exercise their spiritual authority if they are also temporal rulers. The Sovereign Pontiff (he urged) is the necessary, indeed the only and exclusive basis of Christianity. To him belong the promises; without him disappears unity – in other words, the Church (*Du Pape*, vol. 2, p. 594).

De Maistre's principal concern was with his native France, and his hopes of restoring there the confessional state were still alive when Pius IX ascended the papal throne. Hence Pius too seemed, at least at first, to be concerned primarily with what he saw as a renewed Gallicanism and its likely political effects on the French Church during his own papacy – and he took steps intended finally to subvert them. We shall consider these in relation to the infallibility debates which were to come, but nineteenth-century Ultramontanism has a prehistory in Germany as well as in France, and its enemies there had variegated concerns, these being primarily intellectual. For although popes (and ultramontanes more generally) came to realize rather late the radical challenge of new movements in Germany, this German challenge was eventually to prove more serious and enduring than the French, being less concerned with the political than with the intellectual future of the Church and holding above all that the 'new world of Catholicism' was to rest on the increased study of Church history, that being an important branch of new and especially German forms of 'scientific knowledge' (*Wissenschaft*).

The best indication of what was to come in Germany can be recognized in the writings of Johann Nikolaus von Hontheim (1701-90), published under the alias of Justinus Febronius, Febronia being the name of his niece. Hontheim was a canon lawyer who in the later part of his life become suffragan bishop of Trier and, like many of his nineteenth-century successors, especially and significantly in part-Lutheran Germany, hoped for the eventual reunification of a Western Church torn apart at the Reformation.

Hontheim's book, *On the State of the Church and the Lawful Power of the Roman Pontiff*, published in 1763, proved a runaway success, not least among secular rulers and especially with Joseph II of Austria, soon to preside over the strongly anti-Roman movement which came to be named Josephism after him. Hontheim claimed that to approach Church history historically, without any grinding of theological axes, was a necessary preliminary to Christian reunification; hence he sought to understand the position of the Roman see and the Roman bishop in antiquity, hoping to separate truth from the legends and scandalous fabrications which had grown up in the Middle Ages, not least those deriving from the so-called *Decretals* of 'Isidore' and the 'Donation of Constantine': the latter purporting to record the voluntary transference by that Emperor of his authority in the West to Pope Sylvester. All such forgeries, in Hontheim's view, were intended fraudulently to increase the authority of the Roman bishop.

In patristic times, according to Hontheim, the pope was recognized as first among equals, being especially aligned with the patriarchs of Alexandria and Antioch, both of which sees also claimed apostolic authority. Hontheim did not deny infallibility but claimed to find it residing in the Church as a whole, especially in its ecumenical Councils, rather than with the pope alone as ultramontanes were increasingly claiming. That the ancient Church was to a considerable degree decentralized suggested to Hontheim that there was still an important role for national churches, especially in France and Germany, where he thought that the faith was more intelligently studied than in Rome. Real history could resolve theological differences both among Catholics and with the Protestants better than mere polemics, let alone warfare.

Hontheim's immediate hopes were quashed when within a year 'Febronius' (as yet unidentified) was placed on the Index. As a result of the ban, however, enthusiasm for 'Febronianism' (as Hontheim's views came to be designated) increased, despite the efforts of the Jesuit Francesco Zaccaria to trash them. As for Hontheim himself (when his authorship became known), he recanted, but then downplayed the significance of his own recantation: he had, he thought, done his job well.

The German metropolitans (represented by their suffragans) met at Ems in 1786 to consider their position on issues highlighted by Hontheim in light of the growing assertiveness of the papacy; they were particularly irritated by the appointment of a nuncio for Munich. They allowed that 'The Pope of Rome is and remains the principal overseer and primate of the whole Church and the centre of its unity', but also insisted that 'all other privileges and reservations not associated with this primacy in the first centuries but accruing to it from the later Isidorian Decretals to the clear detriment of the bishops, cannot be attributed to the scope of that jurisdiction now that their forgery and falsity have been demonstrated and universally recognized'. For they were (as Hontheim had urged) to be bracketed with other 'manipulations by the Roman Curia', and against all such manipulation episcopal authority needed to be re-established.[10] In this decision Hontheim's 'historical theology' seemed to be vindicated, as providing both a better account of the past and a set of worthy guidelines for the future; but – harbinger of what was to come – some of the bishops, concerned with their social and political status rather than strictly historical and theological questions, soon backed off. Others had never subscribed individually to the offending text.

The ultramontanes recognized Hontheim's book as a serious threat, though not yet understanding the novelty of the challenge it posed. What they 'knew' was that papal infallibility, temporal power and the necessary functioning of the pope as guide to the spiritual and intellectual behaviour of Christians were inextricably bound together. In Germany, with the Holy Roman Empire destroyed by Napoleon and replaced by nationalist kingdoms, they feared – with good reason – continuing pressure from increasingly secularist states to control Church affairs: in effect to 'nationalize' the Church and to profit from its wealth. They concluded, in this agreeing with De Maistre, that the centralizing of Catholicism in Rome to an unparalleled degree would be a powerful

---

10. For recent discussion see M. Printy, *Enlightenment and the Creation of German Catholicism* (Cambridge: Cambridge University Press, 2009), pp. 25-54.

tool to limit such pressures. Though historical problems were eventually to prove of greater importance, they were particularly convinced that maintenance of the papal states was an essential part of the Church's armoury, while freedom of academic enquiry and of religion would damage the status quo, pointing to the end of the confessional state from which they thought the Church had benefited since the Treaty of Westphalia (1648): indeed from the Peace of Augsburg (1555).

Pius IX agreed wholeheartedly, especially over the papal states, regularly claiming that without such political power he would be unable to behave as a pope should. With hindsight, this might seem absurd, not least since Napoleon had already manhandled Pius VI (who died a prisoner in France and whose death was noted as that of Citizen Braschi: profession, pontiff) and Pius VII (from whom he extracted in 1801 a Concordat which lasted till 1905 and which, while allowing the pope the final say on the appointment of bishops, had left their nomination to the secular authorities, as in the *ancien régime* before 1789). Pius VII himself had been dragged off to France in 1809 and kept prisoner until Napoleon's reign came to an end five years later. Such events revealed the reality of the power relationship between popes and secular rulers; nor was there much reason to believe that any future defence of the papal states (or perhaps even of the person of the pope himself) would be any more effective – as of course was to be demonstrated in 1870 when papal control over large tracts of central Italy, including the city of Rome itself, would come to an abrupt and permanent end.

By the time Pius IX took office, the character of the French episcopacy had substantially changed, most of the older bishops having been invited to resign after the Revolution, with successors less prone to 'Gallicanism' tending to replace them. In the longer run France with its fading Gallicanism was, as we have noted, to prove a less enduring problem for the ultramontanes than Germany, where the notion of a national church was more readily to be linked with the increasing intellectual ferment in the universities. For in Germany the early part of the nineteenth century was to see much reorganization of Catholic universities (several of them were refounded) in the wake of the success of the new and instantly prestigious civic university established in 1810 in Protestant Berlin under the guidance of Wilhelm von Humboldt, the friend of Goethe and Schiller, and of the Platonic scholar and radical theologian Friedrich Schleiermacher.

In 1819 at Tübingen Johann Sebastian Drey founded the *Tübinger Theologische Quartalschrift*, a journal heralding Tübingen's becoming the centre of a more 'progressive' Catholic theology increasingly appreciated elsewhere, especially in Munich. In Tübingen itself the growing inter-mingling of Protestant and Catholic populations and traditions led to the establishment of two theological faculties within the same university – with the result that Catholic theologians became increas-ingly aware of the growing historicism already apparent in Hontheim: the search, that is, for what actually happened (*wie es eigentlich gewesen*), accompanied by a growing belief that Catholic philosophy too must expand beyond its traditional and 'Thomist' formulations. While 'Roman' theologians (in Rome and beyond) might prefer to stick with the specu-lative neo-scholastic theology of the post-Tridentine past, having some sort of Thomist ancestry, more 'enlightened' thinkers began to argue that such theology is too abstract and indeed empty: too often mere fan-tasy unless historically intelligible. Perhaps in their zeal for an unchanging understanding of doctrine and ecclesiology the neo-scholastics might find themselves defending the indefensible. Outside Germany, this was a problem apparently recognized by Newman, and by others too: the Church must avoid both a 'metaphysical' contempt for history and the fundamentalism about never-changing teaching which must accom-pany it. Even ultramontanes began to realize that there was a problem about the authenticity of 'Thomism' itself.

That part of our story can most readily be approached by looking at the influential and at times colourful life of yet another Jesuit, Joseph Kleutgen (1811-83),[11] author (among many other titles) of *Die Theologie*

---

11. For a clear account of the Thomistic merits and demerits of Kleutgen see A. MacIntyre, *Three Rival Versions of Moral Enquiry* (London: Duckworth, 1980), pp. 73-75. At a more personal level his colourful earlier life reached its nadir in his involvement as their confessor with the scandalous (and heretical) nuns of S. Ambrogio in Rome, whose novice mistress imposed lesbian initiation rites and frequently entertained Kleutgen alone in her cell at night. See H. Wolf, *The Nuns of Sant'Ambrogio: The True Story of a Convent in Scandal* (New York: Alfred A. Knopf, 2015). After a long investigation by the Inquisition, Kleutgen was convicted in 1862 of moral offences but not of heresy and confined to a monastery in the Alban hills, but Pius IX reduced the sentence against him and in 1870, as we shall see, he was given a major role in drafting the eventual text of *Dei Filius*, Vatican I's constitution on faith and reason. Later, in 1879, he worked on the first draft of *Aeterni Patris* for Leo XIII who dubbed him 'the prince of philos-ophers'. His story matters not only because of his important thesis about the *Vorzeit* and his consequent role in the ongoing development of neo-Thomism, but as an example of the Vatican's (still apparent) willingness to protect its own in matters of sexual morality.

der Vorzeit (1853-70) and *Die Philosophie der Vorzeit* (1863-70). In these massive writings Kleutgen demonstrated for the first time that Western philosophy and theology had by no means progressed in an unbroken line from Socrates to Kant and Hegel; there had been a radical break in the seventeenth century, to be recognized in the success of Descartes in largely transforming metaphysics into epistemology, a move which had led to a new (and to Kleutgen and many others undesirable) shift in the relationship between reason and faith. Now reason was to be the supreme arbiter even in theology.

Kleutgen thought of himself as a genuine Thomist, and his analysis of the *Vorzeit* told him that his Catholic philosophical contemporaries – best represented by Antonio Rosmini (1797-1855) – in accepting the notion of a steady stream of philosophical progress (despite Rosmini's awareness that Kant at least required serious correction) – had imparted to their Thomism a strongly Kantian flavour. Yet for all its insights, Kleutgen's treatment of the history of Western thought was itself seriously defective in an important respect: he assumed that the Thomism which he and his disciples professed (not least, as we shall see, those – to include himself – who at the end of the century took up Leo XIII's challenge to offer a real Thomism in response to more recent philosophical errors) must be distinguished from the still too Kantian Thomism of Rosmini: indeed should be recognized as the Thomism of Thomas himself. In reality Kleutgen's Thomism was heavily indebted to the 'Thomism' of his much earlier fellow Jesuit Francesco Suarez (1548-1617), a thinker sometimes held to be the true originator of 'modern' philosophy and who, like Descartes, tended to transform metaphysics into epistemology, so (among other his mistakes) treating Aquinas as an epistemologist.

That said, the lurking *internal* problems of Thomism were the least of the immediate concerns of popes and their ultramontane supporters as in the first half of the nineteenth century they contemplated the changing German scene. More serious in their eyes even than the political changes around them was the form that the dispute about the relationship between reason and faith and its implications for freedom of thought in philosophy and theology was taking in the gradually more 'enlightened' Catholic universities and seminaries. Especially in Tübingen, then in Munich, Catholic thinkers now tended to replace a neglected Thomism with forms of idealism deriving from Kant and Hegel, variously combining them with remnants of more traditional Catholic theology to suggest that the mysteries of Catholic faith could, if genuine, be reached and must be measured by reason alone. As Pius IX put it in his first encyclical (*Qui pluribus*, 1846) 'These enemies never stop invoking the power and excellence of human reason; they raise it up against the most holy faith of Christ, and they blather with great foolhardiness that this faith is opposed to human reason.'

Among the first of such dissidents, one of the most significant in light of the ever more urgent arguments about the 'Roman question' (i.e. the temporal power of the pope) and papal infallibility, was Johann Adam Möhler, who taught first in Tübingen, then in Munich.[12] Möhler was polemically anti-Protestant and much influenced by German Romanticism. Protestants, he thought, by limiting their theology to the apostolic age of Christianity, rendered themselves unable to construct an intelligible theory of the Church, not taking even the later patristic period into adequate account.

In Möhler's view, however, serious historical study reveals that Catholics had their problems too. Since the Council of Trent especially, too many of them had exaggerated the power and authority of the pope to the detriment of an adequate treatment of the wider Church: thus in effect, though this was not made explicit, being inclined to identify the Church with the pope (or, put differently, to separate the head from the body). This might sound like Hontheim over again, but Möhler's position was more nuanced (even to ambiguity), and he died young, in 1838, before action could be taken against him. His work was to remain an inspiration to 'revisionist' theologians of the twentieth-century such as Henri de Lubac SJ who were to praise his 'Christocentric' approach and his identification of the Church as an organism rather than a mere institution: thus his move away from a post-Tridentine, more formalist account of the Church's hierarchical structure.

Of greater *immediate* significance in the battle between faith and reason was the case of a lesser known philosophy professor at Munich, Jakob Frohschammer (1821-93). After his book, *On the Generation of Human Souls*, deeply indebted to German idealism, had been put on the Index in 1857 – he was later to be one of Kleutgen's targets in *Die Philosophie der Vorzeit* – his dissent from Rome crystallized and he made claims for the necessity of complete academic freedom, for no interference by Roman authorities in academic debate. These ideas were published in *On the Freedom of Science* (1861), a work almost immediately condemned by Pius in the following year in a letter (*Gravissimas inter*) to Archbishop von Scherr, the 'ordinary' of Munich. Pius accused Frohschammer of a radically uncatholic approach in grossly overrating

---

12. Cf. M.J. Himes, *Ongoing Incarnation: Johann Adam Möhler and the Beginning of Modern Ecclesiology* (New York: Crossroad, 1997).

the powers of reason to the detriment of 'the rights, office and authority of the Church': he was advocating not freedom but 'unbridled license', thus betraying sacred theology as well as philosophy. Frohschammer refused to recant and was excommunicated in 1871. His fault, however, was less historicism than the claim to derive the dogmas of the Church by reason alone, thus seriously derogating from Church, and specifically papal, authority.

Demands for academic freedom would obviously have implications for students of scripture. Yet during the middle years of the nineteenth century, though there were worries about the application of new historical techniques to the Bible itself – with which Protestants, predictably, were more concerned – for the Catholics these were in general distant fears. Of more immediate concern – and foreshadowed by Hontheim – was the history of the Church, of the development of its traditions and beliefs, whether formally determined or merely widely accepted; many of these traditions (including claims about an as yet undefined 'papal infallibility') increasingly seemed to many to be insecurely based. That the truth in such disputed questions might be determined not by authority but by unfettered historical reasoning was a source of deep anxiety for ultramontanes, and not least, after his return from 'exile' in Gaeta in 1850, for Pius himself.

* * *

Autocrats rely on a court and some supposed that Pius's shift from hesitant liberal to determined autocrat made him in effect prisoner of the Jesuits Kleutgen, Passaglia, Perrone, Liberatore, Curci, Piccirillo and later successive editors of *La Civiltà Cattolica*, a Jesuit journal founded in 1850 to promote the interests of the Holy See and to encourage neoscholasticism (indeed specifically approved in that role by Pius himself in 1866). Reflecting on the question with benefit of hindsight in 1878, Lord Acton, writing to Ignaz von Döllinger, and speculating that Pius had become convinced that only resort to autocracy would enable him to recover his fading authority, concluded that as a result he 'went over to the Jesuits who were able to exploit his changed circumstances the more easily for their purposes, as the fulfilment of their teaching aims [scil. the teaching of neo-Thomism as they understood it] also involved an increase in papal power'.[13] However, as often in such circumstances, secular or ecclesiastical, we may wonder who exploited whom.

---

13. Cf. V. Conzemius (ed.), *Briefwechsel*, vol. 3 (Munich: C.H. Beck, 1971), p. 207. Döllinger himself is recorded by Luise von Kobell in her *Memories*

*   *   *

Despite the increasing ferment in Germany, Pius's eyes when he returned to Rome in 1850 were still set more fixedly on France, where he (and his supporters) found themselves faced with what they took to be a new upsurge of Gallicanism. The crisis began as early as 1850, when after much provocation Parisian Archbishop Sibour published a pastoral letter attacking the ultramontane journal *L'Univers* and its editor Louis Veuillot, telling his readers not to get their theology from newspapers whose editors had no respect for their local bishop. Veuillot appealed to Rome and the dispute was dampened down for a while but broke out again in 1852 when Sibour, especially incensed by criticism of his appointment of the 'Gallican' Henri Maret as vicar general of his archdiocese, arranged first for the publication of a *Memoire* addressed to the French bishops explaining his views about the relationship of ultramontanism to the French Church., then on 7 February 1853 again severely criticizing *L'Univers* and forbidding his clergy from reading it.

Veuillot looked for and obtained support in Rome, this time with more urgent effect. Soon there appeared an encyclical bearing the same title – *Inter Multiplices* – as that which had declared the Gallican Articles of 1682 null and void. The encyclical, which specifically informed its readers that the pope was greatly grieved when he read Sibour's *Memoire*, thus identified Pius with Veuillot's extreme ultramontanists, and had immediate effect: Sibour withdrew his ruling against *L'Univers*, in effect – as many noted at the time – signalling the end of serious resistance to the 'romanization' of the French Church, not least in the loss of most of its local liturgies.

*   *   *

Meanwhile, as we noted, though in Germany Frohschammer was condemned in 1861 for his ideas on academic freedom within the Church,

---

of Dr. Döllinger as reflecting with some distaste on his (only) visit to Rome that when received in audience he had to kneel three times, 'first in the ante-chamber, then in the middle of the audience room, and finally before the pope, who extended his foot, encased in a white and gold embroidered slipper, towards us to be kissed'. Then Pius addressed his visitors (the others being Acton and the Oratorian Augustin Theiner, Prefect of the Vatican Archives) 'to the effect that the Pope was the supreme authority over all, and that only when the world had learned to bow before the Apostolic Chair would the welfare of mankind be assured'. Quoted in Howard, *The Pope and the Professor*, p. 94.

this was far from bringing peace to German-speaking Catholicism – merely leaving the future of Catholic intellectual activity (at least in the faculties of theology and philosophy) uncertain. For in the same year Döllinger, dean of German, if not of worldwide Catholic theology, threw oil on the fire at a Congress of Catholic scholars in Munich, telling the assembled participants that the temporal power of the papacy was unnecessary, incompetently exercised and should be abandoned. He soon moved further in an increasingly urgent criticism of papal attitudes and of Ultramontanism more generally. Advancing beyond the political question of the papal states, at a second theological Congress in Munich, in an address provocatively titled 'On the Past and Present of Catholic Theology' which was to draw both massive support and massive disapproval throughout the Catholic world and beyond, he argued that the Roman theology which the Vatican was trying to impose on the universal Church had become 'one-eyed'.

That one approved eye was guided by a speculative scholastic philosophy based on the texts of Aristotle, while neglected was the other 'eye', that of history and exegesis, which Döllinger (not entirely accurately) traced back to ancient Antioch and for which he asserted equal claims to antiquity. According to Döllinger, in light of the sad damage inflicted on the French Church by Napoleon, it was now the duty of German theologians, skilled in the new historical sciences, to enable this second eye to see clearly once more. Whether for better or for worse, German theologians would not forget that charge!

In Döllinger's view, one of the effects of Catholics remaining 'one-eyed' would be the further alienation of both Orthodox and Protestant Christians – thus in effect the dismissal of the injunction of Jesus himself to promote unity among his followers – whereas historical enquiry would show that when legends and mistakes are eliminated from Church history, the Churches will be found less far apart than commonly believed. What is more (as Döllinger increasingly came to insist) recognition of the degree to which untruths had contributed to the dangerously misguided 'Roman' mindset would show that papal infallibility was no age-old article of Catholic faith. In this and in Döllinger's 'ecumenical' concerns, the ultramontanes were right to recognize a major threat to traditional Catholic theology, not just to their hoped-for renewal of papal authority in particular.

As Döllinger's second fateful Congress was being planned, the Vatican authorities, guided by Kleutgen and Cardinal August von Reisach, former archbishop of Munich – and urged on by the ultramontane press, especially Veuillot's *L'Univers* and *La Civiltà Cattolica* – became increasingly uneasy. Not without reason, for next, in 1863, Döllinger published his *Fables of the Popes in the Middle Ages*, a book which, as all immediately recognized, struck hard at papal pretensions by suggesting that those to whom the ultramontanes regularly appealed (not least Aquinas[14] and Bellarmine[15]) had been misled by those forgeries to which Hontheim had drawn attention: the Donation of Constantine, the legend of Constantine's baptism by Pope Sylvester, the non-existing Synod of Sinuessa, the Pseudo-Isidorian Decretals accepted as authentic by Pope Nicholas I. Much of this bogus material, Döllinger continued, had been built into canon law and retained even when its authenticity had been disproved. There was also the matter of the misguided behaviour of popes already judged heretical, above all Honorius I – condemned by an Ecumenical Council in 680 – and John XXII (who had recanted at the end of his life). Even to raise the question of whether a pope could be a heretic – let alone to point out that at least one had been (and non-repentant to boot!) – was to cast a deep shadow on claims about infallibility.[16]

At the close of the same year (on 21 December 1863), Pius's response appeared as an Apostolic Letter (*Tuas libenter*) sent to Döllinger's local ordinary. The pope told Archbishop Scherr that 'we cannot be silent about the fact that we have been greatly concerned, because we feared that with this Congress, held without ecclesiastical authorization, a working method would gradually be established that takes something away from the rights of ecclesiastical power and that authentic magisterium which by divine institution belongs to the Roman Pontiff and to the Bishops united and in agreement with the Successor of St. Peter'. With this claim Pius not only distinguished between the two types of 'authentic' magisterium but appealed to the 'conscience' of Catholic scholars

---

14. For Aquinas see G. Rocca, 'Thomas Aquinas on Papal Authority', *Angelicum* 62 (1986), pp. 472-84.
15. For Bellarmine see R.F. Costigan, *The Consensus of the Church and Papal Infallibility: A Study in the Background of Vatican I* (Washington, DC: CUA Press, 2005), pp. 22-28.
16. The problem had already come up with regard to the infallibility claims made in medieval times by Ockham. Ockham's solution was that if a 'pope' (like Honorius) was a manifest heretic, he was in fact no pope and should be removed from office. But the question then arises of who is to judge. In Honorius's case it was the clergy of Rome (later vindicated by the decision of the Sixth Ecumenical Council at Constantinople (680) to excommunicate him posthumously). That judgment was accepted by Leo II, Honorius's papal successor.

to accept all decisions of Pontifical Congregations as well as all others approved 'by common and constant consent of Catholics'.

That left it very unclear how such agreement could be measured and of course assumed that the Vatican – ultimately and if necessarily none too indirectly the pope himself – would do the measuring. To follow one's conscience for a Catholic might thus seem to mean little more than to follow papal directions, certainly when it was a matter of questioning papal decisions and pronouncements. We shall return to this topic more than once – and not least when we consider Joseph Ratzinger's late twentieth-century actions as Prefect of the Congregation for the Doctrine of the Faith, where, or so I shall argue, its urgency contributed to a crisis in the wider Church.

Pius noted that academic theologians rely too much on mere reason, that in particular they take inadequate notice of 'the old school' – that is of Thomism as then understood. Dissent, he continued, was unacceptable both from the 'infallible' judgement of the Church – but whose Church? – and also from everything revealed and taught by the 'ordinary magisterium'. Again, we shall meet debate on this same point a hundred or so years later.

Tuas libenter not only raised the status of the 'ordinary magisterium', tending to identify it simply as *papal* authority (a theme which was to be pursued further at Vatican I); it was also a precursor of wider and more immediate restrictive legislation: the German episcopate was immediately instructed to keep a more careful eye on theological congresses. Yet even now Pius's eyes, still looking for a restoration of the pre-Revolution status quo, were primarily fixed on France. Hence the fury in Rome when in 1863 the prominent French thinker and one-time disciple of de Lammenais, Charles de Montalembert, in widely acclaimed speeches in Malines, repeated the call for freedom of conscience within the Church.

It was time to act and in December 1864, following up a suggestion first made by Gioacchino Pecci (later Leo XIII), Pius promulgated his encyclical *Quanta Cura* as an introduction to the *Syllabus of Errors*, which listed 80 modern theses to be condemned outright. These ranged from pantheism and rationalism to socialism, from religious freedom to the separation of Church and State. The encyclical was not only a challenge to intellectual and political errors in France and Germany but a ferocious onslaught on the modern world in its entirety – and in desperately attempting to put back the clock to pre-revolutionary Europe certain (at least at the political level) to fail. German thinkers would have noticed that Pius also reiterated the rulings of *Tuas libenter*, and perhaps most significantly emphasized that any suggestions that the views of the 'Scholastic Doctors' might need to be corrected in light of changing times or even of scholarly research into Church history, were ruled out.

In Döllinger's judgement (as in that of many others), the *Syllabus* indicated that the pope had declared war on the thinking and educated world – as indeed he had.[17] Our concern here, however, is not with whether such a judgement was justified but with the condition and mentality of a Church which, as we shall see in the following years, largely approved Pius's policies without adequate reflection on what they implied in terms of longer term 'collateral damage'. Our immediate question, therefore, is whether the Church – even before papal infallibility was formally proclaimed, and regardless of its genuine merits – was already, by the panic and intellectual blindness of its supporters and the servility of its opponents, committed to accepting it. In any case, the coming approval of the decree *Pastor Aeternus* in 1870 was to shed further light on the Catholic mentality of the age, and on the fact that such a mentality – with consequences far beyond infallibilism itself, however understood officially – has been bequeathed to later Catholic generations down to our own day.

---

17. In a letter of 1866 to Charlotte von Leyden cited by Howard, *The Pope and the Professor*, p. 112.

Chapter 2

From the *Syllabus of Errors* to *Pastor Aeternus* (1870)

Gatherings of bishops rarely do good and it is lucky if they do not do harm.

Gregory Nazianzen (letter 22)

[The proceedings of Councils] are, with few exceptions, a dreary, unlovely phenomenon in the Church.

Newman (*Letters and Diaries [LD]*, vol. 26, p. 120)

Theologians who sustain the infallibility of the pope, embarrassed by errors into which some have fallen, have recourse to a distinction.

César-Guillaume Cardinal La Luzerne (1738-1821)

It had long been a concern of nineteenth-century Catholic scholars that their writings might be put on the Index, and so their reputations at least damaged, perhaps destroyed. In the 1860s censorship of the writings of Frohschammer, Passaglia and others showed that such fears were far from unfounded; hence the canonization of Pedro de Arbués in 1867 caused consternation among anti-infallibilists, indeed among many who more generally stood for freedom of thought in the Church.

In the mid-fifteenth century Torquemada had appointed Arbués head of the Aragonese Inquisition to spearhead the campaign against Jews and those among Jewish 'conversos' suspected as having only nominally converted to Christianity. In 1485 he was murdered in the Cathedral of Zaragoza, it was alleged by assassins hired by Jews; however, his unpopularity was more widespread. To Döllinger and others opposed to the proposed definition of papal infallibility his canonization appeared as a warning that the Inquisition was still alive, and might be used to 'discourage' anti-infallibilists. For in Pope Pius's eyes, in view of the political and intellectual 'Afflictions of the Church' – that being the title of an encyclical he issued in 1867, the year of the canonization of Arbués – only a massive closure of the ranks around the Chair of Peter and the pope as Universal Pastor could ward off disaster.

That such a muster was to be enshrined in the decisions of a new Council – the first since Trent – seemed increasingly likely. A Council had been mooted in the Curia since 1850 and by 1854 Pius had made the opening moves towards calling one in consulting a group of curial cardinals who largely backed the proposal. In early 1865 the pope accordingly set up a preparatory commission, the members of which, apart from Cardinal Karl-August von Reisach, retired archbishop of Munich, were entirely Italian. The primary task of these (in contradiction to procedures adopted at Trent where such matters had been largely left to the bishops) was to establish the conciliar agenda, a proceeding widely regarded with suspicion, on the assumption that he who sets the agenda controls the ensuing meeting. Pius then consulted a further group of bishops, most of whom were ultramontane; of these the majority approved the general project, though a few, including Félix Dupanloup, the far-from-ultramontane bishop of Orléans, were more cautious.

The preliminary committee then proposed that six (though eventually five) further commissions be set up, each to deal with one particular feature of the proposed agenda. Of these five only the first (*On Faith and Doctrine*) was to matter in the attenuated Council which would eventuate, being given the task of setting the agenda on 'The hierarchical structure of the Church, its infallibility and papal primacy' and on 'Faith and Revelation'. All five commissions were to be staffed almost entirely from the relevant departments of the Roman Curia: another centralizing device which distinguished the coming Council from its predecessor at Trent. Pius approved these proposals and publicly announced in that same year (1867) that the Council would indeed be summoned. As yet, however, there was no specific mention of papal infallibility in the proposed agenda.

Nest year (1868), in his encyclical *Aeterni Patris*, Pius announced that the Council would open on the Feast of the Immaculate Conception – 8 December – of the following year, and invitations were sent out. In a further breach with precedent, no governmental representatives were invited, a decision which aroused the interest and suspicion of 'Catholic Princes' and those in authority in traditionally Catholic states, especially France. The preliminary commission then set about establishing the procedures and rules within which conciliar debates would take place and preparing the agenda – and in a move which was to be of the utmost importance, a 'deputation' *De Postulatis*, was established to facilitate proposals offered by the assembled bishops being considered for debate.

Experts were needed to help with this preliminary work, and when objections were made to the largely curial and ultramontane character of the members of the commission, a few individuals were added as consultants. Among them was the strongly anti-infallibilist Church historian Karl-Josef von Hefele of the University of Tübingen – soon to be appointed bishop of Rottenburg – who duly noted the 'duplicity' implicit in the tokenism of his appointment:[1] that duplicity seeming to reveal Pius's attitude as to how the Council – indeed Church business in general – should proceed, and seemingly to be confirmed when – again contrary to Trent- it was determined that all the expert theologians asked to help with the Council's work were to be appointed by Pius himself.

*   *   *

The first major conflicts which the Council provoked, however, were not in the commission but in the press, in the wake of a highly provocative, but almost certainly papally approved article in *La Civiltà Cattolica* in February 1869. The coming Council, it was urged, should distinguish between 'liberal' Catholics and those who were 'simply Catholics' and should not only define papal infallibility – though the pope himself had as yet not specifically called for this – but also 'canonize' the *Syllabus* and the Assumption of Mary into Heaven. Whether such a definition of the Assumption was as yet part of Pius's programme is also uncertain but not unlikely. In the event, however, the occupation of Rome by troops of the new Italian state ended all possibility of its immediate proclamation; it must wait until Pius XII and the Jubilee of 1950.

Papal infallibility was not of course the only theme intended for Council debate, though as it turned out, only one other text (*Dei filius*) emerged from its perforce shortened activities. This last document

1. Cf. R. McClory, *Power and the Papacy: The People and Politics behind the Doctrine of Papal Infallibility* (Liguori, MO: Triumph Press, 1997), 76. At Vatican II the assembled bishops, as we shall see, seem to have learned their lesson, or were encouraged to do so: the conservative agenda proposed by Cardinal Ottaviani and the Holy Office was quickly rejected.

was intended to put an end to the now longstanding debates on the relationship between faith and reason. Distinguishing the two domains, it was to determine that they cannot be in conflict; the Catholic faith, that is, cannot be in conflict with reliably formed scientific theses – but any intrusion of 'reason' – or rather, as it was then understood, of rationalism – into matters of faith as determined by 'the magisterium' was anathema.

But what (the term being of comparatively recent emphasis) was the 'magisterium'? That question the remaining activity of the Council was to approach, though its debates focussed almost entirely on the mooted infallibility of the *pope*, without getting involved in the wider – and far more complex – question of the infallibility (or form of infallibility) of 'the magisterium' in general, let alone of that of the wider Church: an unintended omission which would put the wider debate off until after Vatican II, and so for circumstances far less likely to allow of a harmonious and intelligible conclusion. At Vatican I there is no doubt that papal infallibility was what the majority of the bishops were intent on establishing – and though Pius himself at the opening of the Council appeared to remain above the fray, he would soon make his opinion clear: to the great embarrassment of the anti-infallibilists.

In Germany Döllinger held the proposed infallibility to be a radical break with tradition, as distinct from those who thought that it was 'inopportune', and he took the article in *La Civiltà Cattolica* as a call to arms, the foe being easily identifiable. 'If the Council', he wrote in Augsburg's *Allgemeine Zeitung*,

> allows itself to be used to bind the wreath of Infallibility around the Pope's brow.... The Jesuits and their pupils ... [will] deploy it for their purposes and the world will look on indifferently. In 449 a synod was held which received the name of the Synod of Robbers: the Council of 1869 will go down as the Synod of Flatterers.

Whether or not he was right in supposing that the world would look on indifferently (though to the surprise of many no significant pressure was put on the Council by secular rulers), he was prescient in his reference to flatterers, and their example and practice would be imitated by later generations: prescient too about Jesuits, whose influence was (again) to grow exponentially as the century proceeded.[2]

---

2. Cf Aubert, *Le pontificat de Pie IX*, pp. 457-58.

Nevertheless, Döllinger was in a small minority among an anti-infallibilist minority, having very few supporters among the bishops – of whom only a few might seem as solid as Bishop Augustin Vérot of Savannah in claiming at the Council itself (to considerable annoyance) that to vote for infallibility would be 'sacrilege'. The concerns of the vast majority of anti-infallibilists were with the bad effects a definition would have on ecumenism and on the relationships between Catholic (and other) states and their citizens. To many of these Döllinger's views seemed largely unhelpful as too extreme: hence Döllinger's growing concern as he came to realize that 'inopportune' was a weasel word covering many shades of opinion, often implying a failure to grasp the historical and theological difficulties with what the ultramontanes wanted to propose. If a definition was only inopportune, not theologically unacceptable, opposition to it could too easily be subverted. He could hardly have failed to notice that most anti-infallibilists bishops, not least Bishop Dupanloup of Orléans, accepted papal infallibility in principle, thus being in his view deaf to history. Dupanloup's doctoral thesis at the University of Rome had been titled 'The Infallibility of the Roman Pontiff' and was concerned to defend it in some form.

If Döllinger thought that 'inopportunist' opposition was not serious, he was certainly mistaken, though not mistaken about the end result he feared. The article in *La Civiltà Cattolica* aroused as much fury in France as it did in Germany. Although the uproar that arose there on its first appearance died down, the resentment had not gone away and in September Henri Louis Charles Maret, former dean of theology in Paris, now titular bishop of Sura and in favour with the government of Louis Napoleon – thus being prime cause, it is usually held, of that revival of a form of Gallicanism which so infuriated Pius and the Roman Curia – published a book (paid for by Napoleon) 'On the General Council and the Peace of the Church'. Maret's primary aim was to emphasize the importance of the episcopacy as a necessary partner of the pope. The college of bishops, he urged, must approve any document which is to be defined 'infallibly'. For Pius, Maret was to become a particular *bête noire*, and his book was immediately referred to the Congregation of the Index; it was also attacked fiercely in France by Abbot Guéranger of Solesmes and in England by Archbishop Manning in the appendix to a pastoral letter.

Manning's contribution was reprinted in French by Veuillot, and that in its turn drew a set of 'Observations' from Dupanloup which amounted to the first sustained attack by a bishop on the opportuneness of a definition of papal infallibility, and which were in their turn savaged by the usual suspects: it was, of course, the proposed *definition*, not infallibility itself, to which Dupanloup objected. But the writings of Maret and Dupanloup changed few minds, serving primarily to heighten the anger the proposed definition of infallibility was now arousing on both sides throughout Catholic Europe.

By now Döllinger, however, had decided on further action. He reprinted his recent articles in the Augsburg paper (variously revised) in a hastily compiled volume to be published immediately under the pseudonym 'Janus'. It was titled *The Pope and the Council*, 'Janus' being presumably chosen because the gates of the Roman Temple of Janus were open in time of war, closed in times of peace. Its overall thesis was that papal infallibility was a fantasy which serious historical study of the Church must reject. The undoubted implication was that those who favoured it were either blind to considerations of truth – hence wilfully immoral – or grossly ignorant; Vatican theology could only deny reality at its peril.

That said, a number of German bishops seemed to agree – as it turned out, provisionally – at least that the infallibilists were making a serious 'political' mistake. Fourteen of them sent a letter to the pope warning him that infallibility was presently 'inopportune'; other bishops, especially in France, agreed with that judgement, as was to become clear at the Council itself; and a similar letter reached Rome from the bishops of Hungary and Bohemia. Nor was his volume 'Janus' Döllinger's final word: apart from writing to a number of bishops in Europe and the United States, he published in October 1869 – this time under his own name – some *Considerations for the Bishops of the Council Respecting the Question of Infallibility* in which he explained that papal infallibility was something 'new', did not command universal assent, would further and unnecessarily infuriate non-Catholic Christians and hence that theologians possessed of adequate historical understanding must reject it. Yet, as he knew, not only the majority of bishops but the vast mass of Catholic public opinion was against him, most wanting infallibility immediately defined.

Döllinger's new book was widely read, but by now infallibilists had had enough. As the papal nuncio in Munich pointed out, Döllinger's position was not merely that infallibility was 'inopportune', but that he rejected it root and branch. He forwarded 'Janus's' text to Rome where it was investigated by the Congregation of the Index. Manning, now emerging as a leading infallibilist in the wider episcopate, told the Congregation of the Inquisition that 'Janus' advocated a number of heretical propositions and that Janus and Döllinger were probably identical. By the end of the year *The Pope and the Council* was on the

Index. But though, inevitably, Döllinger was not invited to participate in the Council, he had far from surrendered when it began.

Acting through his former pupil Lord Acton, who moved to Rome where his house became the unofficial centre of anti-infallibilist scheming, Döllinger, under the new pseudonym 'Quirinus' (that being an epithet attached to the old Roman god Janus) now began to publish a long series of letters between himself and Acton, again in the *Allgemeine Zeitung*. These were to be both a report on the Council's proceedings and a commentary from an increasingly hardline anti-infallibilist perspective. Döllinger and Acton knew that their chances of winning the battle which began with the convening of the Council on 8 December 1969 (feast of the *Immaculata* and day of publication of the *Syllabus of Errors*) were slim, though from time to time they struck a more optimistic note.[3] From the start their principal anxiety was that the 'minority' bishops – divided into those few who rejected infallibilism root and branch and the much larger group who thought its proclamation inopportune – would eventually cave in. This would turn out to be the case, not least because, as we noticed, the very word 'inopportune' suggested that the new doctrine in some form or another is *theologically acceptable*.[4] As Acton put it to Gladstone, we can only win if we have men 'prepared in extremity to defy excommunication, that is … as sure of the fallibility of the Pope as of revealed truth.'[5]

'Quirinus' was soon driven to pin his hopes on the normal requirement in the past that Conciliar decrees pass more or less unanimously. That hope too proved to be easily circumvented, owing to the very 'shakiness' to which Acton had pointed. Indeed, given the composition of the Council, the current social and political turmoil which terrified many of the bishops and the immense sympathy for Pius IX throughout the Catholic world, it was almost inevitable that emotion – not least if whipped up by demagogues like Veuillot – rather than appeals to logic

---

3. For a plausible attempt to identify the division of the material between Acton and Döllinger, cf. V. Conzemius, 'Der Verfasser der "Römischen Briefe vom Konzil" des "Quirinus"', *FS Hans Forster: Freiburger Geschichtsblatter* 52 (1963-64), pp. 229-56.

4. So Acton put it in a letter to Döllinger: see V. Conzemius, 'Lord Acton at the First Vatican Council', *Journal of Ecclesiastical History* 20 (1969), p. 278.

5. The letter is dated to 1 January 1870. See D. McElrath, J.C. Holland, Sue Katzman and W. White (eds), *Lord Acton: The Decisive Decade 1864-1874* (Louvain: Louvain University Press, 1970), p. 170.

and historical precedent would prevail, hence that the chances of success for the anti-infallibilist minority were remote.

*   *   *

Of the more than 700 bishops who arrived in Rome, about half came from France and Italy, the Italians being mostly given to 'Roman theology' and the French often anxious to atone for the historic Gallicanism of their Church. Only about 10 per cent were German speakers,[6] and even among these (as we shall see) none recognized as quickly and clearly as 'Quirinus' that the packing of the preparatory committees appointed to establish the conciliar agenda, coupled with the influence of the Roman Jesuits ('that great ecclesiastical polypus'[7]), would give the infallibilists a free hand. The effect, he insisted, would be a subversion of the ancient Church since the infallibilists would be happily positioned to do anything required of them by the pope. Hence 'Quirinus' opined rhetorically that 'if the Pope ordered them to believe and teach four instead of three persons in the Trinity, they would obey'. They 'were to be recognized', he concluded, 'as mere unprincipled "lackeys"'.[8] This comment by 'Quirinus' might sound prophetic of our own times, when another Jesuit editor of *La Civiltà Cattolica* has – how seriously, how cynically? – quipped that 'in theology two and two make five'.

The serious (and the cynical) business of the Council began at the second general congregation on 10 December, the principal requirement being to elect the members of the commission for doctrine. While the anti-infallibilists failed until too late to recognize how important this election was – for the membership of a committee will largely determine its outcome – the leaders of the infallibilists – Manning, Senestrey of Regensburg and Dechamps of Brussels – set about wangling the election of a group almost entirely of their own persuasion. The results were announced on 20 December, and revealed an overwhelming victory for Manning and his supporters, who had thus foreseen and substantially inhibited any appeal by the 'minority' to the more moderate among their opponents. The result dismayed the 'minority' and delighted the 'majority', though some felt a little embarrassed by the tactics so successfully deployed, Cardinal Bilio (substantial ghost-writer of the

---

6. For the figures see O. Chadwick, *A History of the Popes, 1830-1914* (Oxford: Oxford University Press, 1998), pp. 197-98.

7. In Howard, *The Pope and the Professor*, p. 94.

8. G. Sweeney, 'The Forgotten Council', in A. Hastings (ed.), *Bishops and Writers* (Wheathampstead: Anthony Clarke, 1977).

Syllabus) remarking that such methods were not the right way to transact ecclesiastical business. Be that as it might, the infallibilists could now be sure that whatever they (and the pope) wanted would be largely achieved.

On 28 December the bishops turned their attention to the first draft of what was to become the decree on faith and reason, *Dei Filius*, then still known as *Apostolici Muneris*. Many of the 'minority' were highly critical of what was proposed: not least Cardinal Rauscher of Vienna, Bishop Kenrick of St Louis, Archbishop Connolly of Halifax and the determined Croatian bishop Josip Jurai Strossmayer, who not for the last time tried to upset the apple-cart. His first objection was that the decree was proposed not in the name of the Council but of the pope alone. His objections were largely disregarded and discussion dragged on until 14 January, eventually turning to themes (such as reform of the Curia) which came to nothing.

On 22 February a document was circulated, parts of which were to appear not in *Dei Filius* but in the coming *Supremi Pastoris* (eventually *Pastor Aeternus*) on the hierarchy of the Church. Just in time, and apparently tipped off by Acton, some of the 'minority' grew concerned about its thirteenth provision: that for parts of documents, even those concerned with dogma, a simple majority would suffice. In particular Archbishop Ketteler of Mainz urged that, while this might be appropriate for purely disciplinary matters, on questions of faith something approaching unanimity was essential.

By the end of January the hardline infallibilists set about getting papal infallibility onto the Council's agenda. Matteo Liberatore (Jesuit theological adviser to Manning and on the staff of *La Civiltà Cattolica*) organized a petition to that effect to be presented to the pope; it was signed by 372 bishops, and the version of infallibility it proposed was extreme, so satisfying the aims of Manning and Senestrey and revealing beyond any doubt the intentions of the 'majority'. Liberatore followed up his success on 5 February (probably with the approval of Pius) with an article attacking Döllinger as sounding like a Protestant and a schismatic,[9] his further aim being to smear the more moderate anti-infallibilists as closet deniers of infallibility itself.

Liberatore's petition reached Pius and he duly referred it, as was proper, to the committee *De Postulatis*, who recommended its acceptance, and

---

9. M. Liberatore, 'Il Dottor Döllinger e la petizione dei vescovi al Concilio', *La Civiltà Cattolica* 7-9 (1870), pp. 284-300. For more on the 'reception' of Döllinger's concerns see G. Thils, *L'infaillibilité* (Gembloux: Duculot, 1969), pp. 48-55.

on 6 March, Bishop Fessler, secretary-general of the Council, informed the bishops that Pius had signed up to it and that a basic text dealing with infallibility would be submitted in the form of an additional chapter 11 – to be the work of Kleutgen, now rehabilitated after his indiscretions with the Sant'Ambrogio nuns – in the text of *Supremi Pastoris* already in preparation in the committee *De Fide*. When the additional chapter appeared, it closely reflected writings of two of the most extreme ultramontanists, Manning himself and Dechamps of Brussels,[10] thus confirming their wisdom in fixing the election of the committee. The 'minority' realized that things were getting worse by the day: Cardinal Schwarzenburg of Prague even considered abandoning the Council altogether while Strossmayer, prophetically, lamented the servility of the bishops who had behaved, he noted in a letter, like the servile senators of ancient Rome who had 'decreed the emperor as God'.[11]

On 18 March the bishops returned to *Apostolici Muneris*, now revised by a subcommittee headed by Konrad Martin, Jesuit bishop of Paderborn, and largely drafted not by Johann Baptist Franzelin SJ, who had worked on it earlier, and had urged the Fathers that the German universities were at the root of the new cultural challenge of historical criticism of Bible and Church, but again by Kleutgen. Matters chugged along fairly peacefully until Strossmayer again provoked an uproar, first challenging the document being issued in the pope's name rather than in the name of the Council, then by observing that Protestants were not responsible for all the doctrinal and moral errors now under review: some of them were genuinely Christian. Finally he returned to Ketteler's argument that 'moral unanimity' must be required for dogmatic definitions.

Though the debate at this point was far from directly touching on infallibility, the reaction Strossmayer produced was startling, and it will be helpful to cite Cuthbert Butler's account if we hope to understand the impossible position in which the anti-infallibilists now found themselves. Butler was determined to see as much sweetness and light in the Council as he could squeeze out of the letters of the would-be neutral Bishop Ullathorne.[12] His account runs as follows:

Strossmayer: I protest against every interruption. I…
Fathers rising called out: We protest against you.

---

10. Cf. Thils, *L'infaillibilité*, pp. 111-15.
11. Cf. K. Schatz, *Vaticanum I*, vol. 2, pp. 180-82, cited by J.W. O'Malley, *Vatican I*, p. 184.
12. Butler, *The Vatican Council*, p. 272.

Strossmayer: I protest against any interruption.
The First President rang his bell again and again.
The Fathers generally: We wish him to come down; let him
come down [from the podium].
Strossmayer: I protest against....

And he began to come down. The indignant Fathers left their
seats, all murmuring different things. Some said, 'These people
don't want the infallibility of the Pope; is this man infallible
himself!' Others: 'He is Lucifer, anathema, anathema!' Others:
'He is another Luther, let him be cast out!' And all cried out,
'Come down, come down'. But he kept on saying 'I protest,
I protest', and came down.

Not quite the standard of Chalcedon ('Let Ibas burn', 'Cut in
two the man who divides the Christ'), but a good follow-up act and
indicative of the difficulty of obtaining rational discussion of what was
to be revealed as the extremely complex question of the infallibility
of the Roman pontiff. For one of the points which Strossmayer raised
and many of his colleagues wished to ignore was that if you live in a
partly Protestant country you have different problems from those who
work in largely Catholic states with Catholic rulers. For, as we have
noted, the key 'minority' claim that a definition of papal infallibility
was 'inopportune' usually indicated not a variety of disbelief in papal
infallibility but a much more immediate concern with the political (and
'ecumenical') ramifications of publishing a definition of it in 1870. It
was such considerations which Strossmayer's opponents so vigorously
refused to recognize; some of them – Manning in particular – were even
to claim that to define papal infallibility would encourage conversion
from Protestantism.

Though the anti-infallibilists were largely unwilling to accept it, Pius's
attitude too indicated that he regarded all opposition as mere obstinacy
or even treachery. Maret, he wrote, was a 'viper', Cardinal Guidi (a
moderate infallibilist) was soon to be told that his moderation showed
how closely he was linked with enemies of the Church, Dupanloup that
he was tempted to heresy. Strossmayer of course was beyond the pale.
Summing them up, the pope wrote more generally that 'Some leaders
among the opposing bishops are effeminate, and others are sophistical,
or frivolous [that probably aimed at Augustin Vérot who too often
could not refrain from humorously shocking "pious ears"], or heretical
[perhaps with Strossmayer in mind]. They are ambitious, boastful and
obstinately attached to their own opinion.' In reading this comment we

must recall that the pope is not referring to full-blooded anti-infallibilists like Döllinger but to bishops who believed that pressing for a decision at the present time was a serious error of judgement.[13] As a modern scholar has put it, 'Pius IX had little sense of the pastoral seriousness and important theological objections that underlay the reasoning of the minority bishops.'[14] On the contrary, he was unable to understand how any real Catholic could oppose his wishes.

On 24 April the revised declaration on faith and reason (now styled *Dei Filius*) was ready for final approval. The 'minority' bishops were divided on what to do; Strossmayer, supported by William Clifford of Clifton and a few others and sensing a trap, urged that they should vote *non placet*. This, however, was rejected, most of the group supposing that being obliging at this stage would help secure a measure of reciprocal consideration when papal infallibility came before the assembly. In this they seriously miscalculated, underestimating the ruthless determination of their opponents, as Acton and Döllinger had predicted. Strossmayer decided to absent himself from the final vote which thus passed unanimously.

The anti-infallibilists still had a few cards to play: they could invite the European powers to intervene on the ground that the definition of any form of infallible papal authority would endanger Church–State relations: a threat echoed in the Council by many bishops. Surely problems of conscience would arise for Catholics increasingly called on to obey two conflicting masters. Appeals were variously made not only to the rulers of France, Bavaria and Austria, but even to Britain's Gladstone, himself a close friend of Acton and Döllinger, but to little avail. The British Foreign Secretary, George Villiers, told Gladstone that any action the Powers might take 'would have no more effect in arresting the Juggernaut at Rome than it would have in changing the East wind'.[15]

In desperation, Döllinger appealed for help to another prestigious scholar of the day, John Henry Newman, urging him that now if ever was the time to speak and that neutrality looked like lukewarmness: in effect appealing to Newman's conscience. Unfortunately, it seems, he was unaware not only that Newman, though an inopportunist, was a minimalizing infallibilist but also that he had very different ideas about

---

13. For details of such crude partisanship see O'Malley, *Vatican I*, pp. 142, 146, 188, 212.
14. K. Schatz, *Papal Primacy from its Origins to the Present* (Collegeville, MN: Liturgical Press, 1996), pp. 156-57.
15. Cf. Howard, *The Pope and the Professor*, p. 148.

the nature and authority of conscience itself. In Newman's view appeals to conscience, as ordinarily understood, are appropriate only in the realm of one's actions, not of one's beliefs; hence there can be no clash between prioritizing conscience where 'secular' action would normally be called for and accepting beliefs about the infallibility of the pope, themselves dependent on overriding divine revelation and which will necessarily block any anti-papal ('conscientious') action in the ecclesial domain.[16]

Ian Ker concludes a long chapter of his biography of Newman by saying that for Newman 'conscience, in the last analysis, however misguided, is supreme', thus seeming to reject Aquinas's view that it should not be followed if it is in fact erroneous. As we have noted, Newman sees conscience as specifically relating to action, not to beliefs – and (embarrassingly) Döllinger required him to express a belief. The reader must be left to judge whether Döllinger's disappointment with Newman's decision to remain silent (thus avoiding action) was justified. That said, Newman's prophetic anxiety as to consequences if papal infallibility (or indeed infallibility more generally) were to be misused is palpable: so he writes to Ambrose St John (*LD*, vol. 25, p. 192) that if the present pope (Pius IX) attempts to extend the proposed definition, 'we must hope, for one is obliged to hope it, that the Pope will be driven from Rome, and will not continue the Council, or that there will be another Pope'.

---

16. J. Coulson, *Newman and the Common Tradition* (Oxford: Oxford University Press, 1970), p. 121, notes that Newman's view of conscience differs from Acton's. And the background and nature of Döllinger's view similarly differs from Newman's, not least in reflecting the influence of Rousseau who almost reduces conscience to sincerity. Newman's version starts from British moral sense theories, but he always maintained that the 'moral sense' recognized objective moral truths, though not abstractly, abstraction being the realm of the intellect. For Newman, conscience is formed not only from assembled moral habits but also from religious beliefs. Hence any informed conscience must display the 'correct' view about the role of the Church, while mistaken judgements of the conscience (such as, for Newman, those of Döllinger) can arise from subordinating divine revelation to it: such mistakes are part of what distinguishes real conscience from its 'counterfeit' (*Letter to the Duke of Norfolk*, p. 5, a text to be discussed below). Newman's position has been much distorted in recent debates for ideological reasons; for a balanced account see S.A. Grave, *Conscience in Newman's Thought* (Oxford: Oxford University Press, 1989). I would concur with Grave's judgement that 'Newman, writing on conscience is not, on the whole, at his best' (p. 185).

When approached by Döllinger, Newman evaded the (basic) issue, concentrating in his reply on the fact that the dodgy methods employed by the 'majority' were not at all unusual. Of this Döllinger was well aware – and deeply disapproving – but this was far from what he and others claimed to recognize as the real disaster: not chicanery but doctrinal irregularity with – and contempt for – the demands of conscience in matters theological as well as political.[17]

*   *   *

By late April conciliar discussion of infallibility was moving towards its inevitable conclusion. For some time the ardent infallibilists had begun

---

17. Even after the Council Newman persisted in treating Döllinger's primary concern as with the irregular procedures of the Council rather than the substance of the infallibility thesis itself. He himself had always accepted papal infallibility, but preferred that it not be proclaimed – until it was, when he declared himself 'pleased at its moderation', adopting the line that the ultramontanists had not got what they wanted because the powers now affirmed for the pope were only in faith and morals and did not extend to politics. Perhaps, he claimed, the definition might even 'limit' the pope's power: a curious echo of William of Ockham. Yet Newman simultaneously admitted that there was no special reason for infallibility to be proclaimed when it was and noted that 'you put an enormous power into the hands of one man, without check, and at the very time, by your act, that he may use it without special occasion' (*LD*, vol. 25, p. 175). Presciently he was also concerned at the danger that a pope might 'use his power without necessity, whenever he will, when not called on to do so' (*LD*, vol. 25, p. 192). Although Newman continued to believe that Döllinger's case was 'tragic' and that he came to be harshly treated by Archbishop Scherr, he attributed the blame for the tragedy to Scherr, not to the authorities in Rome who had pressured Scherr to act ((*LD*, vol. 25, p. 341). Papal 'sanctity' was already beginning to show some of its less edifying consequences, tending to verge on that 'impeccability' which some of the anti-infallibilists dreaded. Nevertheless and more prophetically, Newman noted that the phrase *ex cathedra* had not been clearly defined (*LD*, vol. 25, p. 219) and that the mind of the pope and of the people might be adversely affected by infallibility (*LD*, vol. 25, p. 259). He seems also always to have expected (as if this were the whole story) that the 'balance' of authority between pope and bishops would be righted, presumably in a further Council (*LD*, vol. 25, p. 310). For detailed discussion see I. Ker, *John Henry Newman: A Biography* (Oxford: Oxford University Press, 1988), pp. 651-93. For Newman's view that the Jesuits were too powerful (on which he agreed with Döllinger) see Ker, *Newman*, p. 679.

to worry, not least in light of the threatening political situation, that the chance to get papal infallibility defined might slip away; hence, as we noticed, by the end of January a number of petitions had reached the chairmen of the various committees and the pope himself, urging that papal infallibility be *immediately* debated. Cardinal Bilio, however, presiding over the committee *De Fide,* though the pope's man, was not alone among the presidents in disliking suggestions circulating that the order of the agenda be changed to allow the controversial chapter 11 of *Supremi Pastoris* (as the proposed text was still labelled) on papal infallibility to be discussed immediately, thus debating infallibility before treating Church hierarchy more generally – or, as the anti-infallibilists put it, separating the head from the body of the church and dealing with it on its own.

Both sides now recognized that the situation was critical: for the minority Dupanloup, Lajos Haynald, bishop of Kalocsa-Bacs in Hungary, plus a number of Americans headed by Peter Kenrick of St Louis, as well as Darboy of Paris and even Secretary of State Antonelli (himself a member of the majority), argued against any change in the order of proceedings. To no avail. Pius assured a delegation sent by Manning and Senestrey that he 'would do the right thing'; this they rightly took to mean that papal primacy and infallibility would be next on the agenda: a hardly surprising conclusion since months before Pius had told Piccirillo, editor of *La Civiltà Cattolica*, that 'I am so determined to go forward with this matter that if I knew the Council was going to be silent on it, I would dissolve it and define it myself.'[18] Hence on 29 April came the decisive announcement: chapter 11 of *Supremi Pastoris* would be considered immediately.

Debate began on 14 May and continued until 3 June, to resume on 6 June. Little new material was adduced but the arguments were passionate and the conclusion predetermined. The revised document was introduced by Bishop Pie of Poitiers, who tried an irenic approach though to little effect. The very next day his colleague from Dijon rose to claim outright that the whole idea was absurd: no ordinary Catholic would understand exactly what powers the pope enjoyed and, whatever the professionals might say, would tend, scandalously, to think that the papal power was 'personal and absolute': perhaps the first time a bishop had recognized that, whatever the intent of the infallibilists, their proposal, in almost any form, could have very undesirable effects on the mentality of simple believers.

---

18. So Schatz, *Vaticanum I,* vol. 3, pp. 182-83.

The battle raged back and forth with many of the leaders on either side taking to the floor. Manning himself spoke at length on 25 May and was greeted with roars of applause, but on the same day his English colleague Clifford not only rejected his claim that a definition would be helpful among Protestants but noted that even the more hardened infallibilists had little idea of exactly what they were proposing and what its implications would be. He received his reward when two days later Pius asked an English priest whom he happened to meet to tell Clifford that he had acted reprehensibly 'in speaking against the pope and the church': the two apparently in Pius's mind being identical, as later was more unambiguously shown to be the case.[19] On 14 June sections 1 to 3 of the revised text of chapter 11 were approved.

On 17 June Pius himself addressed the bishops, having decided to tell them that they divided into three groups: the first group hardly behaved like bishops at all – this being recognized as aimed especially at Strossmayer who might be seen of an evening out of episcopal dress; the second were collaborators with 'the world'; the third (in line with the much earlier pronouncement already noted in *La Civiltà Cattolica*) were real Catholics who stood firm in Catholic truth.

The following day the pope made his view of himself even clearer. The Dominican Cardinal Archbishop of Bologna, Filippo Maria Guidi, himself a moderate infallibilist, attempted mediation in the spirit (as he argued) of Thomas Aquinas and Cardinal Bellarmine, urging that the intended definition must contain some reference to the authority of the bishops so that the traditions of the various Churches in communion with Rome could be recognized.[20] This looked helpful, and has been interpreted as an attempt by a prominent Dominican to call out the more recent carelessness about tradition which seemed to characterize the now dominant Jesuits around the pope.

Strossmayer ran up to kiss Guidi's hand as he stepped down: not a helpful gesture in the circumstances, as perhaps reminiscent of the Iscariot. Pius, for his part, found Guidi's intervention deeply offensive, and carpeted the cardinal the very same day: he was a jumped-up friar who owed his entire position to the pope, and had shown his gratitude by helping the enemies of the Church. When Guidi persisted that the tradition of the church must be taken into account, Pius's reply (on the

19. Cf. O'Malley, *Vatican I*, p. 206.

20. See in particular, U. Horst, 'Kardinalerzbischof Filippo Maria Guidi OP und das 1 Vatikanischen Konzil', *Archivum Fratrum Praedicatorum* 49 (1979), pp. 429-511.

evidence of Dupanloup in his journal who should have known) was portentous: 'I, I am the tradition; I am the Church': a reiteration of his reprimand to Clifford and to the effect that Church and pope are identical. Further revisions of the text continued and were presented on 9 July, but Pius's words (and his now dominant Jesuit following) were to haunt the Church up to the present day, as we shall see.

The final significant intervention (still cited, as we shall see, as authoritative in Vatican II's *Lumen Gentium*) was by the bishop of Brixen, Vinzenz Gasser, on 11 July. Gasser tried to interpret the upcoming declaration in as modest a sense as could be managed; it was, he argued, to be read as teaching that a final and definitive papal decision should occur only when the bishops were hopelessly divided on a major matter of faith or morals: moreover that the pope is only infallible when his pronouncement indicates the view of the Church as a whole.

Here, of course, is where the continuing ambiguity lay: who was to know (apart, presumably from the pope, as might be hoped) that he was indeed expressing the will of the universal Church? With no consultation with others, how could any assurance that he was aware of the mind of the Church be plausibly given? Nor was Gasser's interpretation the understanding of either the 'majority' bishops or their 'minority' opponents, and there is even less reason to suppose it represented the view of Pius. It must be construed as little more than a sop to the dissenters – though, as we shall see, it provided wriggle-room for those anti-infallibilists who later were to defend their eventual acceptance of the definition. As for Pius himself, his view seems well summarized by Roberto De' Mattei, commenting not only on a pope's now accepted doctrinal supremacy but on his absolute powers of jurisdiction:[21]

> According to this definition the Roman pontiff can do anything in the Church, can exercise this authority over anyone, and can do so without being limited by anyone.... The Vatican I definition had erected an insurmountable bastion against the anti-papal tendencies lurking even within the Catholic Church.

Further attempts at 'damage control' on the Council floor by Darboy and Ketteler were rejected, their intent again being to tie *ex cathedra* judgements (the phrase originated with Archbishop Ullathorne[22]) to

---

21. R. De' Mattei, *The Second Vatican Council* (Fitzwilliam, NH: Loreto Publications, 2012), p. 311.
22. So Thils, *L'infaillibilité*, p. 201.

the traditional witness of the Church. So on 13 July a preliminary vote on the disputed clauses was taken: 88 voted *non placet* and 62 *placet iuxta modum* (that is, requiring amendments) with 451 in favour. The dissidents included three cardinals, two patriarchs and several prominent archbishops, though Pius himself had confided to Darboy that he expected no more than ten *non placets*. Historians of the Council have sometimes argued that to vote *non placet* rather than *extra modum* was a tactical mistake, since it prevented further negotiations, apparently ignoring the fact that such negotiations had gone nowhere and were most unlikely to do so.

The next day Pius received a message ('inspired' presumably) from a comparatively lesser known bishop, Charles-Emile Freppel of Angers, urging that the wording of the text be significantly changed once more: the key phrase was now to read that definitions of the Roman pontiff are binding 'of themselves (*ex sese*) and not by the consensus of the Church (*non ex consensu ecclesiae*)', and it was as such that it was presented to the assembled bishops on 16 July. The addition, of course, cannot be explained as merely a rebuttal of a claim of the French Fourth Gallican Article (of 1682) that 'In controversies concerning the faith, the Sovereign Pontiff takes a leading role. His teaching is the concern of each and every church, but his judgments are not irreformable unless the Church gives its agreement.'[23] Rather, it represented what the pope and his loyalist supporters had been seeking for largely other reasons. Gallicanism apart, what Pius wanted was that his jurisdiction, which he was inviting the bishops to acknowledge – and as a predecessor had attempted to induce the Orthodox to acknowledge at the Council of Florence (1431-49) – was to cover not only faith and morals but all areas of governance of the Church: a power, that is, 'to feed, rule and govern the universal Church'. It must have been clear to all who cared about Eastern Christianity in 1870 that no Orthodox Christian could accept that any more than had most of their predecessors in the fifteenth century. Primacy is one thing, universal jurisdiction quite another. The addition served only to make later appeals to Gasser's 'clarification' the more implausible.

And now the 'minority' made their final, fatal mistake. Forgetting arguments from unanimity, and persuaded largely by Dupanloup, who urged that to vote against the pope would seem scandalous, some 60

---

23. Cf. G. Sweeney, 'Forgotten Council', p. 167 and n. 23 – though the present writer is far from endorsing Sweeney's interpretation of its intent, let alone of its appropriation in Vatican II's *Lumen Gentium*.

of them – by a majority vote of 36 to 25 and following the example of the 36 neo-Arians at Constantinople I – found pressing reasons to leave the Eternal City, being unprepared to follow up what their consciences had previously urged on them, and having declined to follow Haynald's advice to fight on. To the contrary, most on leaving promised to accept whatever decision was reached by the remainder. Among them was Döllinger's archbishop, Gregor von Scherr of Munich, once a determined opponent of the definition.

The departure of the 'minority' leaders opened the way for the elusive near-unanimity (normally required as a determinative feature of valid ecclesiastical decisions on matters of faith) to be achieved, when amid tempestuous fury, two days after the fatal insertion, on 18 July, 533 bishops voted to approve the schema, two (Edward Fitzgerald of Little Rock and Luigi Riccio of Cajazzo) voting *contra*. In his final letter 'Quirinus' summed up the sorry spectacle: 'It only remains to follow up the anathematized enemy, the bishops of the minority, into their lurking-places, and compel each of them to bend under the Caudine yoke amid the scornful laughter of the majority.'[24] And so it was to turn out.

Rome surrendered to the forces of the King of Italy on 20 September, by when the mopping up of the 'minority' bishops – not to speak of their supporters – was well under way. On his return to Munich Archbishop Scherr on 21 July told the theology faculty to submit. Several hesitated and similar resistance was widely apparent in Germany. In some anxiety and sensing danger of a schism – indeed what was to be named the Old Catholic movement was already beginning to take shape – Scherr, together with Ketteler (also, as we have seen, an active spokesman for the inopportunists), called for a meeting of the German episcopate.

This took place on 30 and 31 August. Nine bishops attended and drew up what came to be called the 'Pastoral Letter of Fulda'. At the 'theological' level it suggested a rather minimalist interpretation of the new decree, while more 'politically' arguing that the Council was genuinely ecumenical, that it had proposed no novelties but merely illuminated earlier teachings. The bishops concluded that the dogma was binding since published by the Supreme Pontiff in solemn form and in public session.

In short order, Pius penned his satisfaction and gratitude, and his *Pastoral Letter* encouraged 'minority' bishops in France to follow the example of their German colleagues. The remaining dissenters in

---

24. *Römischen Briefe vom Konzil von Quirinus*, 636; cf. Howard, *The Pope and the Professor*, p. 151.

Germany also quickly fell into line, Hefele being the last to do so – who earlier had expressed surprise that his colleagues Ketteler and Melchers 'appear to have forgotten everything that they did and said in Rome'. Nevertheless, and despite being the bishop most professionally aware of how historical reality had been trampled by the majority of his colleagues, after much agonizing and with the *caveat* that he accepted the interpretation of the definition proposed in a book by Josef Fessler, former secretary of the Council, he too caved in on 17 April 1871. By then the remaining leaders of the 'minority' elsewhere, including Darboy, Dupanloup and Maret, had submitted, though the now isolated Strossmayer held out longer – at least until 1877. The behaviour of the 'minority' bishops can only be assessed as a clear example of the subordination of conscience – at least as normally understood – to obedience.

*   *   *

As already noted, my aim in this book is not to write a detailed history of the decisions of the First Vatican Council, still less to evaluate them theologically. They have thus been summarily recounted only as a necessary preliminary to a speculative analysis of their effects on the subsequent behaviour of popes, bishops and clergy and the great majority of Catholic laity: that is, with the actual and not least the unintended effects of the dogma of papal infallibility as defined and of the behaviour of both its supporters and its varied opponents at the Council itself and in its aftermath.

Such effects can be explained as deriving from three historical realities: first, the unclarity and ambiguity of the definition of papal infallibility itself; second, the behaviour of those who promoted it in so peremptory a series of acts, obeying – and willingly – the implicit commands of the pope; third, the virtual disappearance, after the final vote by which it was approved, of what had seemed in many cases serious conscientious objections of varying sorts. That last fact will require further limited comment on 'conscience' as then (and at times now) understood in the Church. While all three of these historical realities demand immediate discussion, their longer effects on popes, bishops and more generally the mentality of Catholics in later generations will form the subject-matter of the following chapters of this book.

The unclarity of 'papal infallibility' – especially of the interpretation (as noted by Newman) to be put on the phrase *ex cathedra* – is clear in the proceedings of the Council itself and was regularly discussed by the 'minority'. Pius IX may have thought of himself as 'the tradition', but neither infallibilists nor anti-infallibilists were quite sure what had been signed up to: it was not so much a fudge as a theoretical proposal the implications of which had not been properly worked out in the determined rush to get it through. Some feared it had gone too far, others regretting its limitation to faith and morals.

Newman's concern about the effects the Council's decision might have on the future behaviour of both popes and their subjects was little shared. As we have noted, he himself approved the new teaching so far as it went, as a seemingly moderate version of infallibility, although he had earlier considered it inopportune. Almost fatalistically – though, as he would have thought, reliant on providence – he felt sure that its weaknesses would in time be rectified. In the event, its unintended effects were not to be so easily disposed of, though concern that 'infallible' papal judgements would appear on a regular basis has been shown to be premature. Nor, as it has turned out, have the anxieties of the 'minority' about Church–State relations been significantly justified.

As for the behaviour of the bishops in general, their example was something of a prelude to what might appear – as I shall argue, has appeared – in the course of the following century, and indeed down to the present day. Though theological arguments in favour of some form of papal infallibility – indeed that it already existed in embryo in earlier centuries – were not lacking, the major influence on many even 'moderate' bishops among the infallibilists was an intense sympathy with the predicament in which Pius had found himself and a readiness to satisfy his obvious desire to secure his own impregnability – understood as infallibility – in the interests of the Church, particularly in its opposition to the modern world: wholly inadequate though these reasons were, and indeed irresponsible at best, servile at worst. Strossmayer, as we noted, had already spoken of an episcopal servility that was to become a pattern.

Nor was the behaviour of the 'minority' particularly edifying. As we have seen, most of them preferred to disappear rather than vote against the pope's wishes, thus leaving themselves no chance to plead for the near-unanimity on the final document they had urged as essential to it, but as 'Quirinus' had predicted, caving in one after another. Though some realized that they might seem to have forgotten the conscientious objections they had voiced while still in Rome, eventually all – after 'agonizing' in their consciences – subscribed to a decree they had previously thought at the least inopportune. If in good faith, they perhaps concluded that their consciences were insufficiently well formed to provide adequate guidance against the pope's manifest determination.

Analysis of the self-justifying utterances in which the French bishops of the 'minority' indulged after their change of heart shows them inclined to claim that what they really opposed was not an understanding of the definition such that the pope need not always require *immediate* consultation – and could not act without it – but that he could act freely with no respect for the 'mind' of the church however interpreted.[25] That explanation of their behaviour seems implausible, reflecting as it does neither their attitude during the Council nor that of the 'majority', nor even of Pius himself. What they claimed to be concerned about looks on analysis to be little more than a self-justifying straw man, since all knew they had accepted a decision which earlier they had thought unclear, unnecessary and unhelpful – yet now were taking advantage of that 'unclarity' to justify their behaviour. Noting that in their absence a near-unanimous decision had been reached, they claimed that the final determination was merely a new way of expressing the long-accepted infallibility not so much of the pope as of the Church as a whole.

It is not difficult to conclude that while the 'majority' bishops might have been irresponsible, the 'minority' were culpably cowardly, preferring to please the infallibilists in general and the pope in particular rather than following the example of Döllinger, who, rightly or wrongly but certainly on grounds of conscience, declined to submit – convinced as he was that history showed papal infallibility – at least as then defined and as distinct from the infallibility (in some sense) of the Church – to be novel and undemonstrated. Though few among the bishops shared his 'extreme' position, throughout the Council they had insisted that their opposition was not merely pragmatic, but based on principle. Nor, of course, did either the 'minority' or the 'majority' pay much attention to the possibility that in the future a pope might be a heretic (which question had been raised in medieval times, and held to be possible by popes Innocent III and Paul IV); nor *a fortiori* not only how such a one could be infallible but how he could be pope at all. Indeed when the matter did come up (so Archbishop Purcell of Cincinnati recalled[26]) it was dismissed out of hand as impossible; any heretical pope would be immediately deposed!

25. M. O'Gara, *Triumph in Defeat: Infallibility, Vatican I and the French Minority Bishops* (Washington, DC: CUA Press, 1988), pp. 175-255, tries to paint a more edifying picture of the behaviour of the French bishops when they returned home, but the task proves beyond her.
26. Cf. J. McGovern, *The Life and Life Work of Pope Leo XIII* (Chicago: Allied Printing, 1903), p. 241.

Historians have asked whether the decisions of the Council were freely given. Certainly, the bishops were free insofar as the 'minority' had ample chance to express their views. But were they free in the sense that in the end they could have *acted* otherwise? The answer must be that they could – Haynald in fact urged that course – but that they 'felt' that their conscience must, in the final analysis, be submitted to the pope. Would that attitude continue whatever a pope might want to define or command? That question has hung over the papacy and the Church down to our own day. For it remained to be seen how popes would take advantage of the vaguely defined infallibility granted them in 1870. One thing, however, is beyond doubt: many even of the most extreme infallibilists would have been appalled by how a future pope would use his 'defined' authority.

*   *   *

Döllinger was excommunicated on 17 April 1871. Hailed by many as a new Luther, he declined to follow Luther's path – though admired and courted by the 'Old Catholics' and seemingly prepared to move further from Catholic orthodoxy in the interests of what might now ungenerously be described as 'lowest common denominator ecumenism'. In life he refused to align himself with the schism, though at his death in 1890 he received the last rites from Johann Friedrich, an old friend from the Munich theology faculty, now turned Old Catholic. His actions before, during and after the Council left questions as to the role of conscience in the Church unresolved. There is no doubt that his actions were conscience-driven.

*   *   *

In October 1974 William Gladstone, now out of office in Great Britain, published an article decrying the political effects of infallibility, in particular the likelihood of its confronting Catholics in Britain with a dilemma between their civic responsibilities and the commands of an 'infallible' pope – and playing (unfairly) on the ambiguity as to the scope of infallibility itself. In November the former Prime Minister followed this up with a lengthy pamphlet on *The Vatican Decrees in their bearing on Civil allegiance: A Political Expostulation*. That gave Newman the opportunity to expound his views of the truth of infallibility: now no longer of its inopportunity, but of its political consequences, misjudged as he held them to have been by Gladstone. Finally, and more importantly, he could consider the problem the Council decision had raised (or should have raised) for Catholic consciences.

Newman's pamphlet, in the form of a letter to the Duke of Norfolk, gave him the opportunity not only to clarify the evasiveness of his response to Döllinger's appeal, but to explain that, though he accepted the new dogma, yet the sense in which the pope is infallible must be further determined by debate among theologians (thus emphasizing the unclarity of the dogma as promulgated). In such discussions, he insisted, theologians (assumed to be clerics, theology being in his view unsuited to the laity) should normally prefer 'minimalist' interpretations.

The core of Newman's Letter concerned the relationship between conscience and authority. He may have known that in the sixteenth century Philip II of Spain had asked the papal legate, Ugo Boncompagni, whether he would ever disobey the pope. The legate had replied 'Should the pope command me to do something that is against my conscience or is detrimental to the Holy See, I will not obey.'[27] He probably assumed that he would receive no such command (so the Stoic philosopher Blossius supposed when giving a similar answer to the question, 'If Tiberius Gracchus asked you to burn down the Capitol, would you obey?'). That assumption might, however, turn out to be mistaken.

Be that as may, Newman proposed a solution that in some respects recalls the lucubrations of the eighteenth-century Anglican Bishop Butler, concluding with the puzzling assertion 'I shall drink to the Pope if you please, still to Conscience first and to the Pope afterwards'. If that looks as though he should have responded differently to Döllinger's appeal, such an interpretation would be erroneous, for now he was careful to distinguish a specifically religious view of conscience from that current in secular society: a society, he believed, in which for the first time Christianity confronted a prevailing disbelief in God. For the Catholic Christian, he insisted, deliberations about conscience must always be set in the frame of belief in God, while for the secularist that could not be the case: hence the 'domains' of conscience as popularly understood and of conscience on matters of Catholic belief must be kept apart. He might have added (but did not) that, when asking for his support, Döllinger was thinking like a secularist.

Though having earlier passed over that infallibilists, including Pius himself, seemed at the Council to have blurred the distinction between infallible utterances by the pope and those of the ordinary magisterium of the Church, Newman insisted that a Catholic, if 'following his conscience' against papal authority, must be able to say 'in the Presence

---

27. I owe this reference to Cardinal G. Müller's, *The Pope: His Mission and Task* (Washington, DC: CUA Press, 2017), p. 208.

of God that he must not, indeed dare not obey' (*Difficulties of Anglicans*, II, 258). He ignored, of course, that Döllinger at least claimed to be in precisely that position. He also assumed that future conflicts (hence possible applications of enhanced papal authority) would occur only in dogmatic theology – hence in matters of faith, not of morals.[28] For in morals, he vainly imagined, there is 'so little that is unknown and unexplored', thus failing to recognize that in that coming secular age of which he was so unhappily aware, it would no longer be over Trinity or Christology that Catholics would be under pressure to conform to 'Caesar' (or a papal Caesar) but precisely over morality: further that there too popes might deploy their enhanced authority in favour of the secular lead.

---

28. *Difficulties of Anglicans*, II, 332; cf. Ker, *Newman*, p. 688.

Chapter 3

Leo XIII: Top-Down Pastor

I found Rome a city of brick and left it a city of marble.

Caesar Augustus

Ordinations according to the Anglican rite have been and are absolutely null and utterly void.

Pope Leo XIII in *Apostolicae Curae* (1896)[1]

Pius IX died on 8 February 1878; he was beatified by John Paul II in 2000, who noted, hopefully but not entirely accurately, in a homily celebrating the event, that Pius 'had clarified with magisterial authority certain questions disputed at the time'; not least he had confirmed the Immaculate Conception of Mary, the Mother of Jesus. The possibility of his eventual canonization still remains on the table.

Pius's successor, Gioacchino Pecci, who had worked for Pius on his *Syllabus of Errors*, was elected on 20 February and took the name Leo XIII. As his dismissal of Anglican Orders makes clear, the new pope was his own man, never unwilling to use his revitalized authority to explain and enforce doctrine as he understood and determined it: the model of a paternal pastor. He saw his role as pope as twofold: to reaffirm the centralized control of the Church which his predecessor had put in place, and to provide, on his own sole authority, fundamental guidance for the future of Catholic theology in a much-changed

---

1. When teaching in Rome I learned that the two Anglican ordinands who each year were members of the community at the English College were unofficially known as 'Null' and 'Void'.

European political climate. During a lengthy pontificate (1878-1903), he developed the centralizing authority of the revitalized papacy through a record 86 encyclical letters (more than all his predecessors together since encyclical-writing was devised as a pastoral tool by Benedict XIV in 1740). By such letters he promoted radical changes in Catholic attitudes in three crucial areas: in the teaching of philosophy, in the study of scripture and – most substantially innovative – in what came to be referred to as the Church's social teaching.

So wide-ranging a programme imposed from the top on Catholic intellectual life had virtually no precedent. Changes of analogous magnitude had normally been decreed by Councils (most obviously Nicaea, Chalcedon, Lateran IV, Trent and finally Vatican I), usually after decades, even centuries, of debate, the papal voice being added as the final seal on these age-old processes of theological discernment. At Nicaea and Chalcedon, however, perhaps the most important Councils of them all, the pope had not been present, being represented only by legates.

With Leo XIII things were very different; we may therefore reasonably wonder whether this was merely the effect of an unusually intelligent, competent and authoritarian pope or whether it should also be recognized as the first fruit of a new mentality in the Church which his predecessor had generated, wittingly or unwittingly, in virtue of his 'infallible' prestige. From the point of view of our primary concerns in the present book, what is immediately at stake is less whether the actions of Leo (or his immediate successors) were desirable or undesirable, genuinely 'Catholic' or not (though few would want to deny their genuine Catholicity), but to what extent the widespread welcome accorded them depended on the revised prestige of the papal office and the corresponding decline in the influence of other bishops, as well as generally of independent-minded theologians and philosophers.

Whether Leo's 'top-down' approach was a product of his personality or in part at least an effect of the new 'infallible' status of the papacy can only be established with any degree of certainty if we look both at his own actions and also, in due course, at those of his successors. In trying to answer the question thus identified about the nature of the new papacy, I shall therefore consider especially (but not exclusively) three of Leo's encyclicals: *Aeterni Patris* (1880),[2] *Rerum Novarum* (1891) and *Providentissimus Deus* (1893).

---

2. For details of the neo-Thomist revival begun under Leo XIII see R. Aubert, 'Aspects divers du néo-thomisme sous le pontificat de Léon XIII', in G. Rossini (ed.), *Aspetti della cultura cattolica nell'età di Leone XIII* (Rome:

Predictably, the ever-present Jesuit Kleutgen was the principal drafter of *Aeterni Patris*, Leo's prescription for the revival of Catholic philosophy through the study of St Thomas – and it was Kleutgen's understanding of Thomism which Leo set out to replicate throughout the Catholic world. For in 1880 there was as yet little thought given to the historical aspects of the thought of Thomas Aquinas. Although Kleutgen and others recognized that it was not to be taught as the Kantian Thomism of Rosmini, they normally identified it with the epistemological Thomism of Suarez; yet late medieval and early modern Thomisms, including that of Suarez, were often far from the Thomism of Thomas himself.

The substitution of one form of 'epistemological' Thomism for another did little to indicate to the non-Catholic world that Catholic thinkers had anything very different to offer. Thomism smartened up with Descartes or Kant might seem to offer a rather ineffective challenge to *bona fide* versions of Descartes and Kant – and although Kleutgen, as we have seen, had identified a 'break' in Western philosophy at some point after Aquinas, he had got the dates wrong: precursors of the break were already to hand with Scotus and Ockham, while the neo-scholasticism of Suarez and his followers was in many respects already on the 'wrong' side of the philosophical divide. To substitute Suarez (for all his Thomistic virtues in some areas) for Kant was to fail to recognize the real nature of the crisis in Catholic thought.[3] Still, Kleutgen's Thomism was presumably what Leo wanted – and what he wanted he got. Yet when we examine his social thinking, especially where it related to rights and rights claims, we shall see that Catholic thinkers had still not recognized the extent of the 'break' in thought which had arrived in spades not only with the epistemology of the Jesuit Suarez and with

---

Gregorianum, 1961) 133-227; V.B. Brezik (ed.), *One Hundred Years of Thomism: Aeterni Patris and Afterwards* (Houston, TX: Center for Thomistic Studies, 1981); F. Kerr, *After Aquinas: Versions of Thomism* (Oxford: Blackwell, 2002).

3. Although during the twentieth century the historical work of Gilson and others eventually helped recover something nearer to the genuine thought of Aquinas (while also encouraging those Thomists 'of strict observance' who thought that Aquinas had virtually finished the job), the basic error (to a degree recognized by Kleutgen) that there could be a genuine reconciliation between the thought of Aquinas and that of the early modern, Enlightenment and post-Enlightenment ages survived into the twentieth century and beyond, not least in the 'New Natural Law' theory of Germain Grisez, John Finnis and others, whose presupposition was that we must start by accepting much – too much – from Hume and Kant.

Descartes, pupil of the Jesuits at La Flèche, but in the growing tendency to see the heart of moral philosophy not in responsibility and virtue but in claims to an indeterminate number of rights.

In *Aeterni Patris* there is no discussion of what Thomism is – and apart from Thomas himself the only Thomist mentioned in the encyclical is Cajetan – though there is a strong claim that Thomism is a vastly improved summation of an intellectual tradition going back to Plato and Aristotle and Christianized in patristic times, especially by Augustine. The corollary of that implication, however, seems to be that little further philosophical work is necessary and that a Thomism of strict observance is required – which would surely misrepresent the attitude of Thomas himself. Yet Leo's authority was sufficient both to confirm an emphasis on a Thomism which had been building up steam for several decades, and to encourage a lack of interest in other Christian modes of thinking, even apparently that of Augustine, despite Augustine's immense influence on the mind of Thomas. That was to be grist to the mill of anti-Thomists of the twentieth century – mindless or other – and not least of those who wanted to spice up abstract metaphysics with historical specifics. Nor did Leo make clear why Aristotle, the other major influence on Aquinas, was recognized by Aquinas as of such importance, let alone reflect on whether Aquinas had entirely reconciled the Augustinian and Aristotelian aspects of his own thought.

That Leo assumed Thomism to be a closed system needing little further development in light of subsequent philosophy reveals a failure to recognize the importance of those aspects of Christian thought which Thomas undervalued or neglected, not least – and for example – in 'anthropology', for whereas Thomas substantially improved on Augustine's account of the soul–body relationship he concentrated on what men should be, while Augustine's peculiar strength lies in his perceptive comments on what they (and the societies in which they live) actually are.

Nor does Leo suggest the need to understand the reasons why non-Catholics found any form of Thomism inadequate; which would contribute to the comparative isolation of Catholic thinkers from most other philosophical traditions in Europe and elsewhere in the decades which followed. (I once heard a biographer of Gilson – one of the most influential of the more historically minded interpreters of Aquinas – in reply to an enquiry as to whether Gilson entered into 'dialogue' with Sartre and other French existentialists, say that he would not have wanted to be in the same room with them.) Overall, then, Leo did little to discourage a 'manualist' version of Thomism which (in the spirit rather of Suarez than of Aquinas himself) saw Aquinas's work as reduceable to a set of propositions more suited to rote-learning than to thinking.

Aeterni Patris was composed at a very early stage of Leo's pontificate – well before his recognition of the need to analyse and refute the faulty intellectual roots apparent in the political views of 'socialists' (i.e. Marxists), anarchists and liberals in *Rerum Novarum* (1891). Perhaps he had not yet realized how much the world had changed, for when he later reviewed the first 25 years of his pontificate in the Apostolic Letter *Annum Ingressi* (1902), he had learned better. That said, in *Rerum Novarum* he had already castigated the attempts of such 'socialists', anarchists and liberals to construct some radical Utopia in which problems of the relationship between capital and labour, bosses and workers, rich and poor, would disappear, finding disastrous threats to the common good in both the 'class-struggle' of the socialists and the greedy excesses of the capitalists: both in their different ways drawing unjust conclusions about the legitimate right to the ownership of property.

There is no question but that *Rerum Novarum* represents a major development of Catholic thought and a significantly new set of concerns, serving in part to bolster Leo's more wide-ranging ambition to replace the cruder authority of an Italian prince – now lost forever (though Leo himself was still unprepared to accept it) with the amalgamation of the papal states into the kingdom of Italy – with the moral authority of a universal pastor. To achieve that, of course, popes might seem to need to retain not only the moral high ground, which was not always to prove easy, but their authority as the unchallenged spokesmen of the Catholic Church on virtually any topic: the latter would provide an opportunity for an exaggerated 'omniscience' during the latter, more rambling years of Pius XII.

Nevertheless, in charting a new course on 'social' issues, Leo was doing more than expanding Church practice; he was recognizing that any pope who castigated individuals but neglected the corrupt institutions which nourished them was out of touch with modern reality (if not with reality in general). Indeed his new approach marked a major break not only with earlier Church practice but with a habit of thinking deeply rooted in Classical antiquity where what was primarily of concern was to praise the virtuous individual while condemning his vicious counterpart – and assuming that such social institutions as slavery or the subordination of women were a permanent feature of the human condition; they might be ameliorated but not abolished.

Such neglect of systemic injustice (of what John Paul was later to dub 'structures of sin') and attention to the virtues and vices only of individuals probably explains in part the slowness of popes and

Churchmen in general in – for example – condemning slavery and slave-trading as an institution rather than only condemning the normally brutal habits of many slave-owners. From time to time, however, the coming breakthrough to concern with 'structures of sin' can be seen to be in embryonic preparation: thus Eugenius IV in 1435 condemned slave-owning in the Canaries, at least implying that possessing slaves is always wrong: a conclusion further approached by Paul III in *Sublimis Deus* (1537). In Leo's awareness of systemic injustice – especially in the increasingly industrialized West, where the loss to Christianity of the working classes already experienced by the Anglicans in the industrialized Britain of the late eighteenth century was now apparently affecting Catholics too – we must recognize not only novelty but wide acceptance and an effectiveness which only the top-down authority now at papal disposal could so quickly have achieved.

For almost single-handedly Leo had 'invented' a whole new dimension of applied moral concern as a regular feature of Catholic pastoral scrutiny. His success could only encourage those who recognized how much good a more autocratic and centralized governance of the Church – an infallible papacy – could bring about. A traditional (and aristocratic) paternalism had received a new lease on life. Indeed, however incomplete, Leo's frequent and innovative defence of rights – hitherto largely secularist territory (though secularists showed little awareness of how problematic their defence can be unless closely allied with Christian teaching about human dignity) – showcases his authority as universal pastor at its best.

In *Annum Ingressi* Leo returned in sadness to the details of the situation in that European world in which he saw the Church as primarily functioning. The trouble had begun, he argued, with the Reformation, in particular with the denial of the authority of the Supreme Pontiff and the consequent recourse in religion to private judgement. Interestingly, he has nothing to say about nineteenth-century *theological* objections to Roman teachings, though even with Luther these had preceded the rejection of the papacy itself, that being consequence rather than first cause of 'Protestant' concerns. Nevertheless, according to Leo, after the Reformation further disasters unrelated to papal primacy but potentially as dire and threatening as the views of earlier Protestants had overtaken the Church: criticism of the authority of scripture, indeed of revelation in general, the substitution of a 'liberty' seen as licence for social order and rank: in brief a numbing scepticism and atheism.

Misguidedly, Leo at this point went on to conclude (echoing the increasing anxiety of his predecessors since before the French Revolution of 1789) it to be all the fault of the Freemasons; the 'all' apparently including the Revolution itself, and certainly the rise of 'Caesarism', the pretensions of overweening national civil authorities, even communism. Such simplistic explanation of a complex history (still widely peddled especially in Italy and the United States) indicates both that the new papal mentality was strictly 'Roman' and that it was still unfitted for substantial reflection on the *sources* of those problems of the age, whether churchly or more widely social and political, which Leo had so clearly recognized.

Nowhere is that recognition more apparent than in the 'social' encyclical *Rerum Novarum* (1891). For the first time in history a pope published a document covering the whole range of human social endeavour, pointing out human aspirations and human failings. The novelty of Leo's approach was recognized by his papal successors: by Pius XI in *Quadragesimo Anno* (celebrating the fortieth anniversary of Leo's document in 1931); by John XXIII in *Mater et Magistra* in 1961 and *Pacem in Terris* in 1963; by Paul VI in *Populorum Progressio* in 1967; by John Paul II in *Centesimus Annus* in 1991. These texts, founded on Leo's document, dominate Catholic Social Doctrine as summarized in the *Compendium of the Social Doctrine of the Church* offered to John Paul II in 2004. Yet we should notice that in that whole collection, among cited doctors of the Church, Aquinas alone gets significant attention with 26 quotations, Augustine manages a mere brace and no other Doctor or Father of the Church more than one. That would presumably have been to Leo's mind. As would the frequent reference to specifically papal documents.

Leo's third major area of pastoral concern was biblical interpretation. The historical-critical method had long become standard among many Protestant Biblicists and – if harnessed to various ideological assumptions – had already shown itself capable of eviscerating Christianity. Yet there is no reason why the method should produce this effect if its aim is simply to make use of historical, literary and archaeological data to increase our understanding of biblical times: as such it does not commit us to any particular interpretation of facts that we may rediscover in a fuller historical context.

Yet if the historical-critical method is combined with (for example) the assumption (much encouraged by the Scottish philosopher David Hume) that because miracles cannot happen they don't happen, the New Testament cannot be read in a recognizably Catholic manner, for not only the miracles of Jesus but his Resurrection itself could not have occurred, regardless of what the Gospel writers may have claimed. That sets the biblical exegete the task of explaining how the Gospels claim impossibilities, leaving him with the unedifying conclusion either that the apostles – hysterically or fraudulently – invented the whole story or that originally there was a simpler and less miraculous version in circulation which, in the process of gradually assimilating itself to ever-accruing 'folk-memories', became embellished by miracles and other superstitious material.

The unending debate about the so-called Synoptic Problem provides a good example of what is at stake, the problem which developed in the nineteenth century being the relationships between the three 'Synoptic' Gospels (Mark, Matthew, Luke). We need to understand that relationship, so it is argued, since the three texts paint very different versions of Jesus' life and actions. A particularly insidious claim is that Mark, decked out with very few miracles and no post-Resurrection appearances, must be the earliest (and therefore truest) account of Jesus' life, Matthew and Luke being later constructions, embellished by urban-myths and wishful thinking in the gradually expanding Christian community. Of course, even if Mark's gospel is the earliest – which is far from certain – it does not follow that it is the most accurate. Indeed, already in Leo's time other readings of the chronology and other explanations of Gospel variations had been in circulation for centuries and should never have been so easily rejected by Catholics following in the wake of 'enlightened' Protestant exegesis: thus Augustine thought that, far from being earliest, Mark was some sort of summary of Matthew and Luke.

As for miracles, and to take an example, by abuse of the historical-critical method one can argue that if Jesus really did predict the destruction of the Temple, it was merely a guess which happened to turn out correctly; alternatively, since he 'could not' have known what would happen, it is likely that accounts of his prediction were added to the Gospels after the Temple had been destroyed. And so on! It is clear that Leo was right to try to bring a degree of common sense into the jungle of contemporary biblical criticism, while recognizing that the new 'historicism' had real merits.

Unnecessary and often implausible attitudes to the study of scripture – revealing a reasonable historical-critical technique perverted by ideological assumptions which make it useful as a destructive tool rather than a way of deepening our understanding of the world of the New – indeed also of the Old – Testament – had long since underpinned the revised versions of the life of Jesus proposed by such as the Protestant David Strauss in his *Life of Jesus Christ Critically Examined* in 1835. It took longer for them to become dominant in Catholic circles; however, and not least with the founding of the Ecole Biblique in Jerusalem by Marie-Joseph Lagrange OP, things began to change and Leo to worry.

In fact Lagrange himself had no time for the efforts of the 'modernist', Alfred Loisy (pupil of the early Church historian Louis Duchesne at the Institut Catholique in Paris). Loisy himself only published *L'Evangile et l'Eglise* in 1903, so helping to fuel the hostility of Leo's successor. In the first instance it was a reply to the biblicism of the Protestant Adolf von Harnack, but with a more wide-ranging intent. By then Loisy's views were well known, widely diffused and possessed of a contemporary flavour. As he himself was later – and informatively – to explain,[4] his aim was via biblical investigation to show the errors of *Thomistic theology* and the falsity of the Church's claim to the objective truth of its dogmas: indeed to rewrite the whole schema of Catholicism itself, not least its hierarchical structure. Thus we see that Leo's concern about biblical studies is not in fact separate from his insistence on the necessity of Thomism.

Long before *L'Evangile et l'Eglise* appeared in print, Loisy had been fired (in 1893) from his post at the Institut Catholique and the very next day after the firing – in his encyclical *Providentissimus Deus* – Leo attempted by decree to delete all 'Protestantizing' biblical studies from Catholic theology, urging then – as he put it later in the Apostolic Letter *Vigiliantiae Studiique* of 1902,[5] by which he founded the Pontifical Biblical Commission (aiming not least to keep a wary eye on Lagrange in Jerusalem) – that 'God has not delivered the scriptures to the private judgment of the learned, but has confided the interpretation of them to the magisterium of the Church'. This claim blurred the distinction between those of the 'learned' who used and those who abused the historical-critical method. Indeed while thinking his rulings would put an end to any Protestantizing use of the techniques of scriptural exegesis, Leo in effect canonized for a while the alternative (and older) Protestant belief in absolute scriptural inerrancy: not that there was any future in that.

Nevertheless, Leo's solution to the 'biblical problem' could be imposed for a time, and his teaching, in stronger form, was to be rigorously enforced as far as possible by his immediate successor. Ultimately, so crudely unnuanced a policy was doomed to failure: there was no way in which new information about the contexts of the Old and New Testaments, arising from investigations with no blatant ideological presuppositions,

---

4. Especially in *My Duel with the Vatican*: English version by Richard Boynton (New York: E.P. Dutton, 1924).

could forever be kept away from Catholic students of the Bible. As for Lagrange, though suspect in his own order, he managed to avoid condemnation: indication that recourse to the historical-critical method would be beyond the power even of a pope to forbid or even (sadly) to limit to non-ideological practitioners.

*   *   *

Leo XIII was the first pope to put Pius IX's vision of a commanding moral and spiritual papacy to the test: to be, in effect, the 'tradition' in an expansive version. The results of his wide-ranging activities are generally thought to have been beneficial both to the Church and to the society around it, though, as we have seen, on biblical studies they could not endure. Moreover, it is clear that the success of his reforming programme – indeed the generally favorable reception of much of its originality – depended at least as much on his authority as Roman pontiff as on the pertinence of his claims. Leo's pontificate would supply the paradigm for the possibilities of the new 'infallible' papacy at its best.

Chapter 4

Saint Pius X and the Modernist Dragon

If everyone does what they are told, no one will get excommunicated.

A.R.

On the death of Leo XIII in 1903, Giuseppe Sarto was elected as his successor on the fifth ballot, and after the likely election of Cardinal Rampolla, Leo's Secretary of State, was vetoed by the Cardinal Archbishop of Krakow on the instructions of Franz-Josef, Austro-Hungarian Emperor: the last time such a veto was to be exercised by a Catholic ruler. Pius X would be noted for his practice of poverty and his lowering of the age of First Communion, but above all for his determined resistance to what in his encyclical *Pascendi* (1907) he denounced as 'modernism': a clear indication that the autocratic manner of the new papacy of Pius IX and Leo XIII was to continue, with words soon followed by actions which some thought as intended less to convert than to terrorize the pope's mainly clerical opponents.

The origins of 'modernism', dubbed 'the combination of all the heresies', lay with many of the beliefs Pius IX had hoped to annihilate in his *Syllabus of Errors*, but by Pius X's time 'heresy' had taken on a new and more radical form in the writings especially of Loisy and had been provided with a wider theological framework by the Jesuit George Tyrell (1861-1909). The movement was no planned opposition to traditional beliefs but a set of theses variously held by individuals who maintained some kind of communication with one another. Its essence was that all Catholic truth is subjective, based not on tradition or history but on religious experience, reminding us of the 'experiential' theories of religion long associated in the Protestant world with Friedrich Schleiermacher. As Ernesto Buonaiuti – though as yet anonymously – put it in *Programme of the Modernists* (1907), the significance of dogma is not that it is objectively true but that it arouses the appropriately subjective 'religious feelings' in the human psyche.

As Pius understood it – rightly – the strength of the new movement, as well as its novelty, lay in the approach to scripture advocated by Loisy himself and by his disciples. Leo XIII, as we have seen, had tried to head off problems in biblical interpretation deriving from the abuse (and even the use) of the 'historical-critical' method and their wider theological consequences, but scriptural 'modernism' was now to receive new impetus from outside biblical studies. Maurice Blondel's influential *L'action* (1893) strengthened the hands of the modernists by affirming the primacy of action understood with little attention to any transcendent foundational backdrop: dogmatic 'truths' are (again) to be measured not in terms of objective reality but of the immediate response they arouse in the human heart, and the consequent activity of individual believers. This might look like a move towards 'spirituality' without too much concern for scripture or tradition.

Papal reaction to all this was fast and furious. The Holy Office, endorsed by Pius, struck back hard: its decree *Lamentabili* (1903) condemned some 50 'false' claims associated with 'experiential' theology, together with any application of the historical-critical approach to the Bible and tradition. Pius had not yet finished: in the encyclical *Pascendi* (1907) he unveiled a great raft of errors, whether philosophical, theological, historical – even political insofar as they called for the separation of Church and State or any democratization of ecclesiastical practice: these variegated iniquities were now grouped together under the broad heading of 'modernism'.

In many ways Pius's philosophical analysis was accurate, not least in his castigation of those who, developing the ideas of Blondel, substituted human experience for objective belief as the essential core of the Catholic faith. According to Pius, the modernist starts with his religious sentiment, which indicates its vital immanence in his heart: that is, buried in his subconscious self. 'Modernism', as he identified it, is thus a product of nineteenth-century German historicism (often applied ideologically to justify pre-assumed conclusions) plus a new variant of the idealism which had dominated German philosophy since Fichte and Hegel.

Though successful in the short run, Pius failed to destroy the opposition. For developed from the earlier hyper-Kantian 'transcendental

Thomism' of Rousselot and Maréchal, a more moderate version of subjective idealism (with loss of the genuinely 'transcendent') lurks beneath the theories of latter-day Thomist 'transcendentalists', not least Heidegger's Jesuit pupil Karl Rahner, who, hoping to evade the conclusions of his teacher, introduced what he paradoxically dubbed an 'supernatural existential'.[1] Indeed most recent German theologians have been unable to shake off some variety of subjectivism – and German theologians, overemphasizing the necessity of finding common ground with Lutherans, are still (just as in the nineteenth-century) over-represented and overvalued in the theological guild. We shall return to the 'Lutheran problem' later in this study, though the problems of religion as free-floating spirituality go far beyond those of (mere) ecumenism.

Rejecting the 'poisonous' effects of 'modernist' errors, Pius determined that the primary task of the corrected theologian, far from seeking further to understand the workings of God and his relation to humanity – that being already known to the Church – is to explain to the sceptical that Church tradition, viewed as a complete and virtually non-reformable whole, cannot be in conflict with legitimate developments in scientific knowledge. However, the political setting for this corrective project (expressed, as Pius maintained, necessarily in colourful language) assumed the continuation of Catholic states able and willing to enforce Church decrees: which world was already in its death throes in Pius's time and was finally to pass away after the First World War.

Nor did the pope grasp that an inward-looking and debased version of Thomism, however papally authorized, would be ineffective

---

1. Helpful comment on the Jesuit attraction (not only in Germany) to such subjectivism is to be found in S.M. Fields, 'The Reception of Aquinas in Twentieth-Century Transcendental Thomism', in M. Levering and M. Plested (eds), *The Oxford Handbook of the Reception of Aquinas* (Oxford: Oxford University Press, 2021), pp. 408-22. The basically un-Catholic nature of Rahner's thought is revealed by his preference for Heideggerian 'authenticity' (i.e. consideration of what we really are as determined by introspection, self-acceptance and adaption to our immediate circumstances) over the objective truth that our existence, however we are 'thrown into' being, depends on God. Rahner would have been better guided by Augustine's understanding of individual uniqueness among human beings while all remain 'existentially' in the same divine boat than by trying to Christianize Heidegger's account of authenticity which entails the radically un-Christian assumption that authenticity is recognizable when we accept the fact of our extinction. Facing the reality of death is one thing, giving a Christian account of its implications quite another.

in demolishing – let alone replacing – the immanentism which he so vigorously (and often accurately) denounced. Nor perhaps that his attitude – as theologians far from 'modernism' soon came to point out – suggested that Christian faith (and especially Christian morals) consists in little more than obedience to the pope as authorizer (rather than privileged identifier) of 'Thomistic' rules, now to be publicized in burgeoning numbers of manuals. Faith, far from being merely 'experiential' – as to a degree it must be – is to be accepted 'extrinsically' as a collection of injunctions and rejections, and with the premise that the incomplete (indeed – as was to turn out – often misrepresented) thought of Aquinas should form the Church's rule-book.

In brief, Pius knew what he hated, and though he thought (mistakenly) that he had adequate intellectual remedies, he also concluded that sticks as well as carrots were needed if the situation was to be brought under his control. Despite his belief that he had drained the intellectual morass, he was disposed to indulge that absolute spiritual power of suppression which he took to have been confirmed by the Vatican Council. Pressure was to be applied in the first instance to ensure the total control of all seminaries by 'Thomism', however inadequately (as it turned out) presented, and priests must above all be obedient.

Towards the end of his pontificate, Pius published *Doctoris Angelici* (1914); this not only reinforced his insistence in *Pascendi* that the basis of all seminary study should be especially (*praecipue*) the writings of Aquinas, but toughened the language of command: 'We wish, we order, we prescribe', he wrote, that Aquinas's *Summa Theologiae* should become the textbook for all theological teaching; this, of course, meant that it would be indeed taught in 'potted' manualist versions, ensuring that the brand of Thomism then in favour would be served up unnuanced. Deploying the same prejudice, Pius's successor, Benedict XV, affirmed in Canon 1366/2 of the revised Code of Canon Law that Aquinas's writings (as then understood) were to be the foundation of all philosophical and theological instruction in seminaries.

Pius spiced his philosophical and cultural analysis and his direction of the methods required for the teaching of theology with severe action against obstinate individuals, having determined rougher methods than the author of the *Syllabus of Errors* had thought necessary to be now essential – and on a wide scale. Tyrell was excommunicated in 1907, as in the same year were all those involved in the publication of the then still anonymous *Programme of Modernism*; Loisy was out in 1908 (pointedly excommunicated on what was then the feast-day of Aquinas). It being as yet unclear that Buonaiuti had written the larger part of the

Programme, his excommunication had to wait till 1925. His informative autobiography, *Pellegrino in Roma,* an invaluable commentary on the age, set out his version of the story in 1945.

In a final attempt to compel conformity, on 1 September 1910, by the *motu proprio Sacrorum Antistitum,* Pius imposed an anti-modernist oath on all clergy and Catholic educators; this would only be abolished by Paul VI in 1966, though by then it had become largely a dead letter. Acceptance of the commitments prescribed by the oath was to be 'encouraged' by a more sinister instrument, unofficial and 'lay', but with at least tacit papal approval. For in 1909 Umberto Benigni had established the *Sodalitium Pianum* to keep an eye on the thoughts and expressions of presumed dissidents; in particular, seminary professors' lectures were to be monitored, offenders being delated to the appropriate disciplinary authorities: paternalism was beginning to look more like dictatorship, authoritarianism more like totalitarianism. Nevertheless, Pius believed that his teachings were entirely compatible with longstanding tradition, as was his authority to enforce them: an authority so recently confirmed at Vatican I.

Pius's ultimate inability to suppress his 'modernist' adversaries (and anyone even suspected of modernism) was not only the result of his fail-ure to offer a more satisfying intellectual response to the philosophical and theological weaknesses he so ably described, if in somewhat uncouth terms, in *Pascendi,* but also of failing to recognize that for all the absolute power he had been given to suppress and to punish on his own sole authority, the Church was now living in a world which he could not keep out of sight and hearing by the banning of books, purging of dissidents and encouragement of delations; in brief, that his absolute power could not keep the Church isolated from and inoculated against outside influences – or eventually from a laity seemingly harder to control. For long too his successors persisted in that mistaken and ultimately futile belief, seemingly longing for a more deliberately clerical church. Yet mere rejection of non-Catholic thinking plus the exercise of papal power would prove no substitute for careful and deliberative setting forth of the objective truths of Catholic Christianity in their proper historical contexts.

What suppression could do, of course, was to encourage delusions of all-powerful authority in the pope himself and an increasing servility – already evident at Vatican 1 – among his fellow bishops, as also among large sections of the lower clergy and laity – until, that is, Vatican II (against papal wishes, and despite papal 'manipulation') broke the spell and was claimed to demand a revised approach to the by now endemic question of the relationship between conscience and authority. Indeed, the ultimate effect of the spell-breaking, as we shall see, was to compel a pope eventually to conclude he must choose between traditional teaching and papal control: a choice not envisioned by Pius X.

Politics and repression apart, Pius correctly discerned that at the heart of 'modernism' lay a denial of truth as (in Aristotelian language) an identity of the human mind with the 'form' of objective reality, in favour of regarding it as an identification of the mind with the spirit of the age. That denial would persist through the rest of the century in the papacies of Pius XI and Pius XII – who held to the old ways and compelled the church to follow suit – and into the Second Vatican Council where what its opponents called 'neo-modernism' showed up as influencing the thought of those who wanted radical change – though most 'progressives' still hung on to at least a degree of dogmatic objectivity even in the now officially acceptable 'pastoral' version of theology.

For the next Council, with, as we shall see, papal encouragement, sought to add a pastoral dimension to Catholic thinking without abolishing older objective certainties. These were to continue (at least for a while) to run in parallel with a pastoralism always tempted to a view of truth as 'orthopraxy' rather than orthodoxy. And so with our contemporary age we would reach a pope who wants a post-modern account of truth – and the long habit of obedience rather than critical thought constrains many to follow him: again finding it simplest just to obey orders.

The latter conclusion Pius X would have approved, while anathematizing the revised account of veracity and the contempt for tradition increasingly in circulation. But Pius X, now dead and canonized, can, it seems, be safely ignored, as can certain of his successors.

Chapter 5

The 1930s: Fascists, Nazis, 'New Theologians', Condoms

Si jeunesse savait, si vieillesse pouvait.

Anon.

How many divisions has the pope?

Joseph Stalin

On the death of Pius X in 1914 Giacomo della Chiesa, archbishop of Bologna, succeeded as Benedict XV. His main preoccupation was with attempting to save Europe from the catastrophe of the First World War and securing a place as pastoral adviser to the victors when the war concluded four years later. In both these projects he was unsuccessful, but he left an important and compromising political legacy: that of maintaining absolute impartiality between the warring nations. The papacy, as judged fitting for a superhuman institution, was to remain above the fray, attempting only to end the slaughter and help those whose lives were ruined – often by being left stateless – by the collapse of empires around them. As for more strictly ecclesiastical matters, Benedict in the main continued the policies of his predecessors, keeping the lid on dissent.

Benedict also arranged for the Code of Canon Law to enshrine his predecessor's ruling that Thomism be the near-exclusive guide in Catholic education whether in seminaries or papal universities and colleges. Importantly, if disingenuously, he also made sure that the new Code noted that 'bishops are appointed by the pope'; this, fitting appropriately into a Code which replaced the *Corpus iuris canonici*, could be viewed as 'the culmination of a century of ultramontane centralization'.[1] For although papal appointment of bishops was indeed the situation which pertained in 1917, only a hundred years earlier, of the 650 bishops in Europe, less than 100 had been papal appointees.[2] Indeed since the earliest days of the Church, either local communities or powerful secular kings and lords had appointed most of them.

These two important matters having been disposed of (at least for the time being) Benedict's death in 1922 left one thing clear to those who thought seriously about the state of the Catholic world: papal power over academic curricula in Church institutions on the one hand, and the newly established papal control of the appointment of bishops on the other, had become the building blocks required to re-enforce the subordination of the episcopacy to the pope as established at Vatican I. This subordination is still on display today in the 'tradition' of *ad limina* episcopal visits to Rome, where, in what can be an humiliating manner, the past performance of every bishop is reviewed and his future direction firmly indicated. Although this may elicit only nominal assent, for the notorious words of an ancient tragedian – 'my tongue has sworn, my heart remains unsworn' – might be applied to an institutional structure likely to promote a habit of bad faith in the hierarchy, at least among its careerists. As bad faith can easily turn into self-deception, and not merely the deception of others, so self-deception will encourage 'cover-ups', where found necessary to protect oneself and one's institutional world.

*   *   *

By the time Benedict's successor, Achille Ratti, had been elected as Pius XI, the world was growing used to the disappearance of old monarchies and empires swept away by war and revolution; meanwhile Fascists in Italy and Nazis in Germany were setting out to generate the new politics in Europe which would lead to a second round of warfare: the Second World War. Hence Pius found himself confronted politically by two mortal enemies (plus Mussolini): for the Nazis in Germany were soon to rival the threat to humanity he had already identified in the newly formed Soviet Union. Ratti's predecessors had lambasted Communism

---

1. So Printy, *Enlightenment*, p. 31.
2. For summary details on the history of episcopal appointments over time see E. Duffy, *The Papacy: Myth and Reality*, The Michael Richards Memorial Lecture (London: Catholics for a Changing Church, 1997), pp. 7-10.

for the best part of a century and he shared their antipathy, apparently in the early years of his pontificate thinking the Nazis the lesser immediate evil.

This judgement was encouraged by Pietro Gasparri, the Secretary of State he inherited from Benedict XV and whom for a while he retained in office. Gasparri also remained a determined advocate of Benedict's view that, whatever the rights and wrongs of the geopolitical struggles in Europe, the pope, as spiritual father of the whole of humanity, must retain an absolute impartiality in the hope and expectation that he be asked to arbitrate between the contending parties. Yet, and even before the same policy was applied to the Nazis, 'absolute impartiality' sounded to many like appeasement proceeding from moral cowardice. As the now-excommunicated Loisy was to put it, 'No one has the right to be neutral in moral questions.' Nevertheless, for Benedict (and later for Pius XII) it enabled the pope both to avoid the dangers inherent in condemning atrocities and to remain in a position to give aid and comfort to at least some of the actual victims of the violence of war or of domestic tyranny.[3] In the earlier part of the twentieth century it could provide moral consolation – and some hope of moral influence – to offset the still lamented loss of the papal states.

In the early years of Pius XI 'impartiality' was also encouraged by the German-loving Eugenio Pacelli (later Pius XII) who had been sent to Bavaria by Benedict as nuncio in 1917 (before long he was to be accredited to Prussia). In 1930 he succeeded Gasparri – sacked because he resisted Pius's growing concern about Hitler – as Secretary of State: an apparently remarkable decision since Pacelli was protégé of Gasparri and committed to a similar 'impartiality'. Perhaps Pius thought that,

---

3. The policy of impartiality had its origins in the aftermath of Napoleon (or even earlier). Already in 1821 Cardinal Consalvi was to observe that 'because of his position as the visible head of the Church, and an essentially peaceful sovereign [the pope] will continue to maintain ... a perfect neutrality toward all nations'. Leo XIII too had hoped to use impartiality to restore a top-table place for the pope as moral counsellor, replacing the position popes had earlier enjoyed as sovereigns when they still ruled the papal states. For discussion of the origins of 'absolute impartiality' see C.R. Gallagher, 'The Perils of Perception: British Catholics and Papal Neutrality, 1914-1923', in J. Corkery and T. Worcester (eds), *The Papacy since 1850* (Cambridge: Cambridge University Press, 2010), pp. 162-81, esp. 165-74. For Leo XIII see V. Viaene (ed.), *The Papacy and the New World Order; Vatican Diplomacy, Catholic Opinion and International Politics at the time of Leo XIII* (Leuven: Leuven University Press, 2005), p. 14.

careerist as he was, Pacelli would obey orders – a judgement which to an extent proved correct. Perhaps too it was intended as a tactical concession to the 'impartiality' viewed as desirable in the Roman Curia. For Pacelli was far from alone as an 'impartialist' at court; Pietro Tacchi-Venturi SJ, Pius's principal liaison officer with Mussolini, was significantly sympathetic to Fascism, which may have helped when he became the principal negotiator of the Concordat with Italy whereby Vatican City was established as an internationally recognized entity, thus ending the self-identification of the popes as 'prisoners in the Vatican' which had obtained since the time of Pius IX.

The 'impartialist' policy that Pius inherited from his predecessor and his predecessor's Secretary of State implied not only a search for peaceful solutions to conflicts in Europe but strong support for the newly founded League of Nations and hence an opportunity to denounce what might be seen as abuses or atrocities (whether perpetrated by the political left, right or centre); this without naming the perpetrators, meaning the Hitlers and Stalins. The policy was to talk morality while remaining above politics, and a positive aspect of such 'morality' was to be the signing of Concordats, first with Mussolini's Italy, in September 1933 with Hitler's Germany, then with a number of South American dictatorships. For a while the German and Italian dictators were happy enough with this approach, though Pius himself became increasingly uneasy. By 1930 he had sacked Gasparri (though officially Gasparri had 'retired' owing to age). As for Pacelli, he saw himself as primarily the protector of Concordats, as providing at least a hope of protection for Catholic communities, especially those in his beloved Germany, threatened as they were with Nazi reprisals against any hostile declarations from Rome.

Pius himself gradually recognized the impending disaster. Though he had once thought of Mussolini as the man for our times, in 1931 – with the encyclical *Non abbiamo bisogno* – he condemned the dictator's increasingly totalitarian attitude to education and the social upbringing of Italian youth that threatened the Church's educational monopoly. Nor, as soon became clear, had Hitler any intention of keeping his pledge to protect Catholic interests in Germany. By the Concordat he had already obtained a free hand at the strictly political level, leading to the destruction of Germany's centre party and the Catholic trade unions, as to the murder of various Catholic politicians. Hence Pius's anxiety, indeed anger, grew, despite 'impartialist' pressure from Pacelli who would urge that Nazism would not last long – this Gasparri had also believed – and in the meantime could be used to eliminate the Bolsheviks: conclusions which many outside the Church were also happy to draw.

However, as things got worse, and German anti-Semitism and other forms of racism began to spill over into Italy – in a flood by 1938 – Pius determined to speak out. In 1935 he had forbidden Catholics from having anything to do with Charles Maurras's Action Française, an organization headed by an atheist but popular with 'intégriste' Catholics in France. On 14 March 1937, he published in German the encyclical *Mit Brennender Sorge*, roundly denouncing all forms of racism and worship of the state. That document had been in part composed by the pliant Pacelli and was to be read from every pulpit in Germany. But it was too late and was almost inevitably followed five days later by a second encyclical (*Divini Redemptoris*) in which – seemingly as a sop to the Curia – Pius renewed the old condemnations of Communist atheism.

Still Pius declined to abandon the battle with the Nazis, whose barbarism he by now hated unambiguously. Bypassing his own Secretary of State, he instructed three Jesuits, the principal being the American John La Farge, to draw up a further and more comprehensive attack on racism, paganism and other plainly Nazi characteristics – and especially on anti-Semitism – in a third encyclical to be entitled 'The Unity of the Human Race' (*Humani Generis Unitas*). But it was not to be. Delayed first by the Jesuit General Ledochowski, playing politics as was the Jesuit wont, and sharing Pacelli's anxieties as to the destruction Hitler might unleash on the Church in Germany, La Farge's document only reached the Vatican after Pius, now on his death-bed, demanded it be put in his hands immediately. When he died before seeing it, Pacelli and the 'impartialists' breathed a sigh of relief; for a time at least they were safe, though concerned who would be the next pope and what he would do with the intended encyclical.

*   *   *

Pius XI was a worried man, and his anxieties were not only political. It seems clear from the earlier actions of his pontificate that he aimed to combine the repression of dissent achieved by his immediate predecessors – he condemned Buonaiuti in 1925 – with an affirmation of many of the more innovative policies of Leo XIII. Papal authority was thus not to be limited to the renewed 'Tridentinism' of Pius X. However, he continued his predecessors' theological concern with scriptural interpretation where serious problems had already arisen among Protestants. Things seemed to be getting worse. Following on after the earlier magisterial and destructive authority of Adolf von Harnack (himself a target of Loisy, as we have noticed), the 1920s saw the arrival of 'form criticism'.

By form-critical techniques, especially those developed by Martin Dibelius in *Die Formgeschichte der Evangeliums* (1919), the new Biblicists attempted to determine the true sense of the Gospels by placing them within apparently recognizable forms (genres) of the literary world of the ancient Near East. Part of the difficulty of this (rarely recognized at the time) is that the literary forms of antiquity cannot easily be mapped onto the literary forms of modernity: which fact becomes especially clear if we ask in what sense the ancients at the turn of the eras could be said to write biographies, however many biographical features their texts exhibit.

Nor was the situation clarified by some basic hermeneutical claims of Dibelius himself, as also of Rudolf Bultmann who interpreted 'Love thy neighbour as thyself' as 'love your neighbour tomorrow as you love yourself today': a psychologically destructive notion in implying that to love others one need forfeit even that self-love intelligible as self-respect. Dibelius, for his part, believed that all ancient texts which have come down in stylized form (presumably to include all the speeches in Thucydides' history) are largely the reflections of the author rather than any serious record of events. Pericles will never have given that famous funeral oration at the beginning of the Peloponnesian War.

Yet for all his extended and often justified concern about the still unresolved problem of Biblicists, in philosophy at least Pius had no doubt that his immediate predecessors had got things right; his encyclical *Deus Scientiarum Dominus* (1931) is an unmitigated reaffirmation of the need for a virtually exclusively Thomistic theology. Nevertheless, new 'dissent' was bubbling up, not now in the crude rationalism and immanentism of the modernists, but among those concerned about ecumenism and the 'separated brethren' –predilection which had helped to ruin Döllinger. The 'dissidents', mostly Dominicans and (more surprisingly) Jesuits, had somewhat different immediate aims. The Dominicans were concerned in the first instance to rid Aquinas of 'neo-scholastic' accretions derived from Cajetan and Suarez. The Jesuits could be more radical in hoping to replace the 'medievalism', the deformed 'Augustinianism' and for some especially the 'Thomism' of theology (be it in better or worse versions), with renewed emphasis on the patristic age.

The new project, that is, was a 'return to the sources', less perhaps to the scriptures (since the scripture studies 'guild' was already recognized as pointing the Church to what Pius X had called immanentism – indeed to the denial of the most basic historical 'facts' on which Christianity depends) than to a cleaned up Aquinas and particularly to the Church

Fathers, especially the less 'juridical' Greeks. As for 'modernism', the 'dissidents' were generally inclined to see it as a mistaken but inevitable reaction against a régime of faith reduced to obedience and the rote-learning of a deformed Aquinas.

The new 'dissidents' declined the name 'new theologians' – popular-ized with hostile intent by Garrigou-Lagrange[4] – preferring to describe themselves as advocates of 'ressourcement'. They hoped to find in the early church an antidote to a poisoning of Catholic thought beginning with an over-systematized Augustine and continuing through a misread Aquinas, and taking advantage in the early modern age, so its critics thought, of the backing of Western states still usually prepared to acknowledge the supremacy of the pope even in 'worldly' matters. By then, as they saw it, theology had become ossified in the various forms of scholasticism and its accompaniments, that is in canon law and an 'unchanging' liturgy nailed down by the Council of Trent.

The 'new theologians' urged a return to the patristic sources, and generally (especially for the Jesuits) to the Greeks rather than the Latins: indeed it has sometimes seemed to the present writer that for some of those innovators who eventually were to influence the Second Vatican Council the master theologian of the patristic age was not Augustine but Origen – whose universalism might be ecumenically helpful and lead to a more fluid version of Catholic theology. In the longer run, resourcing the less juridical Greeks might also raise doubts about the pope's own juridical as distinct from merely patriarchal power. For the more circumspect, however, perhaps Athanasius, Gregory of Nyssa and Maximus Confessor might be safer bets than Origen, or so such as Jean Daniélou and Hans Urs von Balthasar seem to have concluded.

*   *   *

The two major centres of what came – despite the objections of its advo-cates – to be called the 'New Theology' were the Dominican monastery of Le Saulchoir at Tournai in Belgium (later moved to near Paris) and the Jesuit bases at Fourvière and the nearby university at Lyon. For the student of papal power in the Church the variegated fortunes of members of these two institutions will reveal much about how papal authority – its use and abuse, its favour and disfavour – made all the difference, both doctrinally and personally, in the twentieth-century Church. In the good old days of early Christianity Jerome had commented sardonically on

---

4. See R. Garrigou-Lagrange, 'La nouvelle théologie, où va-t-elle?', *Angelicum* 23 (1946), pp. 126-45.

the rise of Ambrose to the archbishopric of Milan: 'Yesterday the circus, today the altar'. In more recent times it might be, 'Yesterday the doghouse, today the cardinalate'[5] – depending on who is pope.

For many years the community at Le Saulchoir was dominated by Marie-Dominique Chenu OP, one-time pupil of the conservative Garrigou-Lagrange in Rome, but who, contrary to the views of his teacher and following the lead of Ambroise Gardeil, first rector of Le Saulchoir, took upon himself the mission – intelligible enough for a Dominican – to rid Thomism of various deformations deriving from Suarez and more generally to oppose its reduction to 'neo-scholasticism': rather the thought of St Thomas must be read in its time and place and with an eye on the biblical 'signs of the times', the phrase being now fashionably misinterpreted. Reason must not be set in opposition to faith – least of all in deploying the historical-critical method – but be seen not as generating an arid rationalism, rather as enabling an ongoing analysis of the working of the Spirit through time. Incorporating two earlier lesser publications, Chenu's *Une école de théologie: Le Saulchoir*, though at first circulating only in manuscript, may be regarded as the first blast of the new trumpet of a reform which might be characterized broadly as a call for theology to be more closely related to an active, Christ-centred faith, less seen as the acceptance of a mere set of propositions.

Though Chenu seemed to some close to the 'experientialism' of the modernists, his aim was to steer clear of the manualism which reduced Thomas's ideas to a set of such propositions and Catholic morality – indeed faith itself – to mere obedience and the avoidance of sins rather than the practice of virtues. He seems to have recognized that all

---

5. The bibliography on the 'new theology' is immense and ongoing. Among the more helpful introductions to the 'literature' are – apart from M.-D. Chenu, *Une école de théologie: Le Saulchoir*, drafted in 1937 and put on the Index in 1942 – F. Kerr, *Twentieth Century Catholic Theology* (Malden, MA: Blackwell, 2007); H. Boersma, *Nouvelle Théologie and Sacred Ontology* (Oxford: Oxford University Press, 2009); J. Mettepenningen, *Nouvelle Théologie: Inheritor of Modernism, Precursor of Vatican II* (London: T&T Clark, 2010); Janette Gray, *M.-D. Chenu and Le Saulchoir* (Oxford: Oxford University Press, 2011); G. Flynn and P.D. Murray (ed.), *Ressourcement: A Movement for Renewal in Twentieth-Century Catholic Theology* (New York: Oxford University Press, 2012); A. Nichols, *Yves Congar* (Wilton, CT: Morehouse-Barlow, 1989); E. Fouilloux and B. Hours, *Les Jesuites à Lyon, XVIème-XXème siècle* (Lyon: ENS, 2005); C. Potworowski, *Contemplation and Incarnation: The Theology of Marie-Dominique Chenu* (Montréal and Kingston: McGill-Queen's University Press, 2001).

theology, as all philosophy, must attempt – even *per impossibile* – the
avoiding of a reductionist account of human experience. Yet in seeing
Thomism in its thirteenth-century context, Chenu's readers might have
concluded that Thomism is not objectively true (so far as it goes and
always with reference to its foundation in a metaphysic) but simply a
product of the faith-experience of its age; hence needing to be radically
adapted to our own. Such would be the worry of Pius XI.

Rightly Chenu wanted to propose Thomism as a theology in progress, to argue that Aquinas was a stage on the road, or as he put it,
'The absolutization of St Thomas is a first class burial.'[6] That left the
problem of what kind of adaptation would keep anything of the original
objectivism of Aquinas intact, especially as Chenu the Teilhardian
optimist paid limited attention to original sin[7] – though an empirical
as well as a theological datum – and was one of those inclined to hope
that 'orthodoxy' could be defined in terms of 'orthopraxy', i.e. of the
experience of the faith of the Thomist in action from age to age.[8] Yet
though it might be well to emphasize the presence of the Spirit in
theological development, it must be equally important not to ignore the
human tendency – including the tendency of theologians – to pervert:
hence one man's lived experience of the faith might be another's heretical
immanentism.

'Discernment' was certainly required, but who is to do the discerning,
and on what principles? Ultimately it must be the pope, provided with
his near absolute authority by Vatican I, and whether ruling on his
sole initiative, or after serious consultation, if not with bishops, at least
with – one hoped – competent scholar-theologians. Chenu's *Une école
de théologie: Le Saulchoir*, long in disfavour, would be put on the Index
by Pius XII in 1942; however, his emphasis on 'pastoral' theology was
to be highly influential after it gained papal favour at Vatican II. Chenu
had always appeared to reject a theology of obedience, but in any revised
understanding of obedience the problem remains. To what or to whom

---

6. Cited by Potworowski, *Contemplation*, p. 108.
7. The influence of Teilhard on Chenu's optimistic account of humanity
   and human society – and on that of other 'new theologians' – is widely
   recognized; see Potworowski, *Contemplation*, pp. 120-21. For Chenu's
   comparative inattention to the prevalence of sin (as compared e.g. with De
   Lubac) see *Contemplation*, p. 179.
8. For orthopraxy see Potworowski, *Contemplation*, pp. 182-87. For one of
   the more problematic efforts of Chenu on orthopraxy see 'Orthodoxie-
   orthopraxie', in G. Philips (ed.), *Le service théologique dans l'Eglise: Mélanges
   offerts au Père Congar* (Paris: Cerf, 1974), pp. 51-63.

does one afford it? And underlying any possible answer there remain questions of Truth – and again of conscience.

Difficulties about the relation of orthopraxy to fundamental theology help to explain how many Dominicans, following Chenu, failed to recognize that 'Thomisme vécu' (as by worker priests) could easily degenerate into immanentism, usually of some neo-Marxist stripe where the objective truths of 'sacred metaphysics' – term of the age – could be gradually eliminated by pastoral practices of the 'lived' faith-experience. In other words, in recognizing the need to understand and empathize with an increasingly dechristianized society and inhibit the ensuing loss to Catholicism of the working classes as well as the intellectuals, one could easily fall into the same dechristianized – that is anti-transcendental – 'hole' as has the society one is trying to understand.[9] Perhaps Chenu himself can be absolved of immanentism, but at times he comes close enough to it to give a hostage to fortune – and an opportunity for the severe criticism of the 'Roman' authorities, at least during the papacies of Pius XI and his successor. Strangely he seems to have taken no notice of the help his hoped-for 'real Thomism' might have discovered in the early twentieth-century phenomenological movement, eventually in the revisionist Thomism of Edith Stein.

There is no doubt that Chenu was more aware of the problem of a false 'updating' than some of his disciples: certainly than Edward Schillebeeckx, credited by some as a major theological influence on Vatican II, by others as having almost single-handedly destroyed the Dutch Church by apparently coming to deny the historical Resurrection along with transubstantiation and other ecclesial 'baggage'. Among other one-time Chenu pupils, Gustavo Gutiérrez, a secular priest, went on to study with the Jesuits at Lyon and became the primary founder of Liberation Theology – he only became a Dominican in 2009 – while Matthew Fox, inventor of 'creation-centered spirituality' would be expelled from the Dominican Order in 1993. Reformed Thomism might go in strange directions, unless papally or otherwise controlled! Pius's concerns are at least understandable.

Chenu's most influential pupil, Yves Congar OP, came to a more edifying end, being named cardinal by John-Paul II in 1994 after sharing with Chenu a period of marked papal disfavour. In the variations of his career, as of that of his master, one cannot but be aware once again

---

9. A similar problem, as we shall see, was to arise with 'liberation theology'; some claimed that this too might be identified as a legitimate revised version of Thomist orthopraxy.

of the importance of the approval of the Roman pontiff in the decades after Vatican I, indeed, as we shall see, also after Vatican II. Although Congar is often thought of as the godfather of Vatican II – about which his memoirs are highly informative, both for what happened and for what he wanted to happen – it is highly implausible that Pius XI would have approved his later high reputation.

As we have noted, during the papacy of Pius XI the 'new-theological' Dominicans concentrated much of their effort on getting their Aquinas right, on seeing his thought as dynamic and to be updated for a new and contemporary setting (which might also imply necessary improvements in ecclesial structures). By contrast, the Jesuits of Fourvière-Lyon were especially concerned with the recovery of the theology of the ancient Church: not, of course, merely as cultural archaeology – though much of their scholarship was of the highest quality – but to encourage the Church to rethink its theology in the light of the Fathers, and especially, as we noticed, of the Greeks. However, behind their attempts to adapt the thought of the early Church to modern times, and as they always admitted, was the continuing influence (however moderated) of the anti-objectivist ideas of Blondel, and (even less helpful, as in Chenu) of their fellow Jesuit, Pierre Teilhard de Chardin. His book *L'energie humaine*, highly esteemed by Chenu, was already on the Index in 1939, by when he had long been suspended from teaching.

In the longer term, of the many Jesuits engaged in the work of 'renewal', and of the 'recovery of the sources', the most important were Henri de Lubac and his one-time student Jean Daniélou.[10] These 'new *Jesuit* theologians' who emerge in Pius XI's reign, though certainly hostile to 'neo-scholasticism' – De Lubac (like Chenu) had been appalled by what he had been offered as a seminarian – were less concerned with efforts to recover the real Aquinas; indeed Daniélou in particular was markedly

---

10. Contemporary debate about De Lubac is of massive proportions. Perhaps the most helpful introductions in English include D. Grumett, *De Lubac: A Guide for the Perplexed* (London: T&T Clark, 2007) and *Henri de Lubac and the Shaping of Modern Theology* (San Francisco: Ignatius Press, 2020); R. Voderholzer, *Meet Henri de Lubac: His Life and Work*, tr. M.J. Miller (San Francisco: Ignatius Press, 2008); Mettepenningen, *Nouvelle Théologie*; Flynn and Murray, *Ressourcement*; J. Hillebert, *T&T Companion to Henri de Lubac* (London: T&T Clark, 2011); P. McPartlan, *The Eucharist Makes the Church: Henri de Lubac and John Zizioulas* (Fairfax, VA: Eastern Christian Publications, 2005), pp. 75-97. Perhaps most basic, however, is G. Chantraine, *Le cardinal Henri de Lubac: l'homme et l'oeuvre* (Paris: Lethielleux, 1983).

anti-Thomist, believing that medieval philosophy in general operated at too irredeemably abstract a level and with inadequate attention to theological history: that is – and despite the efforts of such as Chenu – to the demands and necessities of particular times and places. To correct such imbalance, as we have noted, De Lubac and his supporters looked for a different – and at very least supplementary – resource among the Greek Fathers, and in particular the disciples or partial disciples of Origen – though even Augustine, Ambrose and Jerome might be rehabilitated if purified of the medieval accretions which deformed their writings, and so restored to their proper early Church milieu.

In their earlier days De Lubac and Daniélou were primarily known outside the theological 'village' whose inhabitants fought over ecclesial reform, by their foundation of the invaluable and influential series of ancient Christian texts 'Sources Chrétiennes'. An 'unofficial' purpose of these was to support a more 'historically' based structure for Christian theology, that is, without too much philosophical (i.e. neo-scholastic) abstraction. (In effect this meant recovering Platonic transcendentalism as a metaphysical support for a more Aristotelian emphasis on concrete human action.)

Although the Dominicans at Le Saulchoir and the Jesuits of Lyon had different specialties and immediate interests – the one, as we have seen, still largely philosophical, even Thomist; the other patristic (though sparingly of Augustine) – they recognized one another as sharing in a common cause: to redeem theology from a debased and potted Suarezian neo-scholasticism and to widen its basis to include the lived experience both of contemporary European man and the Greek Fathers. We should notice, however, that rather little credit was given, at least by the Jesuits, to the fact that Latin medieval philosophy had corrected many of the more unfortunate failures of patristic times, especially by making regular use of the Aristotelian account of the relationship between the human soul and the body. Be that as it may, the Jesuit-Dominican axis in the times of Pius XI and later was well symbolized in that De Lubac's soon to be notorious *Catholicisme* was published in 1938 in the series 'Unam Sanctam' in Paris, the Dominican Yves Congar being the series editor – both being at this stage ecumenically minded and for that too suspect in Rome.

Ecumenism, and deploying the early Church to promote it, involved significant risk, making those who revived the early Church for such purposes liable to be suspected of proposing a Protestantizing rejection of medieval developments in sacramental theology: a charge perhaps not totally unfounded – and strengthened if they could be convicted of hanging about with Protestant scholars of Christian antiquity. Normally, under Pius XI, they were forbidden to do so.

De Lubac, the expert on Origen, though much an object of suspicion under Pius XI (and XII), would eventually receive his cardinal's hat from John Paul in 1983. As for Daniélou, in his earlier days he normally kept his head down, his concerns appearing at first less controversial and more strictly historical, as he was an authority on the less suspect (and recently rediscovered) Gregory of Nyssa. Underneath, he was a somewhat volcanic character, as would be revealed when in the next papacy he would argue that Aquinas had little historical sense – and again in 1969 when, after obeying a virtual order from his friend Paul VI to accept his own cardinal's hat, he revealed in no uncertain terms that he was among those who were convinced that the partisans of the 'Spirit of Vatican II' were corrupting the Church and in particular the religious orders, including his own. This the Society of Jesus, now led by Pedro Arrupe, failed to appreciate, especially when on 23 October 1972, Daniélou broadcast his disillusioned views in an interview on Vatican Radio. His death in startling but in fact honourable circumstances occurred two years later – and many who had been his former friends took occasion to denigrate him, for a while with some success.

Like other 'new theologians', Daniélou had apologized for modernism as the wrong reaction to an unfortunate situation. After his 'turn' in the late 1960s against the ever-expanding progressivism of many of his former collaborators, he would have maintained that his basic theological stance remained largely unchanged; that it was the circumstances that had changed, one bad ecclesial situation having now morphed into something in its own way as bad or worse. Hence he now found himself in company with De Lubac, his old teacher, and Joseph Ratzinger, becoming a stalwart defender of papal authority and optimist about the necessary authoritarianism which that institution must maintain. In a distorted way, Pius XI had got something right after all. He had had to reform his attitude to Fascists, and come to hate Nazis; he had no intention of changing his belief that, in theology in general and on papal authority in particular, his predecessors were on the right road. Authoritarianism (and worse) might be perilous in the secular world; if (and only if) moderated by tradition, it was and is appropriate in the Church.

Which brings us to a final and toxic theme that surfaced in Pius's pontificate, this time in moral theology and easily recognizable as central to the changing attitudes to the rise – and possible fall – of papal power since Vatican II. For Pius determined to confront a problem which in the longer run was to threaten the authority of the Church, and particularly of the pope, among coming generations of both believers and unbelievers more than all the Fascists, Nazis and 'new theologians' put together: an age-old problem in new guise, that of sexual morality.

Aware that in 1930 the Anglican Conference at Lambeth had taken more than tentative steps towards accepting both divorce and contraception for the married, Pius realized that the problem would become, indeed had become, a Catholic problem. Hence on the last day of December in that same year 1930, 'looking', as he put it, 'with paternal eye on the universal world from the Apostolic See', he published what was to prove the fateful encyclical *Casti Connubii,* in which he castigated the 'grave sins' of abortion, adultery, divorce and contraception: sins against the sanctity of marriage as ordained by God.

These were sins increasingly attractive not only to Catholics but, as the Anglicans had already discovered, to the unchurched 'neopagans': nor was neopaganism, in Pius's view, a 'privileged' attribute of Nazis alone. Its developing culture might spill over into the Church. Though the expression 'culture wars' was not yet in vogue, Pius would have recognized it as very relevant to his theme in *Casti Connubii.* What he would not as yet have recognized, even in his nightmares, was that a pope might find it necessary and desirable to come down, however ambiguously, on the 'wrong side' of a cultural divide.

Pius is clear in *Casti Connubii* that sins against God's laws on marriage were now the fashion in the scientistic, disillusioned atmosphere of Europe and beyond that supervened the disasters of the First World War. He appealed against such sins to the traditional account of marriage summarized by Augustine as *proles, fides, sacramentum:* that is (primarily) children, then the mutual loyalty of the spouses, finally the inseparable bond in its Catholic understanding as reflecting the bond between Christ and the Church as expounded by St Paul in Ephesians. The authority of *Casti Connubii* as formal teaching of the 'ordinary magisterium' was to haunt the Church up to the next Vatican Council and well beyond.

Chapter 6

The End of an Era? Pius XII as Past and Future

Tempora mutantur nos et mutamur in illis.

Based on Ovid

Eugenio Pacelli had run into trouble, even opprobrium, as Pius XI's Secretary of State by upholding the policy of 'absolute impartiality' derived more recently, as we have seen, from Benedict XV and his Secretary of State Pietro Gasparri. That policy had worried many when applied to the Kaiser, but Pacelli's application of it to Hitler and the Nazis aroused a much greater unease; however, it was to allow him, transformed into Pius XII, to follow Benedict's lead in helping the persecuted while largely refraining from specific criticism of atrocities.

Pacelli's election as pope in 1939 offered the cardinals a last desperate hope of mitigating, by appeasement, impending Nazi savageries. Among his first acts as pope was the suppression of his predecessor's final attempt to denounce in a new encyclical the neopagan racism of the Third Reich. That had met with initial approval from the Nazi (and the Fascist) leaders: according to *Der Angriff*, propaganda organ of Goebbels, the new pope was 'a good judge of the present times', an accolade Pius was surely to come to regret. Count Ciano, Mussolini's Foreign Minister, added that the Fascists 'could get along well with this pope'.[1] The 'getting along' meant little more for the Church than the chance to protect a

---

1. For details see F.J. Coppa, *The Life and Pontificate of Pope Pius XII: Between History and Controversy* (Washington, DC: CUA Press, 2013), pp. 128-29.

considerable number of Jews in religious houses, mainly in Rome, when the storm came to rage over the Eternal City.

By 1 November 1950, Pius perhaps hoped that such moral ambiguities could be consigned to history – though it would not work out like that. As a much-loved survivor of the abyss, he could make plain that, despite the Nazis, the Fascists and the Communists – despite even *La Nouvelle Théologie* – the 'show' was still on the road. With Mussolini as well as Hitler departed from the scene, he could bask in the approval of the more than a million pilgrims who flocked to Rome in 1950 by land, sea and air from all parts of the globe to witness him carry the Marian programme of Pius IX a stage further by proclaiming as infallible dogma the long-accepted Catholic belief that Mary had been transported body and soul to heaven.

It was to be the only occasion in which such infallible power, authorized by Pius IX and Vatican I almost a hundred years before, had been directly exercised. That might be seen, paradoxically, both as concluding a particular era in Catholic history and as reminder that papal authority was confirmed and still available, whatever doctrines were still to be definitively taught by the 'ordinary magisterium'. As if to confirm the rightness of his decision, Pius had been permitted to see in the Gardens of the Vatican itself the sun dancing in the sky – as earlier witnessed by the children at Fatima during their Marian visions of 1917 – on the two days before the proclamation of the new dogma: and once again a week after.

But even as Pope Pius was carried into St Peter's on the *sedia gestatoria*, even as he blessed an endless stream of pilgrims at the close of his historic day, he knew that, though the Nazi and Fascist dictators were gone (and even Stalin, though destined to survive for three more years, was checked by American atomic power), troubles in the Church – in the form of threatened dissent from traditional Catholic teachings – were likely to bubble up again. He knew that the authority of Leo XIII, the severity of Pius X (the pope with whom he wanted to identify his own reign and whom he was to beatify in the following year) and the continuing pressure exerted in doctrinal matters by Pius XI, had not yet quelled the increasing theological anxieties of Catholic thinkers. His own authority, backed by the favour of the Virgin, must be exercised in a last determined effort to quell 'the murmurers' and prop up the truths of the faith.

Indeed, in 1950 itself, shortly before enjoying his triumph with the Proclamation of the Assumption, Pius had revealed in *Humani Generis* a wide-ranging theological vision in terms of which he hoped to regulate the undisciplined ecclesiastical turbulence he had inherited from his predecessor. That turbulence he now saw as fuelled especially by the new liturgical movements as well as by the continuing concern for ecumenism associated with the usual suspects among Catholic philosophers and theologians: not least the continuing influence of Blondel, still apparent beneath the 'New Christianity' of his determinedly Thomist admirer Jacques Maritain. This 'New Christianity' was a political project intended to replace the outdated concept of Catholic Christendom and, being widely Christian rather than narrowly Catholic, would imply a relationship between Church and State more acceptable to a liberal-democratic age. With hindsight one can recognize one of the roots of a more recent 'cultural Catholicism'.

The immediate and intended effect of *Humani Generis*, seen by many as a revised and slightly more liberal version of Pius X's *Pascendi* – but not followed by a flood of excommunications – was to launch a further persecution against the 'new theologians', about whom Pius was clearly worried as early as 1946. Rallying the once irreproachable Jesuits assembled in Rome, he had remarked that:

> A lot has been said, not always with sufficient reflection, about a 'new theology' which, in a constantly developing world, would itself also be in constant development, always en route and never arriving anywhere. If such a view were thought legitimate, what would happen to the immutable Catholic dogmas and to the unity and stability of faith.[2]

And already in *Mystici Corporis* (1943), Pius had identified relativism as the heart of all errors in philosophy and its theological avatar. Particularly in its ecumenical version, it misrepresented the 'Mystical Body of the Church', not least at the hands of liturgists seeking peace with those now to become known as 'separated brethren'. The Catholic Church, according to Pius's view of such dissidence, would no longer be identified as the sole manifestation of that Mystical Body. Indeed, other doctrines could be modified too, being regarded as merely versions of the truth assumed appropriate from age to age. Perhaps it would have surprised Pius that some of the original radicals of Vatican II, not least Joseph Ratzinger, but especially De Lubac,[3] were to discover in *Mystici*

---

2. *AAS* 43 (1950), p. 389.
3. Cf. P. McPartlan, '*Ressourcement*, Vatican II, and Eucharistic Ecclesiology', in Flynn and Murray, *Ressourcement*, pp. 400-01.

Corporis no mere reassertion of the past but a path for future theological progress if interpreted on more Christological lines, that is, more in accordance with the almost forgotten theology of Tübingen's Johann Adam Möhler.

The problem of the 'separated brethren', at least since the time of Döllinger (if not before), was particularly acute in Germany where, as we have noted, at many of its distinguished centres of learning, Tübingen especially, there were closely related departments of Catholic and of Protestant theology. Understandably, therefore, Catholic ecumenists were especially concerned with those 'brethren' of the Lutheran persuasion – and that drove them to attempt some degree of rehabilitation of Luther himself. Yet before 1939, year of the accession of Pius XII, Catholic historians of Protestantism in Germany, though determinedly critical of the state of the late medieval Church, had been convinced of the absolute iniquity of Martin Luther.[4]

A far-reaching change developed with the appearance of the first volume of Joseph Lortz's *History of the Reformation in Germany*. Lortz was a longtime member of the Nazi Party which he only renounced in 1938 – therefore presumably sympathetic to Hitler's anti-Semitism which echoed that of Luther. As for many of his predecessors, for Lortz the late medieval Church was almost irredeemably corrupt, both in its practices and in its 'Ockhamist' theology offering an apparently extrinsic doctrine of salvation and a seemingly Pelagian account of human moral capacity.

Luther, according to Lortz, had identified many of the problems and their danger to the faith, and after Lortz had broken the ice, other scholars (notably Louis Bouyer and Hans Küng) argued to some effect that Luther's doctrine of justification by faith was more or less a restoration of the original Catholic teaching.[5] It was not that Lortz took Luther to be Catholic, but rather that there was a strong Catholic undertone to his otherwise individualist theology and that his 'apostasy' was very understandable given the dire condition of the German Church. Such sweetening of the Lutheran pill was improved on by Erwin Iserloh, one of Lortz's students, who argued that Luther had never pinned his 95 theses on the Wittenberg church door as a fierce challenge to Catholicism;

---

4. For an admirable summary of Catholic attitudes to Luther in the twentieth century see E. Duffy, 'Luther through Catholic Eyes', in *A People's Tragedy* (London: Bloomsbury, 2020), pp. 125-42, esp. 129ff.

5. The acceptance of this interpretation by many Lutherans and by the Catholic hierarchy was sealed in 1999 by a Joint Declaration on Justification.

rather in the first instance he had submitted his doubts to his bishop, as would be normal practice. Among historians that argument has been widely accepted.

Nevertheless, and as others would be eager to point out, Luther's mischief in Catholic eyes was not limited to his theory of justification; he soon was to offer a more sweeping assault on the whole Catholic system – in particular on the pope, whom he came to view as the Antichrist, the devil incarnate. In Germany, among ecumenists, such problems could easily, it seems, be ignored – at least for a while – and the work of Lortz and his successors, up to and after the Second Vatican Council, suggested that in the interest of ecumenism, and especially of reunion with the Lutherans, dogma should be played down.

Yet despite its partial truth, such revisionism could amount to a further invitation to bad faith among the clergy: Luther and Lutheranism could be presented as, even believed to be, other than what they were, Luther shown to be no heresiarch. More generally, the interests of ecumenism should, so the idea seemed to develop, take precedence over fuddy-duddy doctrinal considerations; orthopraxy (we can get on well with the Lutherans) should take precedence over orthodoxy. What if a pope should one day develop that line of thinking, following his German theological tutors? That question, in Pius's time, was for the future. We shall return to it.

Though Lortz was writing in 1939, the challenge he represented touched Pius XII but little. More pressing in those simpler days was that there still might lurk potential heretics among the Dominicans of Le Saulchoir and the Jesuits of Fourvière, whose fatal brew must be again denounced: there were to be no more mistaken theories of evolution (Teilhard de Chardin SJ being regarded as particularly threatening); no more Marxism, immanentism, German-style idealism, no existentialism. However, Pius's eyes in all this were largely focussed not on his beloved Germany – though problems on that front were soon to crop up – but on France. Relativism summed up all the errors that he again castigated in *Humani Generis*. Yet unlike his predecessors and in parallel to his approach to the scriptures, he was prepared to allow that some of these alien systems of thought might have nuggets of worth to add to the perennial philosophy which he still saw as more or less completed, rather than ongoing, in the work of Thomas Aquinas.

To keep the balance right, to prevent the younger theologians and philosophers, especially among the clergy, from deviating too far, Pius insisted again on the authority of the 'magisterium', citing Pius IX and emphasizing in the spirit of Vatican I that not merely *ex cathedra* determinations but all pronouncements of papal encyclicals should acquire unchallengeable status. But how was that to be done? And how should the Church continue to handle those who like De Lubac and Daniélou were both knowledgeable and sympathetic, as we have seen, to the early Fathers, the Greek Fathers and Origen and his disciples in particular. Such people could not yet be neutralized by being created cardinals, but might that not be a long-term solution? Certainly not for Eugenio Pacelli, but, if it were, what would be the implications, both for the traditions of the Church and for the authority of the Roman pontiff? Origen himself was always too hot for Vatican approval, and though there was a suggestion in Paul VI's time that he be rehabilitated, it did not happen, probably because he is (unjustly) hated by the Orthodox.

In brief, in *Humani Generis*, as already (as we shall see) in the scriptural encyclical *Divino Afflante Spiritu*, a degree of change was to be allowed, but very tight papal control maintained: only the exercise of such authority would suffice, Pius supposed, to achieve such a balancing act, though revising canon law in papal favour could do no harm and hence was arranged. But what if popes were to wish to retain their authority and, in accordance with the spirit of the age, were to change the traditions which that authority since time immemorial had been supposed to defend? We recall again that for Pius IX the pope *is* the tradition. What if his views should be untraditional?

*   *   *

By 1950 a new wave of repression was well under way, its theoretical foundations now displayed in *Humani Generis*, perhaps the last determined papal defence of 'neo-scholasticism'. Indeed, a well-run campaign against the 'new theologians', demanded by Garrigou-Lagrange in the first instance against his fellow Dominicans, had begun as early as 1942 when Chenu's *Une école de théologie* and an *Essai sur le problème théologique* by a Louvain Dominican, Louis Charlier, published in 1938, had been put on the Index.[6] Both Chenu and Charlier were then relieved of their teaching posts.

In the same year a further Dominican, Dominicus De Petter, was dismissed from the faculty at Louvain, along with the historian René Draguet. In the wake of *Humani Generis* the attack was resumed; it was widely believed that the onslaught on the worker-priest movement to be

---

6. The phrase 'new theology' (or rather its immediate predecessor) was first used in comment on Chenu and Charlier by P. Parente, 'Nuove tendenze teologiche', *Osservatore Romano*, 9-10 February 1942, p. 1.

found there was aimed in particular at Chenu and Congar. Chenu was finally 'expelled' from Paris in 1954, along with yet another Dominican, Henri-Marie Féret, last of the so-called 'Three Musketeers', the others being Chenu and Congar. The latter of these lost further official credit for urging that there was need for much greater lay participation in Church affairs. In 1954 he too was deprived of his teaching post, servility being hardly his way, as when he dubbed the instrument of papal control, the Holy Office, 'a police régime of betrayal'.[7] As for lay dissidents, the pope and his advisers probably realized that, in theory, they were harder to control, unless also rendered servile.

Nor were 'dissident' Jesuits to be spared, though the retribution was generally less savage, perhaps because the primary persecutors of the 'new theology' – Garrigou-Lagrange and Marie-Michel Labourdette[8] – being Dominicans, were especially concerned to 'clean up' their own order. That said, Daniélou lost his job as editor of *Etudes* as early as 1946 as a consequence of a strongly worded article 'Orientations présentes de la pensée religieuse',[9] in which he argued that Aquinas had had little historical sense. Then in May 1950, shortly before the publication of *Humani Generis*, De Lubac was told he must leave Fourvière, while in June Henri Bouillard and two others were similarly exiled from Lyon and moved to the Institut Catholique in Paris. Bouillard's revised doctoral dissertation – *Conversion et grace chez S. Thomas d'Aquin* – was regarded as particularly offensive, not least for its apparent criticism of transubstantiation and for Bouillard's distinction between theological affirmations *per se* and our ability fully to grasp them as they are 'represented' to us in our minds.

Perhaps surprisingly De Lubac's masterpiece *Surnaturel*, though much criticized, not least by Garrigou-Lagrange and other Dominicans, escaped formal censure for a while, though the Jesuit General applauded its author for keeping a comparatively low profile, in the end to little avail. In 1950 De Lubac also lost his position as editor of *Recherches de science religieuse* and three of his books and an article – along with a book and the notorious article of Daniélou (1946) – were ordered removed from Jesuit formation houses.

---

7. See Mettepennigen, *Nouvelle Théologie*, p. 42.
8. Labourdette refused to publish Garrigou-Lagrange's polemic against the 'new theology' in *Revue Thomiste* (of which he was the editor), but delivered a more moderate attack himself: M.M. Labourdette, 'La théologie et ses sources', *Revue Thomiste* 46 (1946), pp. 353-71.
9. Published in *Etudes* 249 (1946), pp. 5-21.

On 11 February 1951, the Jesuit General, Jean-Baptiste Janssens, defended the repression: while admitting its severity, he appealed to necessity, given the 'severe' situation in the Church to which the pope's encyclical had drawn attention. In effect, De Lubac and those who followed him were charged with modernism: with failing to appreciate the proper relationship in human nature between the natural and the supernatural, with mistreating Aquinas as a mere product of his age and more generally viewing dogma as relative to time and place. The Jesuit General was surely concerned that the favour recent popes had shown the Society – hence its massive influence in the Church since Vatican I – might now be imperilled.

Of the victims of Pius's reassertion of what he took to be orthodoxy, several were to return to fight another day and three to be especially rewarded for so doing – though the Jesuits were (predictably) treated more generously than the Dominicans. Daniélou, as we have noted, became a cardinal as early as 1969, De Lubac in 1983, the more aggressive Congar only when almost at death's door in 1994, while Chenu missed the red hat altogether. The eventually revised estimate of De Lubac, Daniélou and Congar should remind us that it was when Leo XIII arrived that Newman too had obtained a cardinal's hat. Orthodoxy might seem dependent on the wishes of a pope, and when those wishes are translated into action, most clergy are quick to adopt the official line as to who and what is orthodox.

*   *   *

For all his punishing of supposed 'modernists', Pius himself, a learned and politically cautious man, knew that he must proceed with care. He avoided excommunications in the mode of Pius X, substituting the removal of offenders from their posts and the concluding in some cases of their teaching. By now even an autocrat must watch the wind; top-down force is not enough in a world, or even in a Church, increasingly scrutinized through journalists' eyes, and both Pius and his predecessor had grasped the value of radio messaging for the propagation of their determinations of the Gospel's implications.

Secrecy about the inner workings of the Church (necessary, it was supposed, about the origins of papal policies as also about Vatican finances) must be blended with an awareness of where a traditional fundamentalism must give way to the advances of scholarship – even in the study of the Bible. There could now be no simple return to Leo XIII's already outdated assertion that 'God has not delivered the scriptures to the private judgment of the learned', nor, one might add, to the assertion of the authority of Jerome and the Vulgate as the last word in biblical criticism. Neither repression nor the encouragement of mere ignorance and pigheadedness could work as well as in the past.

Hence as early as 1942, in *Divino afflante Spiritu*, Pius attempted the near impossible task of reconciling the new biblical scholarship with the old claims of the Church to control – through the episcopacy – all interpretation of the scriptures. That involved recognizing the importance of the study of the Bible in the original Greek and Hebrew as well as the help such study can derive from the ongoing work of archaeologists, scholars of ancient Near Eastern texts and historians of the Near East more generally. Such must be encouraged, not just put down, while the ultimate authority of the 'magisterium' – a term increasingly coming to be understood as with reference only to the pope himself – must be maintained.

To a considerable extent Pius was successful in this; at least for several decades Catholic biblical scholars, even the more radical, breathed a sigh of relief, while the more 'conservative' elements in the Curia and elsewhere felt that the magisterium was still in control. That Augustin Bea, Jesuit rector of the Biblical Institute in Rome after 1930, was for many years Pius's confessor reflects the pope's confidence in a man (and a Jesuit) who encouraged him to avoid both extremes: the ultra-rationalism of the more ideologically minded exegetes whose destructive capacity had been a concern of Leo XIII and the recklessness of more subjectivist scholars. These would abandon much of the 'history' represented in both Testaments and replace it by more 'spiritualizing' interpretations that too often might seem pulled out of the desert air.

*   *   *

Shortly before his death in 1958, almost as if by accident and perhaps aware of how threatening it was to become to the authority of the Church, and especially of the pope, Pius turned to the question of artificial contraception. Though reiterating the ban imposed by his predecessor's *Casti Connubii*, in an allocution to Italian midwives, he now allowed limited exceptions for medical reasons and – more significantly – approved the 'use' by married couples of the wife's periods of sterility, thus in effect licensing a 'rhythm' method of birth control intended to control the number of pregnancies but still within the structures of God-given 'natural' law.

Progressives, regarding this as another hopeful straw in the wind, called for more; conservatives, more prophetically, viewed it as portending a slippery slope. All must have realized that the control of fertility was a problem which in contemporary society was not going to go away, even though as yet largely unaware of the upheaval it would cause; 'women's issues' were hardly mainstream by 1958. As yet the demand to use modern medical techniques to resolve the problems arising from too many births was confined to the purview of more educated groups of Catholics: problems of the physical demands on the mother condemned to repeat pregnancies and the financial strain on parents who wished to give their children a more than minimal education.

Eugenio Pacelli passed away in 1958, year of his allocution to the Italian midwives, surrounded by his small, still largely German inner circle, under the careful eye of his ever-protective nun-housekeeper, a survivor from the good old days back in Munich. His mind had been clouded for some time; he revealed its confusion in sporadic and far-reaching pronouncements based on mugged-up dictionary entries. Yet with Cardinal Ottaviani from the Holy Office keeping a wary eye on doctrine and tradition and further dissent reduced to covert mutterings, he may have hoped that he left the Church stable and healthy. He had perhaps just enough tempered tradition with reform, especially over the interpretation of scripture.

There was no obvious successor and, as was to turn out, the water beneath the surface was still very choppy. Pius had not lived long enough to celebrate the passing of many of the more powerful and persistent dissidents; what would happen next would depend almost entirely on the character and will of whoever inherited the papal autocratic power. As for his posthumous fame, as a transitional figure with appeasing skeletons in his cupboard, Pius would be 'merely' declared Venerable (in 2009). To revert to the language of Döllinger, he was a Janus figure, looking largely backwards in *Humani Generis*, but in his attitude to scripture, in his awareness of the approaching problems about sexuality and marriage, even perhaps – if *Mystici Corporis* could be 'interpreted' less institutionally and more Christologically – in aspects of his ecclesiology, a figure pointing to the future.

Chapter 7

Who Changed What at Vatican II?

Collegiality? The only collegiality traceable to the Apostles was in the Garden of Gethsemane; they all ran away.

Cardinal Ottaviani

Perhaps the most startling fact to emerge … is the extraordinary ambivalence of Pope John's own role.

Eamon Duffy

The prediction during the collegiality debate that the pope would lose his freedom of action would hardly be verified by the succeeding decades of papal history.

Aidan Nichols

Only the pope is authorized to call an Ecumenical Council – a rule endorsed by Vatican II – but when Angelo Roncalli was elected and took the name of John XXIII in 1958 on the death of Pius XII, he was a supposedly stopgap pope and few expected him to follow the tentative leads of his two predecessors and actually call one. Yet during the first announcement on 25 January 1959, he stated that he intended to 'come to grips with the spiritual needs of the present time' and in an allocution to the Franciscans on 16 April that he wanted 'to define clearly and distinguish between what is sacred principle and eternal gospel and what belongs to the changing ages'. Though he then referred to an 'updating' and a letting of fresh air into the Church – he is said to have thrown open a window by way of illustration – so that her evangelizing mission could proceed more effectively in the modern world, yet no one really understood then – nor perhaps do we now – quite what he wanted to achieve, though a number of his directives before the Council, together with his encyclical *Pacem in Terris* – a text replete with unexpectedly long lists of rights deriving from human dignity – indicate a desire that more attention be paid to (some sort of) ecumenism and to the needs (as he saw them) of the increasingly dechristianized Western world. They certainly implied less of a siege-mentality in dealings with Orthodox and Protestants.

What the pope did make clear from the very beginning of the Council was that it was to be not primarily 'dogmatic' but 'pastoral', though the word 'pastoral' (soon to become a useful cliché) had not yet assumed – certainly not in John's mind – its later connotation as a device to change Church *doctrine*. According to this, some hoped that newly established 'traditions' would eventually lead to traditional teachings – or some of them – becoming obsolete: in theological (or Marxist) jargon already current in the Church, that new orthopraxy might be able to 'reform' old orthodoxy. Yet for Pope John not only did 'pastoral' imply that no new dogmatic decisions were intended but (perhaps) that, and as it turned out, some of the final decrees of the Council were to be accorded more weight than others: a new feature for Ecumenical Councils.

Uncertainty about the sense of 'updating' was to prove toxic. Perhaps John relied on the Holy Spirit to blow the correct understanding of the term into conciliar minds and wills. Certainly, he seems to have supposed that a few traditional formulae could be changed without the doctrines they were supposed to express being similarly – if not wilfully – altered. Indeed, he appears to have had no idea of the radical cultural changes his updating might demand, and many took him to imply that scores of traditional practices (and even beliefs) should be abandoned. In the upshot the Council never applied itself to determining which should go and which stay. Yet already on 30 September 1964 Cardinal Meyer of Chicago observed that not all traditions should remain unchanged; cases needed to be looked at individually. This did not happen, and as some – not least the then Cardinal Joseph Ratzinger – would later point out, the Council offered no Theology of Culture to which reformers and conservatives alike might appeal in determining what should go and what remain.

At the opening of the Council most delegates were more concerned – whether in hope or dread – that the new pope wanted to return to an apparently major piece of unfinished business from Vatican I: how to restore the balance between pope and bishops. There was a second source of concern, or of puzzlement; it seemed that Pope John had not decided at the outset of the Council what role he himself, as pope, should play in the proceedings. He later and significantly in *The Journal of a Soul* would note that 'the ecumenical Council is entirely the initiative and in principle under the jurisdiction of the pope'. Later too he wrote that, 'It has been on my conscience, I confess, that *contrary* to what happened in the first two months, from October 11 to December 8, the pope should take his proper place, discreetly indeed but as the real president by supreme right, as head of the Catholic Church.'

Perhaps most informative about John's aims and the power he knew he possessed is a conversation he had on 9 February 1963, with yet another Jesuit editor of *La Civiltà Cattolica*. Roberto Tucci noted in his diary that the pope remarked that 'during the first session he had preferred not to intervene in the debates, so as to allow the fathers themselves freedom to discuss and the opportunity to find the right path ... And they had done so.' Tucci also recorded that John said he was 'completely satisfied' with the proceedings of the first session. In other words, he did know at least something of what he wanted and was watching to be sure that his wants were what the Council (or those who most influenced it) wanted. Had the Council gone the 'wrong' way, that is, he would have had to intervene earlier. He knew that all depended in the end on his own will – and certainly not on the will of the curial cardinals. Prominent among these, Alfredo Ottaviani, in command of the then Holy Office, was to be humiliated at the Council's very outset and as the obvious target of a recorded papal comment that members of the Curia 'have a petty, restricted mentality, because they have never been outside of Rome, outside of their village'.

That said, it seems rash to suppose, as have a number of commentators on the Council, that a rethinking of Church teaching on more 'Christological' lines was John's intention from the start. Such an approach certainly became dear to Paul VI when he took over and certainly characterized many of the Council's final decisions, but to suppose that such an expression of *aggiornamento* was always clear in John's mind looks too like an argument from hindsight.

As for the bishops now summoned to Rome, they too seemed puzzled as to what the Council was to do and what their own role was supposed to be. As noted, it was widely believed that Vatican I needed to be completed insofar as it had defined the authority of the pope in detail but had left the powers and authority of the bishops in limbo. Yet, as we shall see, when Vatican II closed, that was still largely the case. Certainly, some bishops – plus many of their favourite theologians, especially those from France, Germany and the Benelux countries – hoped for radical change. It remains unclear how radical many of them would have preferred it to be.

When summoned, then, the bishops seemed uncertain as to what role they were to play. Were they simply to obey orders (once they had discovered what the orders were) or were they were to take a major, even decisive, role in determining the outcome of whatever deliberations they were going to be asked to engage in? Giuseppe Alberigo, a distinguished historian of the Council, has expressed a common view of the situation they faced as follows:

> After the Vatican Council of 1870, Prussian Chancellor von Bismarck had maintained that from then on the Catholic bishops were simply local representatives of the pope; only the pope had effective power and authority over the Catholic church. Even though Pius IX denied this thesis, the bishops until the end of the pontificate of Pius XII appeared increasingly to be subordinate to the pope and the Roman Curia, which the reform of Pius X had strengthened and which had the Holy Office as the supreme congregation. A large part of theology and canon law had provided a doctrinal basis for this attitude. The social philosophy of the modern centralized state also provided an 'analogue' that was very influential and was adopted [by popes].

As we shall see, the bishops were eventually induced to achieve – or drifted into achieving – a combination of two apparently conflicting possibilities: both to obey orders and also to play a major role in determining eventual procedures and outcomes. Going beyond Bismarck, Alberigo nuances what he – and they – believed to be their situation as follows:[1]

> Pius XII's *Mystici Corporis* made up for the fateful omission of Vatican Council I by solemnly affirming the dignity of bishops as successors of the apostles and head of the particular Churches but it also repeated that 'they are not entirely independent, because they are subjects to the rightful authority of the Roman pontiff, even while they enjoy the ordinary power

---

1. G Alberigo, 'Transition to a New Age', in G Alberigo and J.A. Komonchak, *History of Vatican II*, vol. 5 (Maryknoll, NY: Orbis; Leuven: Peeters, 2006), p. 615.

of jurisdiction, which is communicated directly to them by the same Supreme Pontiff'.

One of the aims of the present chapter is to see whether Vatican II eventually changed this situation or merely varied it, and at the outset I should emphasize again that I am less concerned to identify what was intended than with what was effected by Vatican II's conciliar activity.

There were, of course, sociological parameters within which the Council's deliberations began: on the one hand John XXIII's refreshing simplicity – appearing no longer as a prince of the Church handing down a condescending spiritual largesse to his subjects, but as a brother in Christ – won him the kind of popularity and sympathy with which the sufferings of Pius IX or Pius XII at the hands of the political powers of their days had gifted his predecessors. Many Catholics – not least the bishops at the Council itself – wanted to do what the 'good' pope – *il papa buono* – wanted them to do: a goodwill which quickly spread into the world outside the Church, further enhancing its effects within.

But what *did* the good pope want, apart from letting fresh air into what he plainly perceived as a stuffy, inward-looking institution that might seem to have passed its sell-by date? How did he propose to do that? What were to be identified as the specific issues where change was essential? As it turned out, not the relationship between pope and bishops (though that was not ignored) but, along with the language and form of the liturgy, disputes over the relationship between tradition and scripture were to be at the heart of many of the ensuing debates, accompanied by unprecedented discussions of religious freedom: a *right* to religious freedom, that is, as distinct from toleration. There was also, as we shall see, an attempt, clearly in line with Pope John's intentions, to bring the Church into 'dialogue' (a favourite if ambiguous word of John's successor Paul VI) not only with the 'separated brethren' but with the 'modern secular world', though the understanding of that world with which the Conciliar Fathers struggled was already in many significant aspects looking like 'old hat', as new problems (not about justification, grace and the Trinity but about ecclesiastical authority and sex) were coming over the horizon.

One thing is and was clear: many theologians (if not at first bishops) wanted radically to alter the approach of the Church to other Christians, other religions and the secular Western society, and hoped that John's unexpected decision to call a Council would give them that opportunity. They knew that papal support was essential, and were not yet sure what the pope actually wanted. However, apart from such 'political' considerations, we need to recall two substantial, if underlying, theological points at issue.

First, although there was little sympathy for the wishes of some of the more progressive theologians that Aquinas's thought should be altogether sidelined – rather he is recommended as the pre-eminent doctor of the Church in sections 15 and 16 of *Optatam Totius* (the decree on the Training of Priests, 28 October 1965) – the 'progressives' disputed the post-Vatican I version of his account of the relationship between grace and nature, seeing it as a perversion of his thought and as too radically separating the natural from the supernatural. They followed De Lubac in rejecting Cajetan's interpretation of Aquinas's treatment of the relationship between grace and nature (widely taught since Vatican I) which seemed grossly to underestimate the (though limited) goodness of man as created and as to a degree surviving the 'fall'.[2]

The progressive critics were probably right in thinking that Aquinas's view had been perverted, though whether he had been better interpreted by De Lubac than by his opponents (in earlier days principally Garrigou-Lagrange) is (or should be) less important than identifying the right theological account of the matter. Strictly speaking, the view of Aquinas is of historical rather than of urgent theological concern, though if centuries of Catholic teaching had got him wrong that also should have been relevant to the coming debates, not least about infallibility.[3] For if previous centuries have seriously misinterpreted arguably the Church's most authoritative thinker since New Testament times, broader questions about the security of Catholic teaching can hardly be avoided, and nor can the possible need to re-examine whether it was a mistake of the magisterium to put so much trust in even a corrected interpretation of Aquinas.

After Cajetan and his followers, the second target of the progressives was the Jesuit Suarez, another neo-scholastic interpreter of Aquinas – this time as a voluntarist – and accorded much weight, as we have noted, by 'manualist' followers of Leo XIII. According to his critics the effect

---

2. For comment see S.M. Fields, '*Ressourcement* and the Retrieval of Thomism for the Contemporary World', in Flynn and Murray (eds), *Ressourcement*, pp. 356-57. De Lubac's view is not to be confused with that of Rahner, who chooses to speak of a 'supernatural existential'.

3. Debate about the position of Aquinas continues; De Lubac's refutation of Garrigou-Lagrange has been most recently rejected by F. Feingold, *The Natural Desire to See God According to St. Thomas Aquinas and his Interpreters* (Notre Dame, IN: Ave Maria, Sapientia Press, 2010).

of his work had been that in catechesis Christianity had been widely reduced to the learning of propositional truths and commands, so de-emphasizing a personal relationship between Christ and the believer.

At the start of the new pontificate Cardinals Ottaviani of the Holy Office and Ruffini of Palermo – both of whom had been consulted during Pius XII's meditations on a new Council – had urged Pope John to call one. In their view what was required was to confirm the policies of the recently deceased Pius: and to condemn the application of 'form' (or genre) criticism in biblical studies – a particular concern of Ruffini, himself a former professor of Bible at the Lateran and strong critic of the Biblical Institute in Jerusalem. Desired might also be to add a further Marian dogma of Mary as co-redemptrix, Mariology being, as we have seen, especially attractive to ultramontanes – and certainly to renew attacks on the wicked ideologies of the day, meaning a supposedly continuing 'modernism' and especially Communism – and in language with which the Church was by now long familiar. That language, and the ideas it expressed, would certainly have been welcome to most of the members of the Theological Commission set up under Ottaviani's guidance by Pope John before the Council began, in order, it was assumed, to keep a keen eye on any challenges to 'orthodoxy'.

This the new Commission hoped to sustain through a revised 'Profession of Faith': roughly an updated version of the *Syllabus of Errors* and of Pius X's *Pascendi,* and much disliked by many theologians, though seemingly as yet by few bishops. De Lubac was later to summarize this common distaste both for the 'Profession' itself and for the wider vision of the 'Roman theologians'. For him the schemata originally drawn up by the Curia for the Council to debate were controlled by 'the rules of a very strict and shallow scholasticism, concerned almost exclusively with defence and lacking in discernment, tending to condemn all that did not fit perfectly well with its own perspective'.[4] In the event, the 'Profession' attracted little interest. What survived rather longer was the predictable 'Roman' desire for secrecy about the details of the Council's proceedings and a marked hostility to the press whose variegated reports the Vatican failed effectively to control, not least because of a steady drip of leaked information by Council participants, increasingly aware of the power of the press in the contemporary world – if less of the question 'Who is using whom?'

Pope John's actions while the new Council was being prepared might seem contradictory: on the one hand he appeared to want substantial

---

4. H. de Lubac, 'A Theologian Speaks', in *30 Giorni,* July 1985.

change; on the other he was inclined on several occasions to encourage the conservatives – a majority in the Roman Curia – who wanted any change to be largely cosmetic and concerned only with improving the centralized control and dogmatic certainty which had been further developed since the time of Pius IX. Nor were more radical ideas particularly visible as a result of the consultation with bishops, religious superiors and Catholic universities which Pope John's Secretary of State, Cardinal Tardini, organized as the coming Council was announced: a consultation which might have seemed more 'democratic' than the procedures in place for Vatican I, but the results of which – whatever the real beliefs of the respondents – hardly expressed a desire for radical change.

Perhaps John's apparent respect for conservative views at this stage was a guileful attempt to show a certain fairness. Perhaps he hoped that during the Council itself the bishops would assert themselves in a more radical way. Perhaps he thought that Providence would lead them along that path. Perhaps he was increasingly urged in a more populist direction, as some supposed, by his secretary Monsignor Capovilla, who certainly encouraged him to favour the leftward movement in the politics of the Italian Christian Democrats long promoted by Alcide De' Gasperi. Or perhaps by this stage he was still undecided as to how (or how far) to proceed, and to what ultimate end. In any case, for a while at least he indicated that his concern about the conservative agenda proposed by the Curia was limited to its tone rather than its content. Perhaps he eventually concluded the two could not readily be separated.

That said, at the opening of the Council itself, in *Gaudet Mater Ecclesia*, Pope John seemed to invite the assembled Fathers radically to change the regulations which his own preparatory commissions had set up under Ottaviani's guidance. Those among the bishops and their theological advisers who were hoping for such change were greatly encouraged; thus *Gaudet Mater Ecclesia* was to become the constant point of reference whereby it could be knowingly implied that 'conservatives' were thwarting the pope's wishes: a telling blow against those defending (as they thought) papal prerogatives as well as their own.

Gaudet Mater Ecclesia was issued on 11 October 1962, and at the first General Congregation of the Council on 13 October Cardinal Liénart of Lille, in a prepared speech and presumably aware of Manning's manipulation of the agenda at Vatican I, challenged the voting procedures (though officially not allowed to do so) proposed to determine the membership of the commissions whose task would be to scrutinize the 'schemas' being assembled for later debate in the Council itself.

Overriding the protests of the Chairman, Cardinal Tisserant, and immediately supported by Cardinals Frings, Döpfner and König, Liénart forced a closure of the meeting. Tisserant then reported back to Pope John, who according to Cardinal Suenens was 'very happy'.[5] A 'progressive' Dutch bishop was to hail the event as 'our first victory'. The disputed proposals were to be redrafted and two of the more 'progressive' *periti* – Karl Rahner and Joseph Ratzinger, then still on amicable theological terms – were appointed to the redrafting committee of what was eventually to become the Dogmatic Constitution on Divine Revelation (*Dei Verbum*). Importantly, however, the emphasis in this key document was not on recovering the lost role of the episcopacy but on the Church as the body of Christ. That new emphasis was to remain the centre of the Council's more innovative proceedings.

It was becoming clearer what the pope now wanted – and what he would be able to get. The 'progressive' minority of bishops could now control the more inert majority, thus themselves become a 'majority'. What was later to be called the 'Spirit of Vatican II – a mood of 'revolutionary' excitement, Durkheim's 'collective effervescence' or Max Scheler's 'emotional contagion' – and which was never entirely to fade, had been prompted by the recognition in the Council of what many bishops thought John wanted to achieve. According to the progressives the changes were to lead to what already in 1961 Chenu had called 'the end of the Constantinian era' of Christianity and Congar was later to hail as a turning of the page 'on Augustinianism and on the Middle Ages'.[6]

Commentators have spoken of such enthusiasm as effecting a replacement of the truth of tradition by a 'social will', and that 'the will of the conciliar assembly was in essence an ecclesiastical version of the General Will of Rousseau: a sacred and absolute will to which the Fathers, observing the laws that they had made for themselves, felt obliged in conscience to subordinate their own ideas and opinions'.[7] We have

---

5. See De' Mattei, *Second Vatican Council*, p. 179.
6. For Chenu's pre-conciliar position see *Un concile pour notre temps* (Paris: Cerf, 1961), pp. 59-87. For Congar see *Journal*, pp. 825-26. For an analysis of the new dynamic see M. Wilde, *Vatican II: A Sociological Analysis of Religious Change* (Princeton/Oxford: Princeton University Press, 2007), pp. 22-26. Wilde explains the 'effervescence' (citing Durkheim) as 'the state in which men find themselves when ... they believe they have been swept up into a world entirely different from the one they have before their eyes'. She further explains this as 'a result of individuals gathering together ... to engage in changing an ancient institution in which they all fervently believed'.
7. So De' Mattei, *Second Vatican Council*, p. 493. De' Mattei aptly cites J.A. Talmon, *The Rise of Totalitarian Democracy* (Boston: Beacon Press, 1952).

noticed in the cases of Pius IX and Pius XII the ability of the papacy to profit from such enthusiasm.

It was beginning to look as though the pope had changed sides, or else shown his colours: now the approaching battle might concern not the authority of the bishops vis-à-vis that of the pope so much as – given papal permission – a curbing of the dominant theology of the 'Roman' schools. There now seemed to be three, not two, conflicting parties: the pope, (some) radical bishops, the Curia. What if the pope were siding with what many more bishops would tolerate if told to but which few – unless with papal backing – would be prepared to demand?

Of the open or closet 'radicals' most were 'trans-alpines', already organized in (or as cardinals heading) bishops' conferences, primarily German-speaking, with a strong interest in the 'separated brethren', especially the Lutherans. These were Cardinal Bea SJ – former rector of the Pontifical Biblical Institute in Rome and now put in charge of the new Secretariat – later Commission – to promote Christian Unity; also Cardinals Frings, Döpfner and König. To these were added the Benelux's Alfrink and Suenens and the French-speaking Léger of Montréal and Liénart of Lille. There were also a few Italians: notably Lercaro of the gastronomic capital of Italy, Bologna, and – more cautiously in view of his status as 'dauphin', as too of his long earlier curial experience – Montini of Milan.

In many of the debates that were to follow in the Council itself, though Suenens, Alfrink and Frings were perhaps the most vocal of the 'progressives', it was Bea and his ecumenically minded allies in the Secretariat for Christian Unity who often proved most effective against the traditional power of Ottaviani's Holy Office: this at times, and especially over religious freedom (or 'toleration' as Ottaviani preferred to put it), in direct personal clashes. The hand of Pope John himself must, however, be recognized in the new ecumenical Secretariat's invasion of much of the traditional turf of the Holy Office.

It was the same largely North European story with the more actively progressive theologians, many of them already identified with the *Nouvelle Théologie*: Chenu OP, Congar OP, De Lubac SJ, Daniélou SJ. To these were now added Ratzinger, Philips, Rahner SJ, Dossetti, Schillebeeckx OP, and John Courtney Murray; the last, an American Jesuit, was appointed in April 1964 when the debate on religious freedom was hotting up. From this 'prosopography' some might infer that the opening (though not, as we have seen, the continuing) scenario of Vatican II had a certain resemblance to that of Vatican I: in displaying two vigorous and influential factions plus a mass of unknown and perhaps inert quantities.

It is worth noticing, however – and despite later and hagiographical accounts of popes-to-come (significant in light of the 'unintended consequences' of the Council) – that the roles of Joseph Ratzinger and Karol Wojtyla were very different. Ratzinger had so won the confidence of Cardinal Frings of Cologne that he was entrusted with 'ghosting' the Cardinal's interventions and substantially helped to transform a man who hitherto had appeared a pastoral 'conservative' into the symbol – and more than just the symbol – of the substantially German-speaking group whose overriding aim was that the Church present itself less institutionally and more 'Christologically'. (According to Ratzinger the cardinal – for whatever reason – had some qualms of conscience later on about his conciliar activities.) As for Wojtyla, he played no pivotal role in the proceedings; indeed his important counter-proposal on religious freedom was casually rejected in the final session of the Council, a session in which, as Cardinal Ruffini prophetically noted in a letter to Siri of Genoa, there seemed to be a risk of the Church morphing into a copy of the United Nations.[8]

The whole truth about Pope John's intent when calling the Council will never be known for certain, yet one thing is clear: from the outset he had the power, directly or indirectly, to control the direction of his Council's proceedings.[9] If he hesitated on radicalism before the Council, he thus authorized the Curial conservatives to set up regulations that would eventually be undone. If he had changed his mind (or confirmed his constant intent) in his opening speech, he was still – effectively – enacting his authorization.

Since the present study is concerned more with effects than with intentions or even with doctrine, I shall treat less of what was intended to happen at Vatican II than with what actually happened, being primarily concerned to ask not whether the Council succeeded in defying the wishes of either pope or Curia to centralize further (or to confirm a new direction for the centralizing), but rather whether – regardless of actual conciliar teachings – the power relationship between pope and bishops changed, or was intended to change. I shall thus largely concentrate on the comparatively few sections of the eventual Conciliar documents which treat of the confirmed and continuing relationship between the

---

8. See De' Mattei, *Second Vatican Council*, p. 448, citing Ruffini's letter dated 12 August 1965.

9. An excellent treatment of John's pre-conciliar intentions is to be found in J.A. Komonchak, 'The Struggle for the Council during the Preparation of Vatican II (1960-1962)', in Alberigo and Komonchak, *History of Vatican II*, vol 1, pp. 350–56.

pope – 'the office of the Supreme Pontiff' – and the bishops in respect of their general authority, not least of their role in Ecumenical Councils such as Vatican II itself.

These documents are *Lumen Gentium* (The 'Dogmatic Constitution on the Church', 21 November 1964), *Christus Dominus* (The 'Decree on the Pastoral Office of Bishops in the Church', 28 October 1965) and (primarily as introducing wider issues) *Gaudium et Spes* ('The Pastoral Constitution on the Church in the Modern World', 7 December 1965). I shall also attend more perfunctorily to *Nostra Aetate* ('Declaration on the Relation of the Church to non-Christian Religions', 28 October 1965) and more closely to *Dignitatis Humanae* ('Declaration on Religious Liberty', 7 December 1965).

Only after an inspection of parts of these texts (with their relevant implications) shall we be in a position to determine whether – apart from but not excluding the intent of the documents themselves – the actual dynamics of Church governance, especially insofar as concerns the relationship between pope and bishops, changed after a Council which linked the very different papacies of Pius XII and John XXIII. Three of the principal and most obviously significant documents of the Council, *Sacrosanctum Concilium* ('The Constitution on the Sacred Liturgy' of 4 December 1963), *Unitatis Redintegratio* ('The Decree on Ecumenism' of 21 November 1964) and *Dei Verbum* ('The Dogmatic Constitution on Divine Revelation' of 18 November 1965), are less relevant to our present concerns. In treating of the Council's determinations, I shall always examine the final form of our documents, only rarely alluding to the byzantine, bureaucratic and often disingenuous debates which preceded their attaining that final form, and in which those 'dialoguing' talked past one another or for 'strategic' purposes defended the indefensible. For the delectation of connoisseurs, such behaviours have been well exposed in Roberto de' Mattei's *The Second Vatican Council*.

Starting then with *Pastoral Office of Bishops*, we notice that almost at the outset (though without reference to infallible teaching or to infallibility at all) the authority of the bishops is again immediately tied to, and subordinated to, that of the Supreme Pontiff. In the introduction (section 2) we read:[10]

In this Church of Christ the Roman Pontiff… has been granted by God supreme, full, immediate and universal power in the care of souls…. He is therefore endowed with the primacy of

---

10. Texts from Vatican II are cited from *Vatican Council II*, ed. A. Flannery (Leominster: Fowler Wright, 1981).

ordinary power over all the churches. The bishops also have been designated by the Holy Spirit to take the place of the apostles as pastors of souls and together with the Supreme Pontiff and subject to his authority, they are commissioned to perpetuate the work of Christ, the eternal Pastor.[11]

Chapter 3 of the same introduction continues in the same vein (in published form referencing Vatican II's *Dogmatic Constitution on the Church*, chapter 3):

The bishops, sharing in the solicitude of all the churches, exercise this their episcopal function ... In communion with the Supreme Pontiff and subject to his authority.

And again in chapter 1.4, with similar citation:

Together with their head, the Supreme Pontiff, and never apart from him, they [the bishops] have supreme and full authority over the universal Church, but this power cannot be exercised without the agreement of the Roman Pontiff.

Finally and most informatively we move to chapter 2.8 where – infallibility again not being in question – we read that the Supreme Pontiff can regularly act entirely on his own authority, disregarding the bishops as in the case of infallible determinations:

Bishops as the successors of the apostles enjoy as of right in the dioceses assigned to them all ordinary, special and immediate power which is necessary for the exercise of their pastoral office, but always without prejudice to the power which the Roman Pontiff possesses, by virtue of his office, of reserving certain matters to himself or to some other authority.

We shall return to the phrases 'successors of the apostles' and 'reserving matters to himself', but turn first to the key text of the whole Council (referenced above): *Lumen Gentium*, the *Dogmatic Constitution on the Church*. In its endlessly controverted chapter 3, at the very opening

---

11. The latter part of this cites the *Dogmatic Constitution of the Church of Christ* of Vatican I. Cf. Denzinger, *Encheiridion Symbolorum*, 1828 (306) and 1821 (3050).

of the treatment of the authority of bishops (section 22), we meet again agreement with the teachings of Vatican I:

> The Roman Pontiff, by virtue of his office as Vicar of Christ, namely, and as pastor of the entire Church, has full, supreme and universal power over the whole Church, a power which he can exercise unhindered. The order [note the word] of bishops is the successor to the college of the apostles in their role as teachers and pastors, and in it the apostolic college is perpetuated. Together with their head, the Supreme Pontiff, and never apart from him, they [the bishops] have supreme and full authority over the universal Church; but this power cannot be exercised without the agreement of the Roman Pontiff.

And in section 25 although the phrase *obsequium religiosum* (perhaps slightly under-translated below as 'respect') seems to stop short of demanding strict 'internal assent', there is even greater clarity about the overriding force of papal authority – way beyond that attributed to popes by the infallibility debates of Vatican I – that Vatican II is prepared to allot to it, apparently in the interest of establishing the power and authority of bishops.

> Bishops who teach in communion with the Roman Pontiff are to be revered by all as witnesses of divine and Catholic truth; the faithful, for their part, are obliged to submit to their bishops' decision, made in the name of Christ, in matters of faith and morals, and to adhere to it with a ready and respectful allegiance of mind. This loyal submission of the will and intellect must be given, in a special way, to the authentic teaching of the Roman Pontiff, even when he does not speak *ex cathedra* in such wise, indeed, that his supreme teaching authority be acknowledged with respect, and that one sincerely adhere to decisions made by him conformably with his manifest mind and intention, which is made known principally either by the character of the documents in question, or by the frequency with which a certain doctrine is proposed, or by the manner in which the doctrine is formulated.

The high point of this section of *Lumen Gentium* is reached by an extended citation of Vatican I's account of infallibility, with reference to Gasser's intervention at that Council (however understood). The 'ontological' superiority of the papal office could scarcely be made clearer, and it would hardly be surprising if that superiority were treated – *de facto*, if not *de jure* – by the more servile among the bishops (as in Vatican I) as also by the laity, as demanding strict deference to papal authority, whether on matters determined *ex cathedra* or on others, even perhaps the most humdrum. Thus we read:

> The Roman Pontiff, head of the College of bishops, enjoys this infallibility in virtue of his office, when, as supreme pastor and teacher of all the faithful – who confirms his brethren in the faith (Cf. Luke 22:33) – he proclaims in an absolute decision a doctrine pertaining to faith or morals. For that reason his definitions are rightly said to be irreformable by their very nature and not by reason of the assent of the Church, in as much as they were made with the assistance of the Holy Spirit promised to him in the person of blessed Peter himself; and as a consequence they are in no way in need of the approval of others, and do not admit of appeal to any other tribunal. For in such case the Roman Pontiff does not utter a pronouncement as a private person, but rather does he expound and defend the teaching of the Catholic faith as the supreme teacher of the universal Church, in whom the Church's charism of infallibility is present in a singular way.

In fact, the concept of infallibility itself is puzzling – and was soon to be revealed as such – even apart from the special powers of the Roman pontiff. Thus, also in section 25, we read:

> Although the bishops, taken individually, do not enjoy the privilege of infallibility, they do, however, proclaim infallibly the doctrine of Christ on the following conditions: namely, when, even though dispersed throughout the world but preserving for all that amongst themselves and with Peter's successor the bond of communion, in their authoritative teaching concerning matters of faith and morals, they are in agreement that a particular teaching is to be held definitively and absolutely. This is still more clearly the case when, assembled in an ecumenical Council, they are, for the universal Church, teachers of and judges in matters of faith and morals, whose decisions must be adhered to with the loyal and obedient assent of faith.

Perhaps the most important conclusion to be drawn from all this is that Vatican I's account of papal infallibility – and by implication of infallibility in general – was in no way challenged by the bishops at Vatican II, who either did not realize, or did not want to realize, that the supposed correction in the balance of power between the pope and themselves had hardly been effected; indeed in some respects episcopal power had diminished.

Admittedly, one effect of the Council would be the establishment by Paul VI in 1969 of regular synods of bishops, apparently with a view to sharing Church governance, though their membership was to be entirely determined by the pope. In the event, Paul determined that membership would consist of a group elected by bishops' conferences with a number of *ex officio* members (such as the Eastern Catholic patriarchs), and others chosen by the superiors of religious orders; the rest to be papal nominees. Thus, though this might look more 'democratic', the papal nominees were always on hand to ensure that the pope's wishes were made clear.

Paul knew that this less centralized façade need only be that, since the non-papal appointees would view their appointment as an opportunity to display their loyalty to the centre and (eventually at least) to put aside any less than papal-approved concerns. Thus, by controlling the membership of the synods as well the topics to be discussed, Paul offered the Church a more complex version of the rule that he who controls the membership of committees will normally control their decisions. In any case, and as we shall see, the determinations of synods could be rigged if a pope so wished. Arguably, as Cardinal Pell pointed out in an article for the *Spectator* (11 January 2023) written shortly before his death, the introduction of synods, far from increasing the authority of the bishops vis-à-vis the pope, can serve as a new tool for manipulating and degrading them.

Synods aside, as the Council proceeded, we can observe a number of other important occasions when, without questions asked, the bishops allowed the pope (now Paul VI) to act unilaterally and without requesting advice in Council: such were Paul's new opening to Orthodoxy in abandoning the anathemas of 1054 and the newly toxic matter of birth control. If we wonder why their theological advisers, especially if they were 'progressives', did not warn of the risks implicit in such behaviour, it is tempting to believe that the *periti* took the cynical view that it did not matter how but only that they got what they wanted. Some, however, not least Hans Küng, came later to recognize the implications of such a short-sighted attitude for those hoping for more clarity about infallibility, papal or otherwise, and its implications, even its intelligibility.[12] For the wider question of infallibility could not logically be separated from the relationship between the pope and the bishops.

In this chapter I am concerned less with whether or how the teaching pronounced may make sense than with what it is – while noting for further reference the tendency to emphasize, even extend, infallibility beyond that of the Roman pontiff himself, though without much clarity as to how this was to be understood. That would produce problems in the future, to resolve some of which a 'hermeneutic of continuity' would be invoked: this hermeneutic was intended to explain which parts of theoretically infallible Council decrees are to be read as requiring absolute obedience, and which, for various reasons requiring explication, are not so to be read. The problem will become acute where teachings radically opposed to each other – whether of the same Council or of one Council as opposed to another – seem to imply that at some time a Council has erred – with even the possibility of an heretical pope.

*   *   *

Less than a year after the opening of the Council Pope John died and in June 1963 Archbishop Montini of Milan, a cardinal with longtime curial experience and widely held the desirable successor of John XXIII, was duly elected and transformed into Paul VI. But Paul, often thought of as by nature a cautious, if not indecisive man – 'the Hamlet of the Vatican' – who tended to allow seeing all sides of a question to impede his decisions, saw his role in the Council rather differently from his predecessor. In *Ecclesiam Suam* (24 June 1964) he made clear that in some manner he wished the Council to continue on what he saw as its established path and that John's work be completed, but he also indicated a different, perhaps less 'progressive' emphasis, especially in referring to the specifically Catholic nature of the Church. Thus he cited Pius XII's *Mystici Corporis* rather than regularly persisting with the then fashionable phrase 'people of God' – and in so doing, indicated a greater anxiety about at least some of the changes now in the air or on the table. Whether in taking this apparently modifying line Paul was reasserting his predecessor's 'real' intent still remains unclear.

Paul was also determined to put a time-limit on endless and often repetitive debates and thus bring the Council to its conclusions as expeditiously as possible. That was to curb the attempts of the conservative 'minority' to produce a series of often procedural delays in the hope of

---

12. See Hans Küng, *Infallible?* (London: Collins, 1972), 47-52.

wearing down their opponents: a tactic which at times looked as though it might be successful. To put a stop to it, however, seemed to Paul to imply the necessity – other reasons apart – of securing in the Council's final decisions something as near that unanimity needed for securing full magisterial authority as possible: an analogous problem, one will recall, had been resolved at Vatican I by the decision of the inopportunists to get out of Rome before final voting took place.

It also meant making concessions to the conservative 'minority' (if perhaps concessions which Paul himself desired), while claiming that such concessions be regarded as 'suggestions' and as 'house-keeping'. As in Vatican I, the moral problem arising from this strategy was that, out of deference to the Roman pontiff, many members of the Council (both progressives and conservatives) would shrug off their former and conscientiously held beliefs and vote for what the pope required. As we shall see, for those who adopted this approach there could be psychological and moral consequences serving to confirm longstanding habits and tendencies to clericalism.

Nevertheless, despite the now demanded time-frame, 'conservatives' persisted in taking advantage of Paul's apparent indecision – this seeming to raise the possibility of anti-'majority' vetoes – and in 'Black Week' (14-21 November 1964) thought they had managed to torpedo the intent of the proposed decrees on ecumenism and religious freedom. But Paul in the end got what he wanted, which was a slightly less abrasive version of 'majority' opinion on ecumenism – as on the *Dogmatic Constitution on the Church*: a solution the disappointed newly progressive 'majority' chose to take (as Cardinal Döpfner nicely put it) as an exercise of papal diligence and care.[13] As for religious freedom, that was deferred, being as yet too hot to hold, not least because of Muslim and Eastern Church objections to proposals they would regard as too benevolent towards Jews.

In contrast to Pope John, Pope Paul was thus always prepared to intervene more directly, knowing that both rival factions would – in the spirit of Vatican I – fall into line, thus confirming that the current

---

13. Cf. L.A.G. Tagle, 'The "Black Week" of Vatican II', in Alberigo and Komon-chak, *History of Vatican II*, vol. 4, p. 394. As we shall discuss in more detail, the general attitude of both 'majority' and 'minority' is well summarized by Alberigo (*History* of Vatican II, vol. 5, p. 623): 'During this third period the majority of the bishops found themselves, on more than one occasion, spontaneously restraining their own convictions simply to avoid casting any shadow on their relations with the Pope.'

disputes revolved less around papal versus episcopal power than around how to get the pope to give his winning voice to one or other of the options, whether conservative or progressive, and however watered down. The conservatives could be encouraged to view the new changes as comparatively minor adjustments to older ways, though some – in particular Ottaviani, Ruffini of Palermo and Siri of Genoa – were certainly not always so convinced, rather taking the view that they should make the best of a bad job and by following the papal bidding at least be sure that the centralized power of the Roman Curia (though now pursuing very different policies in however bad faith) could be retained with only minor adjustments.

In that they were not entirely mistaken, for though Paul proceeded after the Council to a shake-up of the Curia, its authoritative position, as distinct from the theological views of some of its members, would change rather little. In the longer run, though not immediately, what changed was the authority of the Holy Office (soon to be renamed the Congregation for the Doctrine of the Faith) vis-à-vis the Secretariat of State – with a corresponding decline in concern for theological precision.

As for the 'progressives', some remained disappointed by Paul's drive for uniformity at the expense of more radical change (and hoped to make further progress in the 'spirit of the Council' after the Council itself had concluded), but all accepted that what the pope wants the pope will get and concluded that they had better take such goods as they were now likely to receive rather than risk the (not unknown) papal displeasure. In neither minority nor majority party were behaviours free of 'doublethink' about the relation of the new teachings to the old, a matter we shall treat in more detail.

∗   ∗   ∗

Conservatives always, and especially during the interminable debates on *Lumen Gentium*, thought that their traditional, i.e. post-Vatican I, teaching on papal authority was under threat, and (perhaps not least to placate them) Paul VI, in one of his now regular interventions, decided to add a 'Preliminary Notice' to the final form of the document, thus making clear his own conservative view on the relationship between pope and bishops. His move appears to have been intended at least in part to close a possible loophole for the more conciliar-minded in insisting that 'There is no such thing as the college [of bishops] without its head: [for] it is "the subject of supreme and entire power over the whole Church. This much must be acknowledged lest the fulness of the pope's power be jeopardized.'

Apart from this reassertion of papal power we may also notice a further example of the non-resistance of the bishops to any significant attempt to rebalance their relationship with the Holy See. The 'Preliminary Notice' was accepted with little debate, thus confirming that reform of a papal power however creeping was far from the most pressing concern of the progressives: that indeed, as Ottaviani and his supporters recognized (and, as we shall see Cardinal Siri noted with satisfaction) was from the 'progressive' point of view a serious mistake, indeed a failure to understand, in an important respect, the 'signs of the times'.

The aim of Paul's 'Notice' being less to limit what individual bishops might teach than what in concert they might, as a whole or as groups, command, it points out that all colleges have a head, and that the authority of a college could not be exercised without the approval of this head. As it then clarifies, the important distinction is not between pope and bishops but between the Roman pontiff acting alone and the Roman pontiff acting together with the bishops in giving his approval to 'collegial' action.

Such papal approval was presumably intended to be explicit, though that is not stated unambiguously, and hence a loophole for *joint* episcopal action without papal approval – even against papal wishes – remained. For while in Vatican I the phrase, 'without the assent of the Church' was intended to disallow any possibility of activities by purely *national* Churches – at that time the Church in Germany, though more remotely in mind was the French Gallicanism of the previous century – the omission in Paul's Notice of *explicit* papal approval for collective activities of nationally grouped bishops was – especially in Germany, self-appointed theological heartland of the Church – to become a source of confusion (even of the possibility of schism) both before and during the pontificate/ of Francis I.

For Francis's encouragement of a 'Synodal Path' has allowed the German episcopate to proceed along the very lines seemingly ruled out by Paul's Notice. Probably the fatal omission escaped attention because Paul's intent was to emphasize what the pope alone could do and groups of bishops alone could not do, rather than what they needed his explicit approval to do. The text runs, 'The Pope alone, in fact, being *head* of the college, is qualified to perform certain actions in which the bishops have no competence whatever', and significantly there is no apparent limit to what those actions might be. Nor can the Notice be interpreted as referring only to decisions *ex cathedra*, since it mentions the 'convocation and direction' of the college, and approval of the norms of its activities.

And the Notice goes further, so revealing in the text of *Lumen Gentium* itself an ambiguity in the desires of its drafters. For the authority of the pope as head of the 'College' is also to be embedded in a distinction between the very nature of papal and episcopal authority as handed down from the Apostles: namely that while the pope has received the undiminished power of Peter, the bishops (individually or as a group) have inherited no particular powers from the other Apostles, whose successors they are, neither in apostolic sees nor elsewhere.

This 'ontological' distinction seems sometimes but not always reflected in *Lumen Gentium* itself in its use of less 'authoritative' terms than 'College' to refer to the bishops as a group: at times named only as an 'order' or 'body' – and bodies not only are inactive but hardly exist without heads! (As Aristotle noted, a dead hand is not a hand.) The assertion in Paul's Notice that unlike popes other bishops do not inherit powers of any kind from the other Apostles seems to indicate not a loosening but a substantial tightening of papal control of the episcopacy in Vatican II. Now bishops seem *de facto* to be no longer successors of the Apostles in any significant sense but in practical terms creatures of the pope.

Indeed, although the powers of the bishops, as the Notice allows, are given by episcopal consecration, the exercise of those powers is entirely dependent on 'hierarchical' (i.e. papal) authority: a limitation certainly beyond the imaginings of most bishops in patristic times, let alone surely of Peter himself. That fact is obscured by a (surely disingenuous) comment near the end of the Notice that the 'hierarchical communion of all bishops with the pope is unmistakably hallowed by tradition'.

Understandably, Paul's Notice was greeted by Cardinal Siri with enthusiasm: 'Everything is all right! The Holy Spirit has entered the Council.... The Pope has dug in his heels and only he could have done it.'[14] But what the pope had effectively done was less to promote a better understanding of the relationship between the magisterium of the bishops and that of the pope than to assert that, in matters of both dogma – the *depositum fidei* – and doctrine of every sort, the power of the bishops is simply to propose; decision-making, apparently without episcopal restraint, is always within the authority of the pope alone. That, of course, is authority far more compendious than any assertion of papal infallibility *ex cathedra*; in effect it empowers the pope to act alone not only in pronouncing developments of dogma in the strict sense but wherever he chooses to act. As we shall see, that 'advice' was

---

14. Siri's journal for 17 November 1964, p. 561, cited by Tagle, 'Black Week', p. 439.

to be followed when the time was ripe, whether or not in accordance with a tradition which was in theory supposed to limit papal authority. Curiously enough, by the determinations of Vatican II, the uniqueness of papal power, emphasized once in the relatively innocuous matter of the canonization of saints, had spread over every aspect of ecclesiastical business.

                                        *   *   *

In light of Paul's exercise of authority at the Council, it will be helpful to glance more critically at a remarkable passage addressed in *Gaudium et Spes*, the 'Pastoral Constitution on the Church in the Modern World', to the 'whole of humanity' – and treating of conscience,[15] a theme we have

---

15. Ratzinger comments on this text at some length (citing Newman but seemingly not fully understanding his position) in his introduction to *Gaudium et Spes* in H. Vorgrimler, *Commentary on the Documents of Vatican II*, vol. 5 (London: Burns & Oates, 1967), pp. 134-36. He does point out, however, that the Council is 'rather evasive on the question of an erroneous conscience', though insisting that Metz's view that Aquinas taught that it should be followed is too brusque. The only other place where conscience is treated in the Council documents appears to be the first chapter of *Dignitatis Humanae* (the Declaration on Religious Liberty) where it is stated that restrictions on following one's conscience in matters of religion are contrary to Catholic teaching. Yet there is no comment here or elsewhere about why conscientious Christians in the past were persecuted: perhaps suggesting a lack of thought on vital but dangerous matters of conscience which might seem to cast doubt on the infallibility of earlier Councils and popes in Council. Not least of Vatican I: Döllinger (desperate to deny what he saw as the introduction of novelties in theology rather than wishing to reject dogmas long established) undoubtedly wrestled with his conscience and was consequently excommunicated, while various bishops who shared his views and then recanted just shrugged off any such apparent difficulties of conscience. In the *Declaration on the Relation of the Church to Non-Christian Religions* (*Nostra Aetate*) persecution and attacks on the conscience of other believers are passed over in haste: 'The Sacred Council now pleads with all (section 3) to forget the past (with its Christian-Muslim hostilities) and urges that a sincere effort be made to achieve mutual understanding'. And again (in section 4) we read that 'the Church reproves every form of persecution against whomsoever it be directed'. (The reference is specifically a summary of regret at past hostility to Jews.) Like many other Council documents the Declaration tends to a careless naïveté about other religions, bending over backwards to over-correct the past, not least about Muslims, while ignoring the implications

already found puzzling in the Catholic tradition, not least at Vatican I. We read (1.16) in a text echoing Paul (Romans 2:15-16) that:

> Man has in his heart a law inscribed by God. His dignity lies in observing this law, and by it he will be judged. His conscience is man's most secret core, and his sanctuary. There he is alone with God whose voice [according to Pius XII's radio message to youth of 23 March 1952] echoes in his depths. By conscience, in a wonderful way, that law is made known which is fulfilled in the love of God and of one's neighbour. Through loyalty to conscience Christians are joined to other men in the search for truth...[16]

But there is a catch: conscience may be led astray by unavoidable (or 'invincible') ignorance – or because we do not bother to think on what is good and true, or because we are blinded by habitual sinning. Which begs the question of the situation of those who do think on what is good and true, who are not strikingly blinded by serious and habitual sin, but who may still come up with the 'wrong' answer. Which in turn is to suggest (as Gregory VII already might have wished!) that for the Catholic the only option is obedience to (even faulty) Church, and especially papal decisions (and by implication to wondering how – or if – the Church or the pope *can* teach faulty doctrine). It might be hard to see how in accord with such theorizing, now apparently sanctioned by Vatican II, St Paul would have been able to 'challenge Peter to his face', forcing him to admit his error over the necessity for Gentiles to be circumcised (Galatians 2:14). Perhaps, after all, there are cases where, as we have seen Newman put it (with whatever intent), one should 'drink to Conscience first, then to the Pope'.

---

of such regret not only for truth but for the status of previous teachings. In this case differences between Muslim and Christian understandings of God are minimized, indeed virtually neglected. More generally we can recognize in the Declaration another example of a tendency to slur over doctrinal change comparable with seemingly rectifying the balance between bishops and the Supreme Pontiff while hardly doing any such thing: 'We never make mistakes'. We shall return to this question.

16. This looks like a star Conciliar example of what Matthew Levering in *The Abuse of Conscience* (Grand Rapids, MI: Eerdmans, 2021) deplores as 'conscience-centered morality'. Interestingly, in his catalogue of (usually bad) attempts to clarify the Catholic concept of conscience Levering has little to say of Newman.

Unfortunately, though it is easy to say we should follow our conscience, it is much more difficult, as we have already observed, to understand when (or if) it is well-formed. The 'modern world' was to get no more guidance on this from Vatican II than from Vatican I – and it is not much help even for a willing Catholic to be told to follow a well-formed conscience unless he or she is also told how a well-formed conscience is recognizable. If we are to follow our conscience in recognizing what limits we should set to papal power, whether as officially or unofficially understood, what – apart from reading the relevant but confusing texts of Aquinas or Newman or of Vatican I and Vatican II – are we supposed to do? Accept the authority of the pope and those who follow him when (as we judge) he is following the traditions of the Church, or at least acting in accordance with their spirit, and not when we might judge he is not? Or is that risky? Safer perhaps to follow the pope whatever he teaches!

As we shall see, that dilemma produced some strange results in the decades after Vatican II. For the question has now arisen as to how we should accept or reject the decrees of a pope when he seems out of sync with the traditions of the Church, or with legitimate and intelligible developments of those traditions – let alone if he might seem outright heretical, as has happened historically. That very problem of conscience lurks behind many of the near-unanimous decisions of Vatican II itself.

*   *   *

It is helpful to think of Vatican II as an 'event' in a particular historical context rather than as merely a collection of documents, and like it or not the effects of that event (as of other Councils from Nicaea to Trent and Vatican I) are fixed in the historical record as firmly as the documents themselves. As was to be expected – and as turned out to be the case – almost every bishop and theologian, whatever variety of theology he advocated, would now appeal to the Council as 'authoritative', its apparent ambiguities allowing readily for such variegated appeals. Hence after Vatican II, as after Vatican I, the Catholic world has been significantly changed, partly for the worse, partly for the better. Although it is not my primary purpose in this essay to evaluate the doctrinal/pastoral decisions of Vatican II but rather to consider their effect on later attitudes in the Church among both clergy and laity – and not least to the papacy itself – I would certainly not want to leave the impression that nothing significant and often beneficial was achieved at the Council event.

Much was indeed to change – and much to be further disputed – as a result of the Council's decisions, however implemented: thus there was no reaffirmation of the unique role of the thought of Aquinas in

Catholic seminaries and universities, while on the liturgy the story is more complicated: the Council was comparatively restrained about the replacement of Latin in the liturgy and did not envisage its complete abandonment in favour of vernacular languages. That was the decision of Paul VI[17] and his liturgical advisers, Cardinal Lercaro and Archbishop Bugnini, who (apparently supposing this to be the intent of the Council) produced their *Novus Ordo* for the Mass: thus aiming at what many of us think of as a desirable goal but generating the new product in an incompetent and often wilfully distorted original version open to more or less uncontrolled tampering and slovenly enactment..

As we have seen, there was also a new emphasis on ecumenism – and increasingly (as it turned out) to be carried on by 'dialogue' rather than with main intent to recover members of other Christian communities for Catholicism. The long existing trend toward greater emphasis on scripture and the early Church was also to be further developed – in effect at the expense of Thomism or of 'decadent neo-scholasticism' of whatever flavour – and often with no check on the absurdities perpetrated by members of the biblical studies guild which earlier popes, as we have seen, had tried ineffectually to control. The laity were to be encouraged (or so it seemed) to greater participation in Catholic affairs (though on a couple of occasions it was deemed during the Council itself that it would be premature for women – in one case the distinguished economist Barbara Ward – to address the assembled bishops). Above all the Council must be seen as a truly international gathering, indicating, the presence of the Church in the entire world, and thus being a precursor of the gradual migration of the Church from its ancient and now largely dechristianized European home.

National bishops' conferences were now to be mandatory: this with the aim to satisfy the continuing hopes of at least some of the bishops, and of Catholics more generally, that some sort of episcopal authority be re-established in the spiritual as well as in the bureaucratic aspects of Church guidance. Few foresaw that such conferences might have rather different effect, namely that individual bishops could shelve their spiritual responsibilities in hiding behind the shield of the national

---

17. I shall return to the problem of the relationship between what the Council intended and what Paul VI actually imposed in the next chapter. A good summary of the 'problem' of Paul's activity and its motivation can be found in G. Dipippo, 'Paul VI did Not Exist: A 'Nostalgic' Response to George Weigel', in P.A. Kwasniewski (ed.), *Sixty Years After* (New York: Angelico Press, 2022), pp. 47-58.

group. But perhaps such spiritual responsibility now lay with the pope alone: the newly elected Jesuit General Pedro Arrupe – then urging his Society to return to its traditional role as (papally licensed) scourge of atheists, heretics and unbelievers (in this case the Communists though the Council generally declined to name them) – insisted that the immediate concerns of particular dioceses (and presumably groups of dioceses) should always be sacrificed to 'absolute obedience to the Supreme Pontiff'. Some of his hearers wondered whether he was hoping that the papalist principles he was now advancing – so much in evidence in the Society of Jesus since Vatican I – were to be reaffirmed in 'the spirit of Vatican I' for the whole Church: a fateful if realistic interpretation, though inaccurate about the eventual direction, hence fate, of Arrupe himself.

*   *   *

Though at the Council much was achieved, problems involving the authority of Councils in general lurked beneath the surface as a result of the manner in which many of the decrees were eventually framed. This was particularly clear in the case of attitudes to Jews and Judaism and to the right to religious freedom in general, where submission to papal preferences could easily combine with double-think (conscience notwithstanding). Cardinal Bea himself admitted that what was originally proposed on religious freedom (in February 1961) was 'not traditional' and that, despite later modifications, remained broadly true. The recommendations on the matter, for example of Lateran IV and Vatican II, cannot honestly be reconciled, nor can Vatican II be on this point regarded as a legitimate development but rather a repudiation of Lateran IV.

In the world of Lateran IV rights were urged and protected by differing groups against one another (guilds against magnates, bishops against kings, etc.). No one prated of religious freedom; it was simply assumed that error had no rights – and hence the problem acquired new urgency when in the early modern period *subjective* rights became important. Some, such as the Dominican Las Casas, claimed that everyone has the right to follow his own religion: thus the aim of the missionary is not to deny that right but to seek to convert to the right religion those who have a right to religious freedom: for Las Casas 'rights theory' (if we may anachronistically so name it) is properly to be viewed as a matter not of 'charity', but of justice.

That view – though having precursors in the patristic age – had been for centuries largely unacceptable to the wider Church, and hostility to it was fuelled by the exaggerated rights claims that swept the world after the French Revolution. Despite Leo XIII's enthusiasm for 'rights' more generally, nineteenth-century popes denied the right to religious freedom (even, where possible, to religious toleration), persisting in the view that there could be no such right. Before, at and after Vatican II, however, the situation changed again, with the Church becoming eager to embrace much of the rights-theory flooding Western society, while paying rather little attention to the awkward fact that the acceptance of a *right* to religious freedom must be seen to clash with the assumptions of earlier ages that error in religion had no moral standing at all.

None of this implies that we should blame our predecessors for their mistakes, rather that if past mistakes can be explained by ignorance or mistaken deduction, Truth will now require that we delete them from the list of 'definitive' teachings. Better that than pretend they were not what they were, but then the demonstrable fact will remain that the Church can and does make mistakes in what it accounts as 'definitive'. We should notice that even at Vatican II, where the right to religious freedom was emphasized, the language used was prone to suggest that there had never been a problem.

For although the Declaration on Religious Freedom starts with a fine assertion of a right to it, first in the preamble and then again by chapter 3 we find ourselves involved in the apparent confusion to which we have drawn attention as to the paramount necessity to follow one's conscience. We cannot but also notice that in the Declaration it is judged convenient to claim to be 'developing' the teaching of *recent* popes on the inviolable rights of the person and on the constitutional order of society – while neglecting to recognize that earlier popes not only taught no such thing, but thought along very different lines.

Thus did Vatican II defenders of the revised teachings prefer to forget earlier conciliar and papal determinations and remember only the gradually softening attitudes which began, they claimed, in the days of Gregory XVI. However, Vatican II's teaching is no mere softening. For although there were *signs* of a different approach even before Gregory XVI, especially (as we noted) in Las Casas's claim that the Indians had some sort of right to religious freedom – that is, the right to err – such ideas had no official status. The amnesia at Vatican II about centuries of Catholic tradition indicates a 'double-think' acceptable to the 'majority' in the interests of securing the changes they required and to the conservative 'minority' in so far as it enabled them to accept anything acceptable to the pope.

A belated attempt was made by some at the Council to show that the new attitudes on the right to religious freedom (advocated already by John XXIII in *Pacem in Terris*[18]) depended on a deeper theological understanding of what had to be admitted about the freedom to err if man's role as formed in the image and likeness of God is given wider emphasis than was normally the case in the recent past. Thus in the Declaration on Religious Freedom itself (2) it is pointed out that 'the right to religious freedom has its foundation not in the subjective disposition of the person, but on his very nature'. True enough, only a bit late and a bit overlooked previously.

For if Cardinal Bea was right in admitting that the new teaching was a substantial breach with the past, that can hardly be countered by the admission that bad theology caused past mistakes: a mistake, however caused, is a mistake. Some, of course, claim that there was little change, indeed honest development, at the Council – for the 'good' reason that if change is admitted in the 'definitive' teachings of the universal and ordinary magisterium, how one can explain that past errors really were errors while guaranteeing that present determinations – indeed other past determinations, and not only of popes – are to be held as in some sense infallible (or at least candidates for infallibility)?

*   *   *

After the Council closed, at least three attempts have been made to argue that there has been no substantive change on the right to religious freedom, that at least the more recent popes – but is that enough? – have set out on a path now explicitly recognized and further developed at the Council itself.[19] Thomas Pink claimed that the Council (in *Dignitatis Humanae*) was only concerned that the right to religious freedom be recognized by the state[20] – and that continuity of Catholic teaching on the question is evident from the time of Leo XIII. That seems inadequate:

---

18. *Pacem in Terris* was always suspect among the 'minority', not least because of its repeated emphasis on rights, though notably the right to life of the unborn is not mentioned: Fernandez, Master General of the Dominicans, and Cardinal Browne OP claimed that this encyclical was persistently misused by those wishing to develop/change the tradition; see J. Hamer, 'Histoire du texte de la Déclaration', in J. Hamer and Y. Congar (eds), *La liberté religieuse* (Paris: Cerf, 1967), pp. 69-71.
19. For a good summary see A. Nichols, *Conciliar Octet* (San Francisco: Ignatius, 2019), pp. 140-45.
20. Cf. T. Pink, '*Dignitatis Humanae*: Continuity After Leo XIII', in T. Crean (ed.), *Dignitatis Humanae Colloquium* (Norcia: Dialogos Institute, 2017), pp. 105-45.

Dignitatis Humanae (2) urges that religious coercion should be exercised neither by individuals, nor by social groups, nor by any human power.

To argue that there is continuity since Leo XIII is only to push the problem back a stage further. It is true that Leo introduced massive numbers of 'rights' into Catholic theology, but not the right to religious freedom; in the Middle Ages any form of religious freedom, as we noted, was rejected – and the 'right' to it unknown. The proper conclusion to be drawn from this history is that perhaps Leo and certainly some of his successors, including those at the Council, taught a different doctrine of religious freedom from that of their predecessors: in particular about the *right* to religious freedom. The evidence shows that for whatever reason the Church now understands human nature in a significantly different way and therefore has had to correct (not to expand or modify) the ordinary and universal magisterium as exercised in the past on this issue.

A second attempt to escape the obvious was made by Brian Harrison,[21] who argued that nineteenth-century popes accepted that some (but not all) anti-Catholic writings and teachings should be immune from any attempted repression. This again misses the point about rights. The right to religious freedom, in the case of freedom from suppression of strictly religious material, is now claimed to be an essential gift of God to human nature; rights, including the right to religious freedom, to be part of our freedom as created in the image and likeness of God. This has to entail the right to make mistakes *in good faith*, not least in matters of religion. Again it is the insertion and revised understanding of rights (or some rights) into Catholic discourse which marks a radical departure from ancient practice.

As I shall argue in a later chapter, the only solution would appear to be to allow that decrees of the ordinary and universal magisterium attain to differing degrees of truth, thus authorizing in some cases substantial revision over time; there is a hierarchy of truths which must be the task of theologians to identify. They must explain how in the light of history (for example) earlier decisions of the magisterium about persecution on grounds of religion should have always been low in this hierarchy and now turn out to be in error. Ecumenically, of course, the whole notion of a hierarchy of doctrinal truths is much disliked by the ambiguous Orthodox – one of the reasons why they can seem to be theologically frozen in the distant past.

---

21. B. Harrison, 'Reading *Dignitatis Humanae* within a Hermeneutic of Continuity', in Crean, *Colloquium*, pp. 45-55.

A third attempt to defend continuity over religious freedom was that of Valuet[22] who argues that the Council never asserted that human beings have the right to propagate error. Yet that is by implication – and from a Catholic point of view – precisely what the claim to a right to religious freedom entails. Clearly all religions cannot be free from error, but the Council had no objection to Jews or Muslims propagating doctrines which from a Catholic point of view must be at least in part erroneous.

As for the Council itself, just as earlier attitudes to freedom of religion were thus casually brushed aside, so in the debate on Judaism few took note of the honest comments of Cardinal Ruffini about the anti-Christian material in the Talmud – though it was largely because of the Talmud that in the thirteenth century Augustine's (and Paul's) teaching on leaving the Jews alone had been widely abandoned, not least by popes. Neglect of history can be used not only to deny doctrinal change but to whitewash circumstances which help explain Catholic error but are inadmissible in contemporary 'dialogue'.

Probably some of the bishops recognized that to admit the weaknesses of Lateran IV and other authoritative utterances would in effect be to abandon the pretence of the infallibility of Councils, which in turn might cause further concern about the infallibility of the pope, indeed about how to understand infallibility more generally. Perhaps it would also encourage those inclined to forget about doctrine and think of the Church as just a charitable organization serving the 'modern world' with a limited supernatural or spiritual flavour: concern, as we have noticed, already expressed by some of the more foresighted at the Council and destined to have a substantial afterlife.

Nor was the crumbling of opposition to changes in Church teaching (beside that on the right to religious freedom) the only disturbing feature of episcopal behaviour at the Council. We have already noted that the repeat emphasis on papal power was accepted rather easily by the voting bishops when confronted with Paul VI's 'clarification' of *Lumen Gentium*. For just voting the 'right' way was not the only option available to them – and what happened in this case at Vatican II reminds us of the unconscionable decision of the minority bishops to leave Rome at the end of Vatican I. Apart from declining to debate, a bishop might rather decline to vote *after* debate, – or, yes, even prefer to vote the 'wrong' way. Nor was what happened over Paul's Notice a 'one-off'; it clearly revealed

---

22. B. Valuet, *'Dignitatis humanae* – Contrary to Tradition?'*, in Crean, *Colloquium*, pp. 147-69.

an episcopal mindset. In similar vein, and for no apparently responsible reason, the assembled bishops (presumably supported by their *periti*, progressive or other) also declined even to debate the 'suggestion' of Paul VI that he would reserve decisions about 'the contraceptive pill' for later resolution by himself, dependent as it was on the assertion in *Dei Verbum* (2.8) that popes did indeed have such powers.

That might look like a cynical choice to avoid responsibility for taking (or declining to take) an unpopular decision – and not least in the case of those conservatives who might hope that Paul would delay his decision indefinitely; at least he had already indicated that his mind was not made up in favour of a change in Church teaching. Why that was the case must perhaps remain unclear; the most generous explanation would be that he realized that whereas definitive teachings challenged in the past had been almost entirely matters of dogmatic theology, this time, and importantly, it was to be over the Church's *moral* teaching and authority and whether the Church might or might not be required to 'keep up with the times'.

*   *   *

That said, we cannot leave the Second Vatican Council without further comment on the striking near-unanimity achieved by Pope Paul and the psychology of those who went along with his wishes even against their better judgement. As after Vatican I Döllinger had grounds for lamenting that people who strongly opposed a definition during the Council debates saw the matter completely differently when Pius IX seemed determined to get one, so in the case of Vatican II many commentators have expressed surprise at how apparently conscientious objection, especially to proposals on religious freedom, melted away when the pope showed his hand.

Some few waxed cynical. Thus an anonymous bishop suggested that the Council was 'a sinister comedy of three thousand good-for-nothings, with gold crosses on their chests, who don't even believe in the Trinity or the Virgin, or at least some of them don't'.[23] In light of subsequent developments this evocation cannot be dismissed out of hand, though it judges rather than explains the phenomenon of unanimity. More precise is De' Mattei's comment on the vote on religious freedom after Paul's intervention: 'They proceeded to a vote and, by some mysterious *mechanism* that melted the opposition', there were 1997 *placets* and 224 *non placets*.[24]

23. Cited by De' Mattei, *Second Vatican Council*, pp. 424-25.
24. De' Mattei, *Second Vatican Council*, pp. 445, 494.

De' Mattei explains this 'miracle' in terms of the post-Vatican I mentality whereby 'generations of priests had been trained to obey the Roman pontiff without qualification'. As (St) Louis had put it (surely a little extremely), 'Our Creed is the pope, our morality is the pope, our life is the pope ... for us the pope is Jesus Christ'. Or in summary and less exotically, for many morality had been reduced to obedience. A more basic question, however, is not with what happened at Vatican I or even Vatican II, but rather how even before Vatican I among the ultramontanes – and not only – an extraordinary deference to papal authority was already in place, as best typified by Dupanloup's unwillingness to embarrass the pope by voting against his known wishes. We have pointed to the fear of the encroaching 'modern world' and an outpouring of sympathy for Pius IX in his obvious predicament as encouraging such deference, but perhaps such immediate explanations do not go to the root of the matter. Rather we should consider the nature of ecclesial, and especially clerical, obedience more generally, and ask whether any 'model' for such obedience can be identified.

A model is not far to seek. From its earliest days the Church had been viewed as a spiritual army, and obedience to one's commander is a necessary feature of an efficient and effective military force. The pope, having become after 1054 sole 'commander' in the West, the demands of the military model – by then in a feudal context – could hardly be ignored. Yet with a military model, the question arises as to the limits, if any, of one's obedience to one's commander.

If we now compare the ecclesial situation with secular military structures, we will note that in the ancient world where the Church grew up, and in the medieval world in which it took on the main features of its Western form, the ordinary soldier – even the ordinary officer – would not be held responsible for obeying improper orders from his superior – unless in 'Christian times' they involved actions immediately harmful to the Church. In our world, and especially after the Second World War and the Nuremburg Tribunals, that assumption has changed.

Now we hold that obedience even in an army cannot be absolute; that there can be circumstances in which we are morally bound to disobey the orders even of a legitimate authority. In earlier days that higher authority would be regarded as responsible for whatever atrocities he might order, whereas the ordinary soldier could plead that he was 'just obeying orders' when carrying them out. Perhaps the model of the Church as an army is still functioning on the older model of the requirements of military discipline. If so, what should now happen when 'ecclesial' atrocities are demanded of the 'lower ranks'? If commands of a pope are supposed to be (at least often) in effect divine commands, ought they ever be disobeyed? 'After all', as Di Nardo put it 'he is the pope'.[25] Must we not now argue, however, that, as in an army so in the hierarchical Church, it needs to be recognized that some orders should not be obeyed, even though it may be made very uncomfortable to disobey them – though in modern circumstances disobeying a pope is hardly likely to lead to being put up against a wall and shot!

Problems will arise if we persist with the older model of 'military' obedience, of which three can be immediately noted. First, that once the spell is broken, radical disobedience (analogous to a military mutiny) may ensue. (This was to happen after *Humanae Vitae*.) Second, that conservatives who follow their ('educated') consciences – at Vatican II Siri was a perfect example – will be liable to give way to progressive popes whose followers labour less under such conscientious disadvantage. Third, that a habit of suppressing one's conscience resolves itself into living in two compartments, and bad faith leads to the kind of *de facto* cynicism about truth (including religious truth) which, as we noted, our more cynical bishop identified among the '3000 good-for-nothings'. Given such obedience, if we have a 'good' pope, things will appear to the more conservative to go well, or at least improve; if we have an unorthodox pope to go badly. Yet it seems only reasonable to hold that truth is not whatever a pope wants to proclaim but what, if he does his job, he will proclaim as being objectively the case. As we have seen, Newman's attempt to resolve problems entailed by a possibly arbitrary pope through his special account of the religious conscience must be rejected as a fudge. Rather we should recall that, already at Vatican I, Strossmayer had compared the 'servility' of the bishops to that of the Roman senators who proclaimed the Emperor – the commander-in-chief – a god.

*   *   *

Although Tillard believed that 'at Vatican II [Pope Pius IX's] *Pastor Aeternus* was "received" in the dogmatic sense [desired] by the minority of Vatican I',[26] this judgment is belied by the attitude of the 'progressives' at the Council itself and by the continuing – indeed increasing – assumption (not only of conservatives but also of progressives) that in the Church what matters more than anything else is the support of the Roman pontiff. Indeed, Vatican II tells us that, even on seriously contested doctrinal points where such support directs the

25. Conversation reported to author.
26. Tillard, *Bishop of Rome*, p. 35.

bishops to accept radical change, it remains true that in the last resort it is largely the pope's decision and only the pope's decision that counts. When the legacy of Vatican II is finally clarified, that fact should not be forgotten. Though the initial 'hot' topic of Vatican II – the need to revitalize the role of the bishops in the light of the enhanced and partially elucidated authority of the pope – was never entirely forgotten, it was far from central to the final documents; indeed, on that score little was changed. Important changes – or better 'additions' – are indeed to be noted in church structures as resulting from the Council's work, but any apparent enhancement of the power of the episcopate seems to be at best cosmetic. While the Council developed the concept of the Church as a 'communion' of individual Churches, the question of episcopal as opposed to papal power has in practical terms been dismissed or archived, and so has remained.[27]

---

27. So Tillard, *Bishop of Rome*, p. 41: '*Lumen Gentium* never settled the difficult question of the boundaries in practice between the authority and power of the bishop of Rome and that of the other bishops, whether because of the "minority's" influence, or from having too little time for its theology to ripen, or too little time generally, or from fear of provoking average Catholic opinion.' Or because they preferred to leave it ambiguous?

Chapter 8

The Pope, the 'Pill' and the
'Woman Problem'

Oxford University Demographer: 'What activity do people often
engage in when it gets dark or the lights go out, as they did
recently in New York?'
Disingenuous student: 'I don't know.'
Demographer: 'F**kin', Mr. G….p, f**kin".[1]

We have noticed the determination of Paul VI (always apparently
wishing to reform but nervous about damaging tradition, not least the
more recent version of 'tradition' as to papal authority) to offer generally
welcome 'suggestions' as to how the Council should proceed: not
least in attaching his Notice endorsing papal seniority to the *Dogmatic
Constitution on the Church*. We have also seen how he was prepared to
override the ditherings of the bishops and exert his own authority in
largely undebated actions: examples are his decisions to accomplish a
meeting of reconciliation in Jerusalem with the Ecumenical Patriarch
Athenagoras – to be consummated by the withdrawal of the mutual
excommunications imposed in 1054 at the origins of the 'Great Schism' –
and to proclaim a new title for Mary as Mother of the Church (thus
upstaging the more 'conservative' proposal that she be declared 'Mediatrix
of Graces'). After the Council Paul's willingness to go well beyond its
decisions on his own initiative has already been noticed in his *Novus
Ordo* for the Mass, with its mandatory *abolition* of Latin which would

---

1. Recounted to the author by the 'student' in question.

have surprised many of the Council Fathers, not least (presumably) Pope John, who wanted Latin to be respected and retained in the Church, especially in seminary education.

More widely and immediately important, both inside and outside the Church, Paul decided to reserve to himself a major decision about the legitimacy of a new form of artificial contraception. Contraceptive devices had, as we noted, been condemned by Pius XI, and that condemnation was repeated at the Council itself (*Gaudium et Spes* 51). But the problem was now highlighted by the widespread use by women both Catholic and non-Catholic – and appreciated by many men – of the contraceptive 'pill' which had become available in the United States since 1960. Apart from encouraging fornication and adultery, it was already recognized by the more thoughtful that its widespread use would change the social structure of sexuality, giving women greater power to decide whether or not they wanted at any particular time to become pregnant. That could affect both the opportunities for women in contemporary society and the dynamics of the marital relationship itself.

Paul's decision to disallow conciliar debate on the 'pill' not only failed to end the matter but rather revealed wider ramifications affecting both his own authority and the authority of the Church more generally. In particular it led to an enduring challenge to the whole structure of Catholic sexual morality: indeed, in the light of the intellectual confusion which the debate brought with it, to the structure of Catholic orthodoxy itself. The battle over the 'pill' (indeed about contraception in general) would continue to rage long after Paul's death, ever more urgently raising the question whether, with all the autocratic authority Vatican I had vested in the Roman pontiff, he would be able to see off this new challenge to tradition, to the Church and to that authority itself. But then perhaps Rome might change its tune, here and elsewhere. By 2022 Vatican sources were already hinting that Paul's eventual rejection of the 'pill' would be overturned.

The extent of this danger was plainly unperceived by Paul when he made his fateful decision. Indeed it remains unclear, as we observed, why he took upon himself the responsibility for resolving a problem which so seriously affected the relationship between the Church and the modern world. For the matter had been raised by Cardinal Suenens, a personal friend of the pope, in the third session of the Council itself. Why did Paul not conclude that he could secure the result he wanted then and there (more or less with unanimity) on this issue, as he could on many others, including the very tricky question of religious freedom?

To understand Paul's dilemma we must briefly rehearse traditional Catholic assumptions about the 'practice' of marriage as well as the mentality of those who wished to update those assumptions in what they saw as the light of contemporary biological and social science. Paul's approach to contraception was obviously intended to be primarily relevant to the practice of married Catholics; any other contraceptive activity would be part of a more basic sinfulness. To understand what was traditionally expected of married Catholics – and the problems that ensued from it – it is appropriate to start with the teachings of Augustine which were largely the basis of Church teaching prior to Vatican II.[2] Augustine had tried to find a middle path between the extreme hostility to sexuality as such, represented by the early Jerome, and the more 'permissive' attitude – not least the equation of the holiness of matrimony with that of virginity – as urged by 'heretics' such as Helvidius and Jovinian. He deployed not only biblical – indeed dominical – injunctions (as against divorce) but also the insistence of Roman law that the purpose of marriage is the begetting of legitimate children. As he put it, the parents of the bride given away in marriage intend to become grandparents, not pimps (*Serm.* 51.13.21-22).

Children then are the primary aim of marriage, but Augustine (and the Church which followed him) added two other conditions for Catholics: the *fides*, the loyalty between spouses which was to persist until the death of one of them, and the sacramental aspect (though Augustine's concept of sacrament differs from more recent usage) whereby the bond of indissolubility reflects the covenant between Christ and his Church (Ephesians 5:23). But although the expected children result from the 'friendship' between the parents, both of whom must consent to the marriage, intercourse merely for pleasure is better foregone even in our 'fallen' state. In more Augustinian language, like a just war it is objectively bad but necessary, as affording relief from a concupiscence endemic in both males and females. Nevertheless, even in a fallen world marriage is at the heart of a well-ordered society; in moral terms it 'precedes' our fallen state and would have been desirable even if Adam and Eve had not fallen.

Augustine's position, the foundation of Catholic teaching until the twentieth century, has obvious weaknesses. He seems to afford little or no recognition to the 'marital act' deepening – indeed as sealing – the

---

2. Augustine's treatment of marriage has been endlessly discussed and evaluated; for my own more detailed view see J.M. Rist, *Augustine: Ancient Thought Baptized* (Cambridge: CUP, 1994), pp. 246-52.

'friendship' between the spouses, or that its role is not limited to directing lust into socially acceptable procreation. That weakness would become associated – not in Augustine himself but in many of his successors – with a deep hostility to the body as such: to the belief that sexual sin was an effect of a 'war' between body and soul. Augustine did not hold that view; for him sin is imposed on the body by the sinful soul, but the nuances of his position were generally neglected. In more practical terms the result of the 'old ways' – and not only among Catholics – was the bearing of more children than might be beneficial either to the health of the mother or to the family finances and the chance of a decent education for the offspring.

In the present world there has arisen the question of overpopulation; however, the principal demand for more contraception at the Council and in its aftermath came from the wealthier countries, especially in Europe, where larger families could more generally be afforded and where the greater education of parents was already inclined to lower the chances of the over-generation of children. In fact, one of the effects of the eventual Western disregard for *Humanae Vitae* would be a reduction of the birth-rate such as seriously to risk the size of the national workforce and, in the longer run, the ability of the diminishing cohort of workers to support an increasingly aging population.

In a long speech at the Council, applauded by many and backed especially by Latin-Americans, Cardinal Suenens called in question the traditional emphasis on the primary purpose of the 'marital act' as procreation; insufficient weight, he argued, had been placed on the unitive aspect of sex in marriage and more attention should be paid to recent scientific work on fertility, as also to the problem of overpopulation in many parts of the world. For some this proved too much: Ruffini pounded on his desk with his fist and complained to the Secretary of State, while Paul himself was to reprimand Suenens at an audience for his 'lack of judgment'.[3] That invited contrary interpretations: was Suenens's proposal inopportune or morally objectionable? The latter would turn out eventually to be the pope's view, though at the Council itself that remained uncertain.

Several possible explanations – all of which might have some validity – have been offered for Paul's decision to defer a decision: that he wanted to avoid a massive and in large part hostile debate in the press about birth control to break out during the Council itself, thereby, among other things, distracting bishops, laity and the general public

---

3. For details see De' Mattei, *Second Vatican Council*, pp. 392-97.

from other urgent matters. Perhaps his published view that he wished the matter first to be examined by a special committee provides the real answer to what, as we noted, was a new and substantive question not about 'faith' but about the Church's traditional authoritative teaching (until recently shared by all other mainline Churches) on this 'moral' issue. Or perhaps he was afraid that the bishops might be seriously divided or even vote in favour of a change in the rules which he himself would be unwilling to accept. At the Council itself, in November 1965 (under pressure from Ottaviani and others), he had apparently endorsed the anti-contraceptive teaching of Pius XI's seemingly 'definitive' *Casti Connubii* and of a Pastoral Letter of Pius XII to the English bishops of May 1964.[4]

Paul certainly knew that outside the Council strong arguments for change had already been made, among many others, by the former archbishop of Bombay, Thomas Roberts SJ, and the German theologian Bernard Häring. It might be better to let things be handled more prudently and – immediately at least – less publicly than in open Council debate. As a first step to resolve the matter when the Council ended, Paul set up a Commission, with Ottaviani significantly in the chair and the less conservative Döpfner as his deputy. The other members were mostly moral theologians (which may have been a mistake in view of the wider ramifications of the problem) – though even the married themselves were to be consulted.

The Commission deliberated long and hard, and it was widely assumed that its recommendations would be for change and that Paul would accept them. Such expectations were only partially vindicated. By nine votes to three (with abstentions) the Commission voted in favour of change. Ottaviani, however, refused to present its majority recommendation (preferring with others to submit a minority report), and the pope was handed the majority opinion by Döpfner, who was presumably relieved that the 'right' result had been achieved.

There followed a long silence, but eventually Paul sided with Ottaviani and the minority. As to why he had done so, plausible suggestions can be proposed. First there was the continuing tradition in the Church.[5]

---

4. For details of the frantic discussion before and after Paul's 'counsels' on matrimony were presented, see P. Hünermann, 'The Final Weeks of the Council', in Alberigo and Komonchak, *History of Vatican II*, vol. 5, pp. 408-19.

5. It is clear from John A. Noonan's *Contraception* (Cambridge, MA: Harvard University Press, 1965) that earlier teaching about contraception had been

In earlier times (though not in the twentieth century) the question of contraception had been widely confused with that of abortion, but with Baer's identification in 1827 of the role of ovaries in the process of conception, any notion that the male sperm contained a homunculus which contraception would allow to die and so was in effect murderous, had been relegated to history.

Nevertheless, the teaching about the intrinsic evil of contraception by artificial means continued as before, being especially strengthened by *Casti Connubii*: indeed, Pius XI's forceful restatement of traditional teaching, from long before the 'pill' had been invented, certainly made it hard for Paul to urge, as many expected, that the advent of the 'pill' made a significant difference to the theological (as distinct from the pragmatic) situation. He also knew that supporters of the 'pill' (such as Suenens) looked to rewrite large parts of the traditional teachings on marriage more generally, especially in playing down the older emphasis on the 'generation of legitimate children': something the modern world longed to hear.

Paul had to face the fact that any liberalizing of the moral law in this instance would be a clear indication that Catholic moral teaching – and why not beyond morality? – was open to major revision, indeed to reversal. Of course, a similar problem had arisen at the Council, as conservatives had pointed out, about freedom of religion, but since Paul made it clear that on that question he wanted change, dodgy arguments had to be cobbled together – as we noted are still in some quarters being cobbled together – that no substantial change had been accepted.

But any open admission by Paul that moral teaching on sexuality could be radically changed (rather than merely expanded, as might be said of the new emphasis on the unitive as well as the procreative aspects of sexual intercourse among the married) would not only damage the Church's immediate moral authority but might undermine – or at least reveal – some of the ambiguities, even contradictions, in its (and the pope's) definitive teachings more widely. To defuse so serious a threat would have required far wider analysis than Paul was prepared to embark on when facing his immediate dilemma, though John Paul II was later to attempt it. Paul, therefore, contented himself with following Ottaviani and the traditionalists in insisting that the 'pill' made no

---

invariably hostile – which might be supposed to make the possibility of change less likely and which the conservatives on Paul's committee were able to insist was the well-established position of the infallible ordinary and universal magisterium, and in recent times.

theological difference, that there could be no finessing of Church teaching about contraception. This was to invite further questions about which moral teachings are 'definitively' prescribed by the pope, which 'definitively' prescribed by the ordinary magisterium and which remain open for future generations to address – leaving much scope for future theologians and canonists, if not to fudge, then certainly to mystify the ordinary bloke in the pew.

So Paul made his lonely and almost inevitable (as viewed from hindsight) decision and was aghast at the hostile reception it received, his surprise being one more indication of how far the official Church was out of touch with the rapidly changing 'culture' of a modern world in light of whose practices it was supposed to be being 'updated'. Whatever the reasons for his decision, it is clear that when writing *Humanae Vitae* he seriously misjudged the mentality current in the Church not only about 'the pill' but about sexual morality more generally. Nor did he allow himself to be much influenced by a memorandum from a group of theologians in Krakow, including Cardinal Wojtyla, who expressed the view that an arid restatement of the tradition in terms of natural law alone would win little support; discussion of the 'marital act' should be carried on in a more 'personalized' manner, emphasizing that sexuality be humanized and that the use of the pill was degrading, especially to women who thus risked becoming a mere source of masculine pleasure. When he became pope Wojtyla tried to repair the damage by re-emphasizing the more 'personalist' aspects of sexuality, but the harm had been done.

Paul knew, of course, that a renewed ban on contraception, to include the 'pill', would be castigated in the secular press, but it seems that, despite his apparent concern about what the bishops might do unwisely in the Council, he underestimated the unwillingness both of many clergy and of large swathes of the laity to reject the liceity of the new form of artificial contraception, whether or not condemned by the ordinary and universal – hence assumed to be at least definitive – magisterium. He presumably supposed that, not least because of the heightened authority which papal infallibility had given him, he could assume and enforce acceptance of that ordinary magisterium. Perhaps in his clerical bubble he failed to comprehend that the ordinary magisterium itself could (at least on 'human' questions of sexual morality) have become a dead letter among millions of the lay faithful and a substantial section of the clergy. The lay faithful in particular might accept the Mystery of the Trinity, but would not accept to be deprived of what they saw as legitimate sexual pleasures now separable from that dread of repeated unwanted pregnancies which had plagued previous generations. Perhaps Paul thought that the earthquake he had called up would subside; which in a way it did, as many of the clergy who remained in the Church as celibates would eventually pretend to accept his decree but give very different advice to their flocks. Bad faith again might seem to solve the problem.

If Paul thought that at least the clergy would *immediately* cave in (as they had done before, not least at Vatican I over infallibility and at Vatican II over his desire for an eventual near-uniformity of the bishops on what were to be the published Council documents), he was seriously mistaken: many bishops and much of the laity were inclined to put a wholly different complexion on the wishes of popes when more personal matters than abstract debate about Church traditions in dogmatic theology or papal authority itself were in question. A less 'dogmatic', more 'pastoral' (i.e. ambiguous) papal approach to sexuality – the Council, remember, had always been billed as 'pastoral', not 'dogmatic'- would have been appreciated by many both clergy and laity who might for a while at least remain unworried as to whether, on paper, the old rigidities were still in place.

There was also a certain serious philosophico-theological difficulty in the encyclical itself, or at least a presentation of the problem which introduced much unnecessary confusion into the ensuing debates. The traditional Catholic belief in the priority of procreation, always interpreted as leaving every 'marital act' open to the possibility of new life, has two features which have often been united but theoretically need not be. Catholic theologians would agree that – biology permitting – being willing, indeed wishing, to produce children, is an essential attitude for those intending to marry; that can certainly be defended as scriptural. |However, as the 'majority' in Paul's commission argued, to be open to children does not entail being open to children every time the 'marital act' is performed, which is the position that *Humanae Vitae* and successive papal documents uphold. As we noted, when Wojtyla became pope as John Paul II, his argument that all forms of artificial contraception are in themselves degrading, especially to the wife, goes some way toward meeting this objection.

The argument that every 'marital act' should be open to children is defended in terms of 'natural' law, not scripture, and of course natural law has always, and necessarily, formed part of the basis for Catholic moral theology. Hence the papal argument had to be that it is unnatural – and therefore sinful – in any way and on any occasion to inhibit the possibility of pregnancy by artificial means – as indeed that any interference with the normal procreative process, including the artificial insemination of a wife by her husband already forbidden as early as 1897 by Leo XIII,[6] must similarly be ruled out, this on grounds of 'onanism' – i.e. only sexual intercourse should transfer the seed.

Prescinding from the question of how far the opponents of *Humanae Vitae* were aware of the long-term effects of ignoring it, whether on the birthrate, the economy or the moral authority of the Church itself – or indeed of the subtleties necessary to critique it coherently – 200 theologians signed a letter to the *New York Times* condemning the encyclical, while serious objections to it were raised first by the Belgian episcopate, then at a meeting in Essen at which were present Cardinals Suenens, Alfrink, Heenan, Döpfner and König, and where the majority of the participants voted that it must be radically revised. That meeting occurred against a background of the publication of a new (and more obviously heretical) Dutch catechism in 1966 which called in question traditional teachings not just about sex but more generally: as about the Eucharist, the virginity of Mary and much more. Some of Paul's nightmares about what would happen if traditional teachings in any 'fundamental' area of theology were to be called in question seemed to be coming into a very regrettable light of day.

Be that as it may, other national episcopates tried to hedge their bets on *Humanae Vitae*, proposing no outright rejection of the encyclical but arguments to the effect that individuals must let their consciences decide what to do – after, of course, taking the proposals of the magisterium seriously: such fence-sitting was especially common in Europe and North America. Pope Paul, seemingly realizing that the situation in the Church had spiralled out of control, the doors opened wide enough for almost any novelty, especially in morals, to be admitted, seems to have been at a loss: he never wrote another encyclical, nor did he make any serious attempt to punish the naysayers.[7] The pill had, in effect, reduced a pope to a silence desired, but never entirely achieved, by Napoleon, Mussolini, Stalin and Hitler.

We now know that Paul's ruling, added to other effects of the Council, not least in its 'pastoral' aspects, in suggesting that traditional beliefs,

---

6. *AAS* 29 (1896-97), p. 704.

7. For papal inaction see C.B. Keely, 'Limits to Papal Power: Vatican Inaction after Humanae Vitae', *Population and Development Review* 20 (1994), supplement: *The New Politics of Population: Conflict and Consensus in Family Planning*. For details see V. Joannes, *The Bitter Pill: Worldwide Reaction to the Encyclical Humanae Vitae* (Philadelphia: Pilgrim Press, 1970), pp. 220-40.

especially in morals, might be up for revision for 'pastoral reasons', was to prove damaging for the Church as a whole. Thus, according to published accounts, there were 329,799 male religious in the major institutes of religion in 1965, 214,913 in 2005. In many cases the contraceptive pill and the new emphasis on the 'unitive' effects of the 'marital act' proved too tempting to resist; colleagues and I used to call the resulting ex-clergy 'late bloomers', while wondering about their attitudes before their 'liberation'. If Pope Paul could control the Council itself, he could not control its effects in the modern world – or the fate of the Church therein. Indeed, apart from the actual loss of clergy, the post-conciliar age would witness a massive burgeoning of clerical homosexuality, with the abuse of minors (and the predictable cover-ups); sexual 'unorthodoxy' was not to be limited to 'straight' irregularity.

Thus one of the prime results of the *Humanae Vitae* debate was that, despite Vatican II's insistence on a very traditional account of papal authority in both 'faith' and 'morals', at least in matters of 'morals', the wishes of popes and of those bishops who (often apparently unwillingly) accepted *Humanae Vitae* – despite in some cases their strong support for contraceptives for population control – were to be widely ignored. Indeed in the aftermath of the encyclical we see a virtual if unofficial schism in the Church between those who would obey *any* papal instruction – in that spirit of total obedience prescribed, if unwittingly, by both Vatican Councils – and those who would obey only those instructions which they approved: thus it all might now depend on what instruction was thought to be a 'good', even a 'Catholic', instruction. Popes in effect might now be compelled to decide which way to go if their control over their flocks was to be retained; they could either reaffirm (with what-ever pressures seemed to be appropriate) what had always more or less been affirmed about sexual morality, or – to stanch the haemorrhaging of believers – 'go with the flow', with whatever loss of moral authority that would induce in the more traditionally minded among their flock.

Though few realized what the wider implications of the massive non-acceptance among Catholics of *Humanae Vitae* would be, the encyclical was to prove the first act of a drama by which papal authority – indeed the authority of the wider 'traditions' of the Church – was to become a matter of major debate within the Church itself. As we shall see, that debate would produce acclaim – indeed sainthood – for John Paul II[8] and great respect for Benedict XVI – while many of the same people

---

8. As we noted, John Paul explained *Humanae Vitae* less impersonally (that is less in terms of natural law) but rather in terms of his version of personalism.

were to view Francis I with great suspicion. 'Good' popes were now to be welcomed by those who thought them 'good', 'bad' popes were to be castigated by those who judged them 'uncatholic', even heretical. In a strange way Pius IX's claim to be the tradition was working itself out in a very untraditional way as the belief not that the Truth is taught by the pope but that the 'truth' is taught according to the varying wishes of individual popes, all of whom, for a while at least, are right about the truth in question.

*   *   *

At first sight *Humanae Vitae* looks to be an encyclical about contraception. Viewed more thoughtfully, however, it has, as we have seen, significant implications for the wider theology of marriage – some of which were to be developed at a more philosophical level by John Paul II. Beyond marriage it raised by implication more fundamental questions about the differing – if they were to be differing – roles for men and women not only in society but in the Church itself. Already in Paul's time such deeper concerns had led to the first significant debates about the possibility of women priests: Paul and his curial advisers again handled this 'internally', that is without raising it as part of wider debate among the bishops, let alone debate against a background of reflection on the nature of infallibility, whether papal or other. Paul had already made clear that he had issued *Humanae Vitae* in terms of the ordinary magisterium of the Church; it was in no way to affect (or so it seemed) problems about papal infallibility itself.

Debate about the role of women in the Church, with all its possible ramifications, went on apace. In 1976, still during Paul's term of office, the Congregation for the Doctrine of the Faith (now led by its new prefect, Cardinal Seper) published the Declaration *Inter Insigniores*, teaching that the Church had no authority to ordain women, appealing to constant Church practice in both East and West, to the exclusion of Mary from the Twelve and women from their successors, and the iconic value of the priest as acting *in persona Christi* being male, as was Christ himself. It specifically dismissed claims that women had a right to be ordained (without mentioning that no one had such a right). As yet no one claimed that Jesus was 'trans'.

Nevertheless, the new ruling again failed to end the matter, thus not only handing it on unresolved to Paul's successors, but necessarily again raising the question of the authority of a papally endorsed document – leading eventually to further attempts better to explain the various sorts of 'infallibility' and definitive teaching. Accompanying the problems raised by *Humanae Vitae* itself, *Inter Insigniores* pointed to a time when 'women's issues' would not only challenge papal authority as rewritten by Vatican I – indeed papal authority in general – but raise the wider and more fundamental question of how the Church might be 'updated' to satisfy the demand for the 'empowerment' of women – not to speak of the claims of those earlier regarded as sexual deviants but increasingly encouraged by the modern (or post-modern) world. By the twenty-first century, problems of the nature of continuing papal authority were to become inextricably entwined with ecclesiastical attitudes to Western phallocracy and its desiderate female equivalent, as exemplified by *The Vagina Monologues*: a play always guaranteed to foment dissension on 'Catholic' campuses.

Chapter 9

Celebrity Autocracy: John Paul II

To whom could I offer my resignation?

John Paul II

I don't see a priest.

John Paul to a distinguished Benedictine
spotted in 'civvies' in Rome

1978 was the 'Year of the three Popes'. Paul VI died on 6 August; the frail John Paul I was elected on 25 August – one of his few acts as pope was to drop the royal 'we' in favour of 'I' – and died of a massive heart-attack on 28 September, leaving the impression of a kindly man, perhaps too kindly for the post to which he was elected; as Patriarch of Venice his coat of arms bore the single word *Humilitas*. In the ensuing conclave opinion was divided between supporters of the notably conservative Cardinal Siri of Genoa and the rather less conservative Cardinal Benelli of Florence, deputy at the Secretariat of State under Paul VI and organizer of the election of John Paul I.

The deadlock was broken by the choice of Karol Wojtyla, Cardinal Archbishop of Krakow and first non-Italian to be chosen for 455 years. In 1979 he was hailed in the *Annuario Pontificio* as 'universal pastor of the Church', a description which again might suggest that lesser pastors were rather like subordinate officers or middle managers: a suggestion doubtless hyperbolical, yet raising from the outset of the new reign the question of whether the declared intent of Vatican II – to restore the balance between pope and bishops lost at Vatican I – had not already been superseded.[1]

It seems that the principal mover behind the unexpected choice of Wojtyla was Cardinal König of Vienna, one of the more prominent 'progressive' cardinals at Vatican II. König was apparently convinced that his candidate, possessed of the reputation of being an effective pastoral bishop and an enthusiast for what he understood to be the teachings of Vatican II, was doctrinally sound. That would appeal in the Third World, and as a bishop living under Communism Wojtyla would be very hesitant about the *Ostpolitik* of John XXIII and (more emphatically) of Paul VI which, being an avatar of the 'absolute neutrality' of earlier popes and now orchestrated by Cardinal Casaroli, was intended to appease the Kremlin but had brought little long-term benefit to the Church. Immediately upon his election, the comparatively youthful Polish pope made clear in his first address to the Roman faithful assembled in St Peter's Square that some sort of new – and populist – order had arrived. His performance won the hearts of the crowd, many of whom initially had no idea who he was.

But the 'political' scene in the Church had changed much since Vatican II and its immediate sequels. The unity of the Church and even respect for the papacy had been in different ways put at risk by the failure to persuade large numbers of the laity (and indeed many of the bishops and clergy) to accept the teachings of *Humanae Vitae*, as also by the unwillingness of many 'traditional' Catholics to accept Pope Paul's *Novus Ordo* Mass: this despite the enduring popularity of 'good' Pope John and to a degree Paul himself. But though the idea of theologians – let off the leash by John XXIII – forming an alternative magisterium had taken hold in some quarters, the 'progressive' theologians of the Council had by now gone their different ways.

---

1. Throughout this chapter I am indebted (as are all who write about John Paul II) to the writings of G. Weigel, especially his *Witness to Hope: The Biography of Pope John Paul II* (New York: Harper Collins, 1999). My reading of the data Weigel so generously and indeed exuberantly provides will, however, at times differ from his: perhaps in part indicating reflection some twenty years on. Weigel's more recent assessment of John Paul II and the Council can be found in vol. 2 of the biography, *The End and the Beginning* (New York: Doubleday, 2010) – until January 2023 unfortunately unavailable in any university library in the UK – and *To Sanctify the World: The Vital Legacy of Vatican II* (New York: Basic Books, 2022).

Some, such as Küng and Schillebeeckx, thought that the Council was merely a start, that far more needed to be changed, certainly in moral teachings, but also organizationally. For Küng especially – he would eventually be duly penalized for this and other presumed failings – the whole concept of infallibility was urgently in need of clarification, while specifically papal infallibility should be reconstructed if not abandoned. The stage was thus set for a new era in the Church (foreshadowed by the reaction to *Humanae Vitae*) with rejections of definitive teaching developing not, as normally in the past, in dogmatic theology – being problems, that is, in Christology or with the Trinity – but in morals (where Newman had predicted they would not arise, all being safe in that domain) and behind that the 'anthropology' which underlies moral theorizing – and where the status of Church teachings was as yet very imprecisely explained – as well as in the theory of the Church itself, so-called ecclesiology.

All seemed to agree that the writ of Church and pope runs in both faith and morals, with little thought yet given to the fact that, though there is a close relationship between the two, they are conceptually distinct – that suggesting that problems and solutions in the one might differ from problems and solutions in the other. Perhaps it might be possible to hang on to traditional teachings on faith (which now seeming merely quaint might provoke little concern), while radically so changing moral teachings as to demonstrate the Church as updated and acceptable in the modern world.

The problem with that is that, though dogmatic theology and moral theology are conceptually distinct, the Catholic account of morality relies on a metaphysical and theological infrastructure. If the two are to be treated as separable in 'real' terms, the Church's moral teachings will have little more foundational support than the secular and foundationless moralities she rejects. As for moral teachings, as on the indissolubility of marriage, though they are not dogmas defined *de fide,* if they are abandoned, that will entail a direct rejection either of the teaching of Jesus himself – hence of his divinity – or of the clear authority of scripture (as with homosexual acts) or at very least an outright denial of Catholic interpretations of natural law as understood by reason.

A second group of former 'progressives' – including Ratzinger, De Lubac, Daniélou, von Balthasar and even Congar – recognized that the revolutionary dynamic, the 'emotional contagion' of the Council, had (as was predictable) got out of hand. Originally associated with the 'Spirit of the Council' journal *Concilium,* these broke ranks and founded a counterblast, *Communio* – the title suggesting religious life rather than conciliar intrigue, a correct interpretation of the Council rather than an attempt to use it as a first step to further 'reform'. Congar hung on at *Concilium* in the hope of moderating his more radical colleagues and many longstanding friendships were ended forever, as some thought their confrères had sold out to unreformed authoritarianism, others that quasi-Protestantizing, even secularizing, had gone far enough.

The results were intriguing. De Lubac was to be created cardinal by John Paul in 1983, Congar in 1994, while Ratzinger was to morph into Pope Benedict XVI. Von Balthasar too, forgiven (perhaps even appreciated) for abandoning the Jesuits, was named cardinal (by John Paul) in 1988 but died two days before he was due to receive the red hat. Daniélou, as we noted, was already in possession of his by act of Paul VI, but died of a heart-attack, unfortunately for his reputation, while on a journey of mercy to the house of a Parisian prostitute whose pimp-husband was looking for money to pay for bail.

The new pope, eventually to be styled 'John Paul the Great', knew – indeed had always known – what he wanted. His papacy can be roughly divided into two phases, in the first of which his primary concern was with materialist Communism in Eastern Europe. In the second phase he was increasingly preoccupied with 'culture wars', urging a Catholic 'Culture of Life' supported by a 'personalist' version of Thomism as an alternative to the Western and more hedonistic variety of materialism self-revealing itself as a Culture of Death and increasingly exported to the Third World. In both phases John Paul was eager to follow his predecessors in their pursuit of that Christian unity (especially with the Orthodox Churches) which had proved so attractive and so dangerous at least since the time of Döllinger.

In the opening years of his pontificate, when his celebrity status was already established by his extraordinary ability to work the crowds (often in their hundreds of thousands) and dazzle the journalists who increasingly turned to popes and popes alone to provide the 'lowdown' on what mattered in the Catholic Church, John Paul's most consistent, even primary concern was with the Communist bloc, above all with the atrocities it was perpetrating (after the Nazis had done their worst) in his native and beloved Poland. Yet even here we can see beneath his patent contempt for Communist tyranny the insistent drumbeat that it can only be defeated by a cultural revival – if not only among Catholics, at least in the spirit of Catholic culture and the respect for the human person which Catholic culture engenders, never by mere force: the same call for a rejection of any kind of secularism, whether obviously totalitarian or other, which he was also to deploy in his criticism of the post-Christian materialist West. For there too, he believed, the Catholic past that had made of the West a great civilization was the only hope of continuing greatness. As in the intimacies of marriage and family life to which he was later to pay close attention, so in dealing with the threat of totalitarian or materialist societies, the theological approach must be 'personalist'. In both public and private life (insofar as they can be distinguished) the same principles of the dignity of human beings (not least of women) must be affirmed and protected.

It would be absurd to deny that John Paul's constant attention to the problems of Eastern Europe, his rejection of the failed and appeasing *Ostpolitik* of Paul VI, paid off. For he recognized what we might call the law of appeasement, whereby seldom will the appeaser gain much for his pains. By heartening the Poles (and indirectly other Central and Eastern Europeans) as Soviet Communism increasingly sank into an economic morass – eventually running into the sands when it attempted to match the massive military expenditure cannily promoted by President Reagan – John Paul became an inspiration to his countrymen and an object of dread (and even occasionally of respect) to his Soviet opponents. The fall of Communism, to which he contributed in no small measure, would heighten the prestige of the Catholic Church throughout the world – unless it was his personal charisma that seemed to win hearts and minds.

John Paul's political achievements – they were mainly during the earlier years of his papacy; he was less effective when required to act beyond the parameters of the Cold War[2] – serve to provide the background to other and eventually more time-consuming activities, especially the war with secularism in the West and with its growing influence within the Church itself. In so viewing these questions, we can notice that John Paul's political stance in one respect differed substantially from, say, that of Pius IX or Pius X. Nineteenth-century popes regarded democracy as little more than the political face of modernity, and their criticisms of it were delivered in an adversarial spirit. To the contrary, John Paul, knowing only too well the nature of non-democratic governments, was a democrat (though not, of course, in his view of authority within the Church), so his critique of the soullessness, barbarity and materialism of liberal democracies was less that of an enemy than of a would-be reformer: a critical and disappointed friend.

---

2. That said, John Paul also helped to improve the quality of political life in other parts of the world, notably the Philippines and various parts of Latin America, though his attempt to moderate the anti-Catholic Sandinistas in Nicaragua (see further below) had only limited success.

As for Western 'barbarism' and cultural neopaganism, it had been an ecclesiastical concern long before Wojtyla became pope, being a root cause of the hostility aroused by Paul's *Humanae Vitae*. Eventually John Paul was to see the cultural problem as especially instantiated in demands for the killing of the unwanted unborn (firmly if rarely condemned at Vatican II), for the scrapping of traditional teachings on marriage and sexuality and for an increasing readiness to eliminate the elderly, or encourage them to eliminate themselves or one another. His more immediate problem, however, was less with 'the world' than with the Church itself, for in what would amount to a 'last hurrah' his predecessor Paul VI had been challenged to face it by Cardinal Ottaviani, then still head of what had now been renamed the Congregation for the Doctrine of the Faith. Ottaviani in a letter to the world's bishops had listed ten areas in which the documents of Vatican II had, in his opinion, been perverted to non-Catholic purposes, in such a challenge anticipating the coming disputes about what the Council really taught: whether urging a renewal or rather a radical reconstruction of traditional doctrine. The challenge of Ottaviani's letter still remained to be faced.

Hence before turning to the new pope's attempt to revitalize (and remoralize) the Church – and indeed Western society more generally – we must return to interpretations of the work of the Council itself. On the surface, apart from a few diehards, almost all bishops and theologians (as indicated by the near-unanimity which Paul VI had achieved in the final voting on Council documents) approved of what had been done. A substantial group still hoped that the process of change had only begun: that further and more radical innovation might turn the Council's activity into an ongoing process. Those who rejected this view mostly failed at the outset to realize that the continuing 'progressives' had a particularly powerful weapon in their armoury.

For, as we have seen, the documents of the Council themselves (apart from their references to papal power) were often ambiguous, the fruit, that is, of compromises judged necessary to acquire massive consent. Hence although those, let us say, associated with *Communio* could argue that their reading of the relevant documents – and especially of *selected* parts of *Gaudium et Spes*, the Constitution on the Church in the Modern World – did not depart from traditional teaching, they ignored the fact that their opponents could appeal to other parts of the same text. Thus the basic problem was what was the *overall* intent of the Council Fathers, if indeed there was one. Did they want to reassert tradition with only superficial changes in wording and correspondingly in practice? Did they understand why many *periti* wanted the changes they wanted, or did they, when push came to shove, just decide to do what the pope wanted or would accept, remaining largely unaware of the underlying problems in the texts they debated?

More specifically – and with immediate reference to our present discussion – did *Gaudium et Spes*, in its possible accommodation to the modern world, undercut hierarchical authority in the Church (as some, such as the influential German theologian Johannes Baptist Metz, believed), or did it allow definitive doctrine to be changed, but only if popes agreed to change it? As we shall see when in the next chapter we review the work of John Paul's right-hand man, Joseph Ratzinger, before and after he became pope, this question was to have a future long after the heady days of the Council had receded into the past. For the difficulties, especially about *Gaudium et Spes*, are deep-seated. Might it not – not least in its tolerance of ambiguities – in effect encourage those who held views similar to Döllinger's, that a counter-magisterium of theologians would do a better job than the more traditional *Roman* magisterium? Given that few bishops read much theology or Church history after their student days, this might seem a reasonable conclusion, but it would come with possibly disastrous if unintended consequences.

In the years immediately after the Council the predominant interpretation of its documents was that radical change was intended, though no one knew how radical such change should be. But at the synod of bishops summoned by John Paul in 1985 to review how the Council had been received, a new reading (long in the mind of Ratzinger and a few others, including De Lubac, but now also associated with John Paul himself) emerged into the clear light of day. Its basis (as Paul VI's first conciliar speech as pope was interpreted) was that the thrust of the Council was Christocentric (implying that moral teaching should be read less directly as a set of deductions from natural law). This interpretation was primarily based on section 22 of *Gaudium et Spes* itself, much of which depended, at times almost literally, on De Lubac's *Catholicisme*. Its opening sentence taught that 'only in the mystery of the incarnate Word does the mystery of man take on light'.[3]

However, other sections of the same conciliar document (especially 36) speak a different language and can be interpreted as proposing a radical separation between religious and secular life (as between theology and philosophy); that might be read as emphasizing the fundamental goodness of modern society as such and thus as encouraging the Church

---

3. See further T. Rowland, *Culture and the Thomist Tradition: After Vatican II* (London/New York: Routledge, 2003), pp. 92-93 (with reference to John Paul II's *Redemptor Hominis*).

to 'accommodate' itself to that society ('warts and all'). According to Cardinal Kasper *Gaudium et Spes* recognizes 'that secular matters are to be discussed in a secular manner':[4] a thesis wholly appropriate for the claim that secular authority must be free from Church control, but also open to the interpretation that the Church has no business in the public sphere and no need to be there. Though only justifiable by an atheist (or at best Pelagian) account of virtue without grace, this thesis would more or less inform the policy of John F. Kennedy and his 'Catholic' successors in the American Democratic party and was to be upheld in many Catholic universities, especially American and Jesuit-run.

In light of such seeming contradictions in the text of *Gaudium et Spes* – or at least in how it could be interpreted – how could one be sure what in their ambiguities the Council Fathers – endorsed by the then pope – had intended? Eventually, and as already noticed, this difficulty was to lead, especially when Ratzinger became pope as Benedict XVI, to the construction of a 'hermeneutic of continuity' according to which we are to believe that only those interpretations of the Council which square with traditional teaching (now read 'Christologically') are valid: a thesis which leaves problematic and unsettling, as we have seen, the 'correct' attitude to be adopted to those radical corrections of earlier teachings (especially on religious freedom and Judaism) so enthusiastically accepted by the Fathers. But the 'hermeneutic of continuity', an apparently desperate – even disingenuous – solution to the problem had been far from fully developed when John Paul II set about his renewal of the Church in accordance with what he saw as the enlightened teaching of Vatican II.

What *was* still on the table, as a legacy of both the Council and of Paul VI, was the call for 'dialogue': which happily undefined word for some might mean discussions with others so that they might see the rational errors of their ways, for others simply a call to 'listen' to alien voices, whether secular or religious, and for yet others a willingness to tolerate views however radically uncatholic without desire to 'proselytize': the latter term coming to indicate an obscenity attributable to those who

---

4. W. Kasper, *Faith and the Future* (London: Burns & Oates, 1985), p. 4. For more on disillusion with *Gaudium et Spes* see A. Nichols, *The Thought of Benedict XVI: An Introduction* (London: Burns & Oates, 2007), pp. 69-71. For the idea that the dispute over how *Gaudium et Spes* should be read as reflecting the rival accounts of de Lubac and pre-conciliar Thomists of the relationship between nature and grace see T. Rowland, *Ratzinger's Faith* (Oxford: Oxford University Press, 2008), pp. 150-51.

sought conversions to the Catholic faith, such being unnecessary since all good men and women are on the path to heaven in their own equally effective ways.

Few noticed the risk in such attitudes of two phenomena: the 'Patty Hearst Syndrome', whereby a weak captive embraces, through enforced familiarity with her captors, their ideology and even joins them in violent actions; alternatively the 'chin-in-armpit syndrome' recognized as useful in labour-management negotiations: a reconciler may, by putting the parties in close and comparatively friendly extended meetings, induce one or both to compromise their initial bargaining position in ways which those they represent may consider ambiguous and even misguided, but which can be interpreted by each party as presenting a successful result.

A further difficulty lurked unseen: not just about the quality of the Council's teachings but about the effects of 'enforcing' them. For if enforcement were to depend on the pope's personal reading of the Council's intent, and a subsequent pope were to take a very different view of this, it would again appear that Catholic truth as enforced depended not on the truth of what a pope in Council (fortified by his quasi-infallible status) taught, but on the mere fact that he chose to teach it. That might lead to the dilemma already raised above: that a pope might teach, indeed might attempt to enforce, heresy – hence arousing anxiety as to what could be done if such a circumstance were to arise – and how to prevent its coming to pass.

In the case of John Paul, no one was going to suggest that what he taught was heretical; his admirers can easily point to legitimately developed tradition as inherent in his approach and to his constant awareness of traditional teachings of the Church. The objections brought against him would rather be that the tradition itself had become substantially outworn and that a pope – any pope – had the right and duty to change it, or at least encourage those with that intent. Vatican II had pointed the way to how such change could be accomplished: distinguishing itself as 'pastoral', it enabled pastoral practices to be developed which were, in truth, dependent on doctrinal change, even if such change were unacknowledged. Eventually, it might be hoped, the new situation 'on the ground' could be assumed to be the result of 'doctrinal' change in the right direction; thus real doctrinal change could be secured by default or by stealth, as pastoral procedures came to pass (and were perhaps intended to pass) as possessed of dogmatic or doctrinal weight.

*   *   *

No one should deny that John Paul II was an extraordinary figure: survivor of Nazis and Communists in Poland, erstwhile professional philosopher, erstwhile near professional actor, writer of poetry and plays, wholeheartedly devoted to a Catholicism he preached with absolute self-confidence, urgent advocate of legitimate rights as dependent on human dignity, alpha-male celebrity, traverser of the globe in dozens of 'pilgrimages', most of which – Ireland and Germany perhaps apart – were hugely successful, making him known to millions on every continent, not least via the various Youth Days which drew hundreds of thousands of 'Papa-boys' from over the world: in at least one case – Denver, Colorado (1993) – overwhelmingly defying the expectations of the pundits.

Canonizer of almost 500 saints world-wide – including Padre Pio, Josemaria Escrivà, founder of Opus Dei, and Gianna Molla, heroine of the seriously pro-life party within the Church – and reviser of canon law in 1983 and of the rosary in 2002, John Paul was the first pope to enter the principal synagogue in Rome (in 1990), and to open full diplomatic relations in 1993 with the State of Israel. (As part of his celebration of the Millennium Jubilee year (2000) he visited the Holy Land, expressing his horror at the Nazi Holocaust of the Jews in a visit to Yad Vashem and prayed at the Western Wall.) But above all – and, as we noted, increasingly – he wanted to replace the Western 'culture of death' with a new vision both Catholic and humanist: hence it is appropriate to begin a more detailed analysis of his 'cultural' work and its effects with his approach to Catholic higher education. That will reveal the extent of his problems (both within and without the Church) in the 'West' as well his determination to use a reinvigorated papacy as a spearhead for a revitalized Catholicism: above all his concern that the priesthood, in crisis since the 1960s, should be more fully endowed with the missionary spirit.

In 1967 the presidents of many Catholic universities and colleges in the United States met at Land O'Lakes in Wisconsin to determine their policies in light of what they supposed to be the spirit of Vatican II. Many of them, not least those from prosperous and fashionable foundations such as Notre Dame or politically influential Jesuit institutions like Georgetown, had apparently come to believe that the only way to improve their academic standards and reputation was by weakening their Catholic character: to take a more 'pastoral' approach, while remaining nominally Catholic. In effect, this would mean striving to follow the habits and mentality of radically secularized American institutions – primarily those in New England and California – at a time of great turbulence in those institutions.

This situation did not pass unnoticed by John Paul, whose attempts to correct the secularizing process in Catholic universities were primarily aimed at – and primarily opposed in – the United States. In 1979 he issued the apostolic constitution *Sapientia Christiana* which proposed new regulations for all universities chartered by the Holy See as possessing 'pontifical faculties'. In 1990, he widened his attempt at reform, showing in *Ex Corde Ecclesiae* determination to restore the fading Catholicism of a wide group of Catholic universities and colleges. Compared with its predecessor it was (and increasingly is) an 'incomplete success', and notably in the more affluent institutions: perhaps not least because, abjuring the dated policies of Pius X, John Paul recognized that hurling excommunications could no longer secure the required effect, and would bring the danger of unnecessarily provoking hostility in a secular world still entranced by his populist and thespian skills.

With the same goal of improving the 'Catholicism' of Catholic institutions, especially of their departments of theology (particularly if Jesuit) – and following in the footsteps of Leo XIII – in 1998 John Paul published an encyclical, *Fides et Ratio*, on what he saw as the prerequisites for Catholic philosophy and theology, while declining to endorse Leo's insistence on the absolute priority of some sort of Thomism. Perhaps it was in similar spirit that a few days previously, he had canonized his phenomenological predecessor, Edith Stein (turned Carmelite nun as Sr Benedicta of the Cross), though in his more philosophical writings, not least about women, he had failed to give her the credit she clearly was due as inaugurating a reforming combination of phenomenology and Thomism. To cap all this activity, in 1992 he presided over the publication of a massive new *Catechism of the Catholic Church* (organized under Ratzinger's guidance and resulting from the work of the synod of bishops held in 1985 to review interpretations of the Second Vatican Council): a document intended to set out in detail the character and goals proper to a revised and updated Catholic humanism, not least by acting as a key to what John Paul and Ratzinger saw as correct interpretations of the Council itself.

Again reverting to policies advocated by Leo XIII and following up the efforts of John XXIII and Paul VI, John Paul hoped to develop his predecessors' concern with social teaching, extending Paul's analysis in *Sollicitudo Rei Socialis* (1988) by drawing attention to the contribution of corrupt local governments (rather than mere inadequate distribution of resources) to problems of underdevelopment. In 1991 he celebrated Leo's *Rerum Novarum* on its hundredth anniversary in *Centesimus Annus*, though less than adroitly managing to give ill-wishers the impression that the old and discredited papal 'impartiality' in politics was still active in seeming to allot blame equally to both democratic and totalitarian rulers. For while he not unreasonably wanted to maintain that the policies of both the Eastern and the Western 'blocs' needed cleaning up, he neglected to emphasize what he certainly believed, namely that one bloc (that Communist world he detested) was worse than the other. Which said, it is clear that the chief point he wanted to make is that social problems are at bottom moral and cultural, arising, where they do, in no small measure from a faulty theory of human nature and neglect, if not contempt, for human dignity.

In criticizing the West John Paul particularly aimed to persuade us to look again at those problems of sexuality, marriage and family that had baffled Paul VI and which, in his view, underlie a great deal of the ills both of the 'world' and of the Church itself, being rooted in a false account of human nature, and which only a revitalized Catholic theology could remedy. But to ask if he could be successful in so mammoth a task, whether inside the Church or beyond, is to ask whether he was able to pass on a legacy dependent on the charismatic deployment of post-Vatican I authority available to him as universal pastor to future generations. Or would that possible success, like that of the televangelist (even of that master of the craft, Billy Graham) fade on the maestro's demise?

Even before being elected pope, John Paul had been concerned about developing changes in Western attitudes to marriage, and while still a simple priest in Poland had devoted much time to counselling married couples. He knew, of course, that abortion was encouraged in Communist Poland as a mere form of birth control, but Poland being still staunchly Catholic, the problem did not yet loom large on his horizon. Yet he was certainly aware that much of the traditional theology of marriage and the relationship between the sexes would need to be re-evaluated and adjusted to a world where the growing empowerment of women was already affecting that 'world's' attitude to marriage, thus requiring some sort of Catholic response. Merely rejecting artificial contraception for all, but especially for Catholic married couples, was clearly no adequate response to wider problems.

John Paul's first substantial treatment of marriage and sexuality in an official document is to be found in *Familiaris Consortio* (1981) which, though an apostolic exhortation issued to summarize the debates of the previous year in a synod of bishops about the family, bears throughout the stamp of his own 'personalist' phenomenology. That enabled him both to confirm and to adapt traditional teaching on marriage so as to place more emphasis on responsible parenthood than on the simple procreation of children, with the persistent aim of harmonizing the biological purposes of nature with personalist ideas as to how such natural necessity should be enacted in ways consonant with the dignity of the human person, and especially (at last) of the wife. As we have already observed, his defence of *Humanae Vitae* followed similar 'personalist' lines. In brief, the pope urged that sexuality be 'humanized'.

The primary aim of *Familiaris Consortio* is to defend marriage by pointing out its intrinsic goodness as an expression of the love of God and its fundamental importance in the formation of a just society – though John Paul surprisingly omitted to consider that one reason (at least in the West) for confusions about marriage is the widespread (individualistic) belief that it is not (as in the past) largely a matter of the union of families and so of the good of society but simply a private arrangement between the spouses. Nevertheless, *Familiaris Consortio* emphasizes the essential role marriage plays in promoting the common good and therefore proposes fourteen 'rights' it must be allowed if it is to perform that role most effectively.

Early in his Exhortation John Paul lists the lights and shades of marriage in the contemporary world. As he proceeds, it becomes clear that his primary concerns are to condemn the exploitation of spouses by one another – that is by the instrumentalization of sexuality – and with the immorality of any interference by the state (such as he knew too well as a marked feature of the Communist world) in what is a primary responsibility of the spouses alone, namely the education of their children: thus also ruling out state pressure for contraception, abortion or sterilization: it is not for the state to arrange the circumstances and practicalities of marriage but for married couples to determine how their union can best promote the common good.

John Paul's Exhortation was, as we have noted, intended as a summary of the work of a synod of bishops; however, before its promulgation the pope had already embarked on his own more personal and theological account of the 'marriage problem' in a series of 130 addresses to general audiences in Rome, eventually to be put together to form a *Theology of the Body*, a *magnum opus* intended as a more reflective account of the truths that lay behind the Exhortation. Simultaneously this aimed to set the teaching of Paul's *Humanae Vitae,* which had failed to win much approval as a set of prohibitions, in a more positive context and to lay to rest any 'traditional' objections to Catholic teachings on marriage and sexuality as in effect 'Manichaean', that is, based on a deep hostility to the body itself and a view of sexuality as at best a necessary evil.

John Paul's tactic, based on blending the early chapters of Genesis with the Sermon on the Mount, is intended to give 'pastoral' form to the thesis that, since as persons we are 'composed' of soul and body, the body is no unavoidable encumbrance on the soul but rather its expression: a specific feature of man's createdness as an image and likeness of God. Perhaps the most original part of his teaching is his interpretation of the fall: the subsequent shame at nakedness which infected Adam and Eve is an allegorical representation of a fear of the 'other's' motives, that being a mark of fallen sexuality. Thus whereas before the Fall Adam and Eve recognized one another as God's gift and each made no attempt to 'instrumentalize' the another, after the Fall they are ashamed because they are inclined to use their sexuality to exploit: original sin is thus to be seen in this case as the desire, become endemic in the human race, to use others for self-gratification, that is, as a sexual variant of Augustine's *libido dominandi*. The pope could have been thinking of (and perhaps should have been aware of) the (then fashionable) Sartre-De Beauvoir account of sexuality which has had such a huge impact on the modern world.

Be that as may, notice that this revised account of sexuality and sexual morality is John Paul speaking, however splendidly, on his own initiative, and it would be wrong to suppose that his interpretation of scripture arose from significant consultation with other bishops or indeed anybody else. For although the pope was constantly talking to the learned and the less learned, what he produced on sexuality was a very personal attempt to correct a longstanding misinterpretation of Catholic teaching, doubtless much influenced by his personal experience of married couples when a pastor in Poland. In the 'outside world', though much admired, it was little heeded, and being the product of a pope endowed with papal authority, was open to repudiation – and would be substantially repudiated – by a successor similarly endowed.

The difficulty future critics would run into is that, although John Paul acted without much formal consultation, his work takes its place firmly within legitimate traditions of Catholic morality. That said, the use of authority for one reason can be copied by those whose intentions are quite other. John Paul apparently assumed that his autocratic manner would not – even could not – be adapted to opposing purposes. But as we shall later observe, he tended to overestimate human (and even 'Catholic') good will (as seen in his dealings with the Jesuits, not to mention his decisions about suitable episcopal appointees).

In his encyclicals John Paul would offer a 'cultural' assessment of the *economic* ills of society (*Centesimus Annus*), and an application of the same cultural principles to marriage and family (*Familiaris Consortio* and its accompanying *Theology of the Body*). But the public battle was still to come and was to follow upon two further foundational (and very personal) encyclicals: *Veritatis Splendor* (1993), aimed especially at theories of proportionalism in moral theology, and *Evangelium Vitae* (inaugurated in 1991 and published in 1995), to which latter the public background was two UN conferences concerned with women, population control, 'reproductive rights' and related problems of moral theology, those held in Cairo (1994) and Beijing (1995): confrontations which, as we shall see, would arouse renewed debate about the nature and extent of papal authority and the binding force on Catholics of papal pronouncements.[5]

These UN Conferences in Cairo and Beijing provided a stage for sharp clashes between John Paul's views on the 'Culture of Life' and modernity's 'Culture of Death', the latter being promoted (in the pope's view) by the administration of Bill Clinton in Washington and the European Union. The basic theology which the Vatican, under John Paul's personal direction, opposed to the advocates of 'reproductive rights' (that is to say, of abortion on demand world-wide) had been developed in *Veritatis Splendor* (1993), published not long before the Cairo World Conference on Population and Development opened. *Evangelium Vitae* (March 1995) appeared a few months before the Fourth World Conference on Women got under way in Beijing in the following September. Perhaps surprisingly, these two encyclicals – though of related character and content – provoked very different reactions in both the Church and the 'world', the first being widely execrated, the second widely admired (even where not accepted).

From John Paul's perspective the Cairo Conference was a disaster only narrowly avoided. At meetings of the preparatory committee Vatican representatives were abused by the chairman, himself President of the International Planned Parenthood Federation, and an extreme 'anti-Catholic' agenda was proposed for the conference itself: marriage was mentioned only to be insulted, sex for teenagers was advocated as a right (whether or not approved by parents), little attention was paid to the disadvantages for children of a marriage-free environment. In response, John Paul tried to strengthen his position within the Church itself by founding the Academy for Life (though this institution was later to become even anti-Catholic under a different pontiff). His campaign

---

5. For a detailed account of these actions and events see Weigel, *Witness to Hope*, pp. 686-95, 715-27, 756-60.

at the conference itself brought limited relief: the American proposal that abortion on demand be mandated was abandoned, and the Vatican delegation enjoyed a fair measure of support from the Islamic world as well as from a number of other Third World states. But the pope's enemies did not give up; Beijing's conference on women was to be the next battleground.

However, this time, as Islamic views on women in society differed from John Paul's, support for Vatican positions was harder to come by, and many Third World states were bullied into believing that economic aid would be cut off if 'reproductive rights' were not part of the final package. This time not Bill Clinton's White House but the European Union – an organization whose anti-Christianity, typified by its proposed charter which contained no reference to the role of Christianity in the formation of European civilization and which was to be a primary target of John Paul's moral crusade for the rest of his life – led the anti-human charge. Luckily for the Vatican, however, its delegation was led by Mary Ann Glendon, a Harvard professor of European constitutional and family law, who deployed her expertise to argue that the European position was radically contradictory; hence the final declaration was not as bad as it might have been, and Glendon, following papal advice to accept what was good and condemn what was not, did so to considerable effect.

The result was certainly no victory, but at best, as everyone knew, an armistice. It was clear that not political manoeuvring at UN conferences but the convincing of hearts was the only way in the long term that the war might be successfully concluded. That convincing has, of course, not yet been secured; papal authority outside the Church is limited to short-term emotional impact, though the two encyclicals – *Veritatis Splendor* and *Evangelium Vitae* – were intended as the first and (at least in hope) not the last broadsides for the papal cause. It remained to be seen whether, on the wider and more intimate issues of marriage and sexuality in a post-modern world of self-serving and hedonist despair, papal charisma was going to be any more effective than the arid reasoning of Paul VI – even among believing Catholics.

The prime target of *Veritatis Splendor* is contemporary relativism about moral values, a theme intimated though scarcely examined at Vatican II, but dear to the heart of a pope who in his earlier days had challenged the moral philosophy of Max Scheler on the ground that, being over-Kantian, it lacks adequate metaphysical and objective foundations. In his new encyclical he taught that it is impossible to separate objective truth from moral thinking, that some standard must be identified if one moral 'truth' is to recognized as superior to another; hence that absolute and objective moral norms must exist.

Such norms had, of course, been proposed at least as early as the Ten Commandments, but John Paul was not satisfied to read these as mere prohibitions; his argument in *Veritatis Splendor* is that the purpose of the prohibitions is to enable each person to live a life directed to goodness and concern for others, and hence 'freer'. His morality is no mere legalism; laws are there to promote the good of oneself and of others and to enable individual persons to pursue those goods not out of fear of the consequences but because these goods are good *in themselves*. As for those he challenges, he argues that their mistaken notion of truth is always associated with a mistaken notion of freedom, which they treat (in effect if not explicitly) as freedom from restraint. Such freedom, in the long run, can only lead to a struggle of all against all, as each individual asserts his 'will to power'.

John Paul was particularly concerned to refute what since Elizabeth Anscombe has been called 'consequentialism' or in theological jargon 'proportionalism'. Proportionalists, at best, propose an apparently kindly pastoralism, concerning themselves not with what is objectively right and wrong, good and bad, but with the intentions of agents and the consequences of their actions. Focus on consequences is open to the objection that it points to a subordination of means to ends and to a lack of attention to the 'virtue' of the moral agent; focus on intentions to the objection that those who do bad things may, even genuinely, believe their intentions to be good. For intentions can relate only to the object intended – and some objects can seem a great deal better than others.

A difficulty with John Paul's position, as maintaining that one should never perform an intrinsically bad act, is that it seems to treat all offences as equally sinful and therefore equally prohibited. Although it is not difficult to think of cases where John Paul's position seems obvious (such as with rape or the torture of children), it is easy to think of other cases where doing something which is intrinsically and objectively wrong might save us from consequences so horrible that no one should feel happy to ignore them. It is hard to tell a woman whose children will starve if she is unwilling even temporarily to be a prostitute that she should let them die. The underlying difficulty with John Paul's approach – to be adopted, he held, by all Catholics – would seem to be that it leaves insufficient place for the virtue of prudence in genuinely difficult cases.

John Paul is on less problematic ground when he insists that one's moral worth is not determined by whether one makes a 'fundamental option' for the good but whether, in particular cases, one tries to act as well as one can. This becomes particularly clear in cases with which he was especially concerned: it is mere humbug to say that I regard abortion as killing the innocent if I make no attempt (legally) to stop people killing the unborn. As Aristotle had put it, the end of practical reasoning is an action.

There are further problems about the moral aspects of public life. Morality by contract with no foundational agreement on principles can easily be discarded when either party finds the contract unhelpful; morality thus becomes provisional. By contrast, *Veritatis Splendor* emphasizes the reality of evil and the slavery it generates: thus John Paul would conclude that the Holocaust was not just irrational, not just contrary to the good of the greatest number or a neglect of the moral law qua law; that beyond all that it was just evil, the vile product of those who had no respect for truth or freedom. In a post-modern world where all acts may be reduced to exemplifying the will to power, it is all of us – not just those who are Christian – who are threatened by the dissolution and rejection of moral truth.

Many both in and outside the Church failed to grasp that in this encyclical John Paul was not merely reasserting a series of prohibitions deriving from an outdated religion, but arguing that such traditional prohibitions are everywhere defensible because they represent a component of the history of man's desire for the freedom to do good and for the truth about what the good really is. He can hardly have been pleased to hear of moral theologians still pushing the view that a 'fundamental option' was, despite his warnings, still to be used as a pretext for condoning individual vicious behaviour. Yet in his displeasure he can only have been made more aware that for all his authority to teach 'dogmatic theology' – matters of faith – his claim to be the universal teacher of morals was much harder to establish, not least if Catholics who care little about, say, details of the theology of the Trinity or the Eucharist, much resent any papal objection to their using contraceptives.

Evangelium Vitae should be viewed as the application of the principles of *Veritatis Splendor* to a specific contemporary moral problem with vast social implications: the contempt for human life viewed as a continuum from conception to natural death: the very problem, as we have seen, which the Vatican delegates had tried and failed to induce world leaders to accept at the conferences at Cairo and Beijing. But applying the principles of truth and goodness to sexual morality after the Sexual Revolution of 1968 and the years following could not possibly be expected to have immediate effect in the contemporary West: *Evangelium Vitae* is essentially a manifesto for the love of all humanity (especially the weak and defenceless) and a challenge to the 'natural' desire for pleasure and immediate convenience. If the conclusions – or something like them – of *Veritatis Splendor* are rejected, the arguments of *Evangelium Vitae*, a corollary of the earlier text, will similarly fall by the wayside: or rather will be ignored because in our 'unfree' state many will not want to listen to them.

Philosophically powerful though both *Veritatis Splendor* and *Evangelium Vitae* are, many Catholics – not least those in departments of theology – refused to accept them. John Paul, for all his charisma – not to speak of his philosophical and exegetical acumen – could not convince those who did not want to be convinced. Some attempted to evade direct criticism of the pope by alleging that the texts were composites put together by various 'Roman' theologians with the pope's signature at the bottom, though a careful reading readily reveals that, while the pope has consulted a number of others in achieving the final form of both documents, they are, as was the theology of the body, very much his own work, proposed to the Church and to the world as such.

A second way of evading the content of the encyclicals was to raise questions about the abuse of power; some claimed that John Paul originally intended to proclaim *Veritatis Splendor* as taught infallibly on his own initiative, making it the first dogmatic pronouncement on morals (as distinct from faith), but was persuaded not to do so by Cardinal Ratzinger. Ratzinger himself has denied this, and the truth of the matter seems to be (as with other documents emanating from this period of the papacy) that John Paul thought of himself as able to assume the infallibility of the encyclical not through exercise of any specially papal authority but as a universal teaching of the ordinary magisterium as determined at Vatican I and confirmed at Vatican II by *Lumen Gentium* (25). That might seem to blur the distinction between dogmas (matters of faith) and moral teachings which, though definitive, are not held to be infallible. This problem with the definitive teaching of infallibility was now more clearly revealed as primarily arising less from *ex cathedra* teachings of popes than with the teachings (perhaps all the moral and social teachings) of the ordinary magisterium, some past examples of which have been revoked.

The same record would be played over *Evangelium Vitae*, it being again claimed that Ratzinger dissuaded John Paul from declaring it infallible teaching by virtue of his absolute (post-Vatican I) authority, and again Ratzinger would deny any such discussion had occurred, this time explaining in more detail that his Congregation for the Doctrine of the Faith had worked hand in hand with the pope on the assumption that the 'new' infallibility was not required because (again in light of *Lumen Gentium* 25) the pope was merely affirming what was infallible already as teaching of the 'ordinary magisterium'. Which again left the question, to which we shall return in the next chapter, as to how far the 'infallibility' of the ordinary magisterium has extended in the past, how far its role was now being extended and what are the implications either way?

Thus did *Veritatis Splendor* and *Evangelium Vitae* call forth a storm of dissent, with desperate efforts, as noted, to explain them away as not having been issued infallibly in line with the pope's infallible authority. There were to be analogous reactions to another of John Paul's projects, attempted only two months after the appearance of *Evangelium Vitae*: this time to break the deadlock between Christians – more especially between Catholics and Orthodox – over Christian unity.

We have seen Paul VI meeting Patriarch Athenagoras in Jerusalem, and the lifting of the mutual anathemas of 1054. John Paul, equally concerned for communion with the Orthodox Churches, first met the next patriarch, Dimitrios I, in Istanbul and in 1987 Dimitrios came to Rome where he shared altar – though not Eucharistic celebration – with the pope. John Paul apparently hoped that inter-communion could be agreed before the turn of the millennium; Dimitrios seemed rather to think in terms of the last times. Nevertheless, the pope pushed on, and in 1995 published a further encyclical – *Ut Unum Sint* – on those very problems of ecumenism which had substantially caused the defeat and defection of Döllinger. Largely dismissed during the modernist crisis, these had been renewed by the 'new theologians' and became a central feature of the teaching of Vatican II.

But there was no further progress with the Orthodox. There are many reasons, doctrinal and historical, why this, though not apparently evident to the pope, was the reality: and not least because the rivalry – indeed the power struggle – between Constantinople and the Moscow patriarchate impeded the Orthodox from speaking with a united voice. As Evelyn Waugh liked to point out, while in the West few remember the sack of Constantinople by the Crusaders of 1204, the memory of that event remains green in the minds of many Orthodox believers. That said, the principal theological difficulty to reunion – seemingly hardly noticed by John Paul and his biographers, despite the rather frosty reception he received during his 'millennial' pilgrimage to Greece (where he was condemned outright by the Athonite monks) – is the papal office itself. Yet in his encyclical (*Ut Unum Sint* 95) the pope claimed to be 'heeding the request made of me to find a way of exercising the primacy which, while in no way renouncing what is essential to its mission, is nonetheless open to a new situation'.

In light of the revised papal authority established by Vatican I and confirmed by Vatican II, it is hard to imagine how any such reconciliation could be achieved without such 'renouncing': in other words, if ecumenism, understood primarily as unity with the Orthodox, is required, the kind of primacy which the Orthodox might envisage, and which more or less existed in patristic times, could not be achieved without frank recognition that Vatican II (even more than Vatican I) had been majorly mistaken. Thus it is hard to understand how in this instance John Paul was not expressing either delusions of grandeur or mere wishful thinking. Rather, as he had failed to understand how radically different his moral philosophy was from that to which almost the entire 'Western' intelligentsia is committed (from their point of view for good reasons), so his view of papal authority differed from anything remotely acceptable to the vast majority of Orthodox, at least for the foreseeable future. .

What about Anglicans? John Paul's interest in these was markedly less than with Orthodoxy. In the event Christian unification in this quarter was to be killed off altogether by the Anglican ordination of women to the hierarchical priesthood. For until that challenge came into the open, there remained a residual hope in some Catholic circles that – despite Leo XIII's declaration that Anglican orders were absolutely null and utterly void – some sort of significant theological reconciliation between the two Churches could be found. Before the Sexual Revolution, many Anglicans still prided themselves on being not Protestants but one branch of a 'Three Branched Church' consisting of Catholics, Orthodox and themselves. In the mid-1980s that fantasy was to be blown away over their determination (in defiance of both the other branches with whom they claimed to cooperate) to ordain women to the priesthood (and eventually to the episcopate).

In an exchange of letters in 1985 between Cardinal Willebrands and Anglican Archbishop Runcie it became clear that differences on women's ordination could not be resolved. Although the Anglican arguments were of a sociological as much as a theological nature, both sides claimed that traditional theology supported them: the Anglicans often held that the principle 'What is not taken up is not saved' implied that unless women could represent Christ at the altar, we would have to conclude that they cannot be saved. The Catholics dismissed this: Christ, as male, represents the whole of humanity, but his human maleness is to be represented in his priests. Thus did another part of the ecumenical drive fall apart.

Matters came to a head in 1994 when John Paul concluded that, since Paul's VI's *Inter Insigniores* had not laid the problem to rest, he must put an end to debate about the ordination of women once and for all, and settle it 'in a definitive way'. He decided on a short document – *Ordinatio Sacerdotalis* – in which he summarized earlier arguments, insisting in what the cynical might dismiss as a sweetener intended to blur the issues at stake that the most important people in the Church were not office-holders but saints, and concluding that 'I declare that the Church has no authority whatsoever to confer priestly ordination on women and that this judgment is to be definitively held by all the Church's faithful'.

That still did not settle the matter. Some claimed that the status of the document remained unclear. That what was clear was that it was not declared infallible teaching in virtue of simple papal ruling. Some thought that, priesthood for women being now excluded, they should concentrate on women's ordination to the diaconate; this we may leave aside, noting instead that the Congregation for the Doctrine of the Faith was asked to determine whether (or perhaps how) John Paul's ruling was 'to be understood as belonging to the deposit of faith'. This would lead to the most serious attempt to clarify 'infallibility' and the status of Catholic teachings more generally in recent times – not only of popes *ex cathedra*.

After some delay the CDF ruled that *Ordinatio Sacerdotalis* is to be held definitively because it merely reiterates what has always been taught, thus (again) being a declaration of the 'ordinary magisterium'. *Lumen Gentium* 25 was again invoked – and the same reaction, though more violently, provoked. In *The Tablet* Professor Nicholas Lash pontificated that the pope was guilty of a 'scandalous abuse of power'; Richard McBrien, a theologian of Notre Dame, wrote that the form of the text was 'utterly irresponsible', while the Catholic Theological Society of America rejected both the pope's assertions and Ratzinger's CDF defence of them. John Paul in effect asserted his position but failed to follow it up. Those who dissented were more or less left in place; some, being laity, could not easily be disciplined.

John Paul's failure to put the matter to rest and his unwillingness to turn to significant punitive measures against dissenters should be seen in light of other disciplinary lapses, further revealing the effective limits of papal authority even within the Church itself. Nevertheless, a few obvious dissidents were suppressed – presumably *pour encourager les autres* – Küng being declared by the CDF (where Ratzinger was now Prefect) not a Catholic theologian, while 'Liberation Theology' (identified correctly as spiritually flavoured Marxism) was condemned as an inappropriate form of Christian 'liberation'. Priests holding office in the Sandinista régime in Nicaragua were corrected and it was noted that, when Fathers Boff and Gutiérrez were reprimanded by the CDF issuing its *Instruction on Certain aspects of the Theology of Liberation* in 1984, vocations to the priesthood in parts of Latin America increased considerably.

It would prove comparatively easy to neutralize a few dissidents, including Küng and Charles Curran, though as a 'scandal' this was widely observed. Importantly, Curran had argued – in this case correctly – that he was not disputing infallible papal pronouncements; however, by that he seemed to imply that all other apparently infallible teachings must exist in some kind of logical limbo, their status being quite uncertain, just as Vatican I and *Lumen Gentium* had left them. The influence of Curran and Küng would hardly survive their being disowned and prevented from teaching as Catholics in good standing; they had always been parasitic on the theological guild to which they belonged, and once outside the fold appeared much less alluring.

The problem of *en masse* enforcement (necessary if traditional moral teaching was to be maintained) – at the expense of an entrenched and powerful body – can be seen in the clearest light if we turn to John Paul's relationship with the Jesuits: often, as we have seen, the most powerful intellectual organization in the Church, normally committed to absolute obedience to the pope and certainly the most apt to grasp at power and perhaps now assumed by many to be 'too big to be allowed to fail'. We have already noticed their pre-eminence at the courts of Pius IX, Leo XIII and Pius XI (to which we might add that of Pius XII), but new 'ecclesial' difficulties would follow John Paul's attempt to rein them in. For though in the quite recent past the Society (with a few dissenters) had still been ardent papalists; now apparently they were to be the subject of severe papal displeasure. Time would come, however, when they would happily return to their traditional support for the papacy; when, that is, a pope was to urge the sort of doctrinal 'reforms' they themselves had already promoted, and for which John Paul reproached them.

In the 1960s the Society could boast over 30,000 members, and as early as 1965 at their 31st General Congregation Paul VI had intervened to warn them about an excessive worldliness in their concern to solve the world's political and social problems by compounding a blend of Catholic teaching and Marxist class-consciousness (*ergo* class-warfare), this to be indulged with little reference to such fundamental Catholic beliefs such as the existence and worship of a transcendent deity. Paul's concern was in evidence again at the proceedings of the next (32nd) General Congregation in 1974, held under the continuing charismatic leadership of Arrupe, General since first elected in 1965. We have already met him intervening at Vatican II, pushing for absolute submission to the will of a pope from whom he expected to find the support he needed radically to change the nature of Jesuit thinking.

It is clear that in Paul's view there was plenty about the Jesuits to worry over. By the time of John Paul II there was even more; Jesuit formation had been radically overhauled in ways which diminished both discipline and intellectual rigour; in Nicaragua two Fathers Cardenal and others held office in the anti-Catholic Ortega régime, while in Latin America more widely Jesuits were advocating liberationism understood as commitment to class-struggle as an expression of Christian love. In Jesuit colleges and universities (especially in the United States) Catholic doctrine was (and still is at date of writing) more or less openly rejected, especially but not only in moral theology. While not all Jesuits agreed with this sort of 'reforming' zeal, the radical orientation of Jesuit theology was overwhelmingly endorsed at the 32nd General Congregation of the Society.

The most unpleasant and uncatholic paradigm case of all this 'reformism' in the Society of Jesus can be recognized in the political career of Father Robert Drinan SJ.[6] Elected to the American House of Representatives in 1971, he served until 1981, and in 1980, as part of a project to keep the clergy out of active participation in partisan politics, was ordered by John Paul not to seek re-election. Throughout his time in Congress Drinan established himself as the 'godfather' of pro-abortion 'Catholic' politicians often deriving from the New England 'Irish mafia'. Among such were numbered Edward Kennedy, John Kerry, Mario Cuomo, Joe Biden and perhaps most emphatically Nancy Pelosi, who 'learned' from Drinan to believe the lie that both Augustine and Aquinas favoured abortion.

In Drinan's case such direct political participation was regularly discouraged even by Arrupe, the by now problematic General of the Society. Nearer to home, in the United States, however, Drinan was supported with lies from the New England Provincial, and when the

---

6. Details of the Drinan case have long been in the public domain, being first widely publicized by Professor James Hitchcock in 1996 in the *Catholic World Report*. For Paul Mankowski's role in the story and his interpretation of it, see now G. Weigel (ed.), *Jesuit at Large: Essays and Reviews* (San Francisco: Ignatius Press, 2022).

truth came to light, thanks to the admirable honesty of a fellow Jesuit, Paul Mankowski, it was to be the honest man who was seriously penalized by his superiors – an outcome not unusual among Jesuits in the United States. (Another American Jesuit who should remain unnamed confided to the present author his desire to have inscribed on his tombstone the words, 'The only Jesuit disciplined by his superiors for preaching against abortion'. Perhaps he was not the only one!)

As for Drinan he was unrepentant and in 1996 in an op-ed piece in the *New York Times* praised the Clinton administration's support for 'partial-birth' abortions. That aroused the fury of Cardinal O'Connor who denounced him as a partisan of the culture of death, but there the matter ended as Drinan soon after passed on to his eternal reward, leaving his confrères a legacy of anti-Catholic moral teaching on which in related areas many of them – and most notoriously in more recent times Father James Martin SJ – would follow suit. Nor indeed was Drinan's opposition to Catholic sexual ethics limited to the Society; an influential number of Dominicans in England and France would become known as supportive of homosexuality; and many others sedulously avoid committing themselves to unambiguous objection to abortion.[7]

Aware of the influence of such thinking not only among the Jesuits themselves but in the wider Church, not least on other religious orders, in 1979 John Paul decided to act. At a meeting with Jesuit Conference presidents he observed, 'I want to tell you that you were a matter of concern to my predecessors and you are to the Pope who is addressing you.' This was accompanied by sending Arrupe a copy of a message to the Jesuits which John Paul I, had he not died, intended to give them. John Paul II said he agreed entirely with the criticisms it made. At this point Arrupe was considering resignation on grounds of ill health.

Had Arrupe pursued his plan to resign, he would have had to call a further General Congregation which, after accepting his resignation, would have elected a successor with similar views. That John Paul decided to prevent, telling Arrupe that he did not want him to resign or

---

7. For partial evidence see J.M.Rist's review of the Dominican Father Gareth Moore's *A Question of Truth*, in what – unexpectedly – was to prove the final edition of the journal *Priests and People* in 2004. Recently another Dominican friar, in a letter to the *Tablet* (12 April 2022), has defended as 'highly moral' a book containing a 'gay' travesty of the Lord's Prayer (so rejecting a diocesan bishop's ruling that its author is unwelcome as a speaker in Catholic schools).

call a General Congregation. In 1981 Arrupe was felled by a stroke and instead of now permitting such a Congregation, John Paul appointed the near-blind Paolo Dezza as his 'personal delegate' to head the Society until further notice. The idea seemed to be that the Jesuits would be shocked into changing their ways: shock that would be second only to the suppression of the Society in disgraceful circumstances by Pope Clement XIV two centuries earlier, in 1773.

Two years on, John Paul met with all the Jesuit provincials near Rome. He lauded the Society's past work, urged them to persist with a rigorous doctrinal discipline which would enable them to 'dialogue' with other Christian groups and with atheists, and to work for justice world-wide. Things were getting better, so the pope said, and there might be a General Congregation comparatively shortly. Indeed Father Dezza and his deputy, Father Pittau, seem to have supposed that the pope had achieved what was intended, though others thought (rightly) that little had changed. In any case, in October 1989 at the now approved 33rd General Congregation, Father Kolvenbach, from Holland, was elected General, the Society having managed to avoid selecting anyone known to be the pope's man.

The pope's intervention thus could be seen to have secured nothing substantial; probably, as elsewhere, his optimism about human nature had let him down. Perhaps he was to rue his failure when in 1992 he had to distance himself from an anti-American editorial in *La Civiltà Cattolica* (normally, as we have noticed, regarded as a papal voice – and soon to be so again), since it might be taken to imply that the pope was an out-and-out pacifist. In 1992, the era of the first Gulf War, that at least had to be denied, though only after the Jesuits had got away with putting it into the public domain. Had John Paul returned to life 30 years later, might he have realized that he had made a terrible mistake in not remaining forcibly watchful?

If we ask how even then he failed to understand that he had dropped the baton, the answer is perhaps two-fold: part of John Paul's success depended on his overwhelming self-confidence – no doubt helpful in manipulating media attention focused on himself (though at times risking his being manipulated in return by those willing to flatter). Another factor lay in his assumption of a higher degree of sanctity among his ecclesiastical colleagues than he realistically could expect: some of them being placemen rather than true believers, others possibly 'plants' of hostile entities. Both these facets of his character can be recognized elsewhere: in his neglect of the moral condition of the Vatican

Curia – an error his successor was bitterly to regret; in his frequent failure to appoint the right kind of bishop: here he seems to have judged loyalty to his papal person more important than doctrinal stability, and many of his appointees shifted their theological ground when a different sort of individual occupied the papal throne. Indeed some of those he promoted – not least Father Marcial Maciel, founder of the Legionaries of Christ – turned out to be moral failures of the highest order, capable of obtaining massive funding by uncertain means; others, like Father 'Ted' McCarrick, limited their vices to young males, though were perhaps also among those in hock to Chinese Communists.

In 'post-ecumenist' matters too, the pope was doubtless encouraged by his sense of the sacred significance of his rank to take risks which his successors had to correct – or further exaggerate. Thus in 1986 a World Day of Prayer for Peace was organized (not without the assistance of the ever pliant papalists of the Sant' Egidio community whose chaplain, Vincenzo Paglia, was later to reach wider notoriety). Not emboldened enough to invite various religious leaders of many faiths world-wide to pray together – thus risking a charge of 'indifferentism', that is, of obscuring the all-important mission of Christ as mankind's Saviour – John Paul planned that at Assisi the different religious leaders should pray in different parts of the city and then assemble for a final meeting of minds – or what some less politely referred to as an 'ecumenical zoo'. A second – and more moderated – version of such diversified praying would follow in John Paul's time, with a final further-watered-down version under his successor.

*   *   *

John Paul always thought of himself as an embodiment of the authentic interpretation of Vatican II, one of the supposed goals of which was to enhance the authority of the bishops, perforce overlooked at Vatican I. Certainly in the Church of John Paul the synods of bishops, inaugurated by Paul VI, continued on a regular basis – but all called at papal command and to debate subjects papally proposed. At the end of each synod a papal summation of the results achieved was produced in an experiment which, while not seriously abused by John Paul, was certainly open to such manifest abuse as later would occur when synods – particularly, as we shall see, on the Family – would be more or less openly rigged and the views of dissenting bishops suppressed.

What then are we to make of this pontificate? From the point of view of conservatives John Paul could be (and was) hailed – as Jerome had hailed Augustine – as the man 'who restored the ancient Church': soon after his death shouts of 'Santo Subito' (i.e. 'Canonize him right now') were raised in the purlieus of Vatican City. From another angle John Paul had used his immense mediatic talents to put the clock back, to delay the more substantial 'updating' – or was it to impede inevitable secularization? – which, according to one view of the intentions of John XXIII, was required. But above all when John Paul eventually died – after a very public period of pain and suffering which a cynical ancient Roman (and many a modern secularist) would have decried as a 'self-promoting' death (*ambitiosa mors*) and the generous would attribute, as John Paul certainly himself intended, to a partaking in the sufferings of Christ – problems with curial vice, both sexual and financial, and with ever more bureaucratic bishops now encouraged to think that doctrine is what the pope says it is, remained on the ecclesiastical table.

Two further and continuing problems remained for John Paul's successor: first the Jesuits, untamed in their defiance of traditional teachings in moral theology, and still inclined to Marxist-flavored solutions to social divisions; then the liturgy. The *Novus Ordo* of Paul VI offended many traditionalists who held it not merely a radical break with past practice, but verging on heresy in its understatement of the sacrificial offering of the Mass: that apart from its often being (sometimes apparently willfully) badly rendered in various vernaculars. If John Paul had, in the eyes of many, restored what they saw as the ancient Church, how easy would it be for another pope – relying on the same enhanced vision of his authority – to set the train moving in the opposite direction? After John Paul the Great, Pastor of the Universal Church and teacher of humanity, with papal infallibility assumed and the infallibility of the ordinary magisterium unclearly defined, who could do what for an encore? Yet another version of the revised papacy of Vatican I had been on display. There were further possibilities to come.

Chapter 10

Joseph Ratzinger:
Poacher Turned Gamekeeper?

But what about that dreadful Pope?
German Lutheran pastor (female) encountered in Iceland

Best pope for 300 years.

John M. Rist

On the eventual death of John Paul II, Joseph Ratzinger, the late pope's primary theological consultant and designated enforcer, was elected in a short conclave; liberal hopes that his demise would soon follow were to be disappointed; and the end of his active papacy was marked by his resignation, after years of failing to achieve what his predecessor had more or less declined to handle: the cleaning up of the 'Augean stables' of the Vatican. In this his reputation as the *Panzerkardinal* might have led some to think he would be successful, but in a curious way his personal history, and his limited return to some, but by no means all, of the orthodoxies he had apparently wished to reform in his younger days, did much to block his path. His resignation, however well intentioned, would afford a further shock to the Church, after the shock of Vatican II and its radical aftermath, and contributed substantially to a growing sense of uncertainty and insecurity among Catholics.

Ratzinger's reputation as Prefect of the Congregation for the Doctrine of the Faith was of the hard man who battled 'heretics' to their knees – not least 'liberation theologians' and former colleagues in the German theological guild, now grown confident they had replaced the 'Roman theologians' of Ottaviani's time as the guardians of real theology. Already at the Council one writer had observed in his book-title that *The Rhine has Flowed into the Tiber.* Yet although the savage and widespread caricature of Ratzinger as Prefect did him an injustice, it helps to explain the hostility which his election generated. As we have seen, in the early years of his theological career he was rated a 'progressive' and at Vatican II was *peritus* or expert adviser to Cardinal Frings of Cologne, one of the more outspoken of the 'progressive' bishops and whose place in the history of the Council was secured not least by his open challenge to Ottaviani, whose understanding of the work of the Holy Office he characterized as a scandal. That at the time Ratzinger presumably agreed with that assessment might make his behaviour as Prefect of the renamed 'successor' Office the more striking and puzzling.

But only at a facile first glance. Already during the Council itself Ratzinger had recognized that the various Council documents – often the product, as we have seen, of committee management and horse-trading, plus Paul VI's insistence on a required near-unanimity – may seem incompatible, and even at times internally incoherent: unless read with that 'hermeneutic of continuity' whereby we must look at the thrust of the whole body of the Council's work to see its real intent, and then ignore, reinterpret or explain away those sections which show themselves manifestly contrary to that intent. In this judgement, as we noted, Ratzinger was joined by a number of other 'progressives', in particular De Lubac and *in absentia* von Balthasar, then in theological limbo having left the Jesuits and it seems in thrall to the mysticism of Adrienne von Speyr. Underlying this more specific problem – and in part explaining it – was the fact, pointed out most clearly by Kenneth Schmitz and increasingly recognized by Ratzinger, that at the Conciliar debates on updating, greater attention had been paid to the more academic and simply historical theme of 'modern philosophy' than to the wider cultural concept of 'modernity'.[1]

We have observed that the problem of incoherence seems most striking if we compare and contrast chapters 22 and 36 of *Gaudium et Spes*, the Conciliar text on the Church in the Modern World. According to the 'hermeneutic of continuity', section 36 must be interpreted in light of section 22; otherwise it is out of touch with traditional teaching – unless of course one is to suppose that a 'paradigm shift' – the phrase is that of Cardinal Cupich – was required by some at least of those who

---

1. K.L. Schmitz, 'Postmodernism and the Catholic Tradition', *American Catholic Philosophical Quarterly* 73 (1969), p. 235.

devised the text of 36, for whom, to the contrary, 36 should determine the properly progressive sense of 22. On similar lines, for advocates of the hermeneutic of continuity, the absence of any reference to love in chapters 15-17 of *Gaudium et Spes* should be read as a casual error requiring correction in light of the older view, deriving from scripture and long tradition, that love is the source of the virtues.

It is clear that Ratzinger and many other 'progressives' were happy with the silencing at the Council of the old Roman pseudo-Thomism and hoped to promote a more Christ-centred theology, based especially on more serious recourse to the Bible and the early Church Fathers, in this following that *Nouvelle Théologie* which many of them had been struggling for decades to promote – until they came to recognize a serious and still unresolved problem about what John XXIII meant (or thought he meant) by updating (*aggiornamento*). For in some respects John, as we have noted, had been a conservative; he wanted Latin retained for all seminary instruction, for example, and is surely to be primarily understood as hoping that fresh air should be let into the Church to guide her in whatever direction the Holy Spirit – rather than the hot air of bishops and cardinals – might blow.

Thus *aggiornamento* was an ill-defined project: to some, as to John himself, it implied a certain rephrasing of traditional teaching to make it intelligible to contemporary Western society; he seems hardly to have realized that, if you change the words and concepts, not to speak of the language itself, you need to be very careful you are not simultaneously changing the basic doctrine. Furthermore, to 'update' could mean more than making Church teaching intelligible to the apparently more sophisticated world of the West; it could mean adopting some – or many – of the ideas of that world which had previously been considered alien to Catholic thought and tradition.

Such an approach could be given and was given, especially but not only by German speakers, a certain Hegelian philosophical support, Hegel having taught that 'truth' depends on the relationship between earlier 'facts' and the culture of succeeding ages. That would imply that Catholic doctrine would need constant reforming. Indeed, the influence of Hegel – as of other nineteenth-century German idealists – has elsewhere too been strong: not least among a recent breed of Jesuit 'transcendental Thomists', anxious, as so many Jesuits in the past, to be up to date (as they supposed) with the latest philosophical fashion, however ephemeral: one thinks of Bernard Lonergan and Karl Rahner, the latter Ratzinger's erstwhile friend and close collaborator. Of course, doctrinal 'development', Hegelian-style, would be a help to those who wish to modernize moral theology, though few of the then modernizers seemed aware that in non-clerical circles Hegel himself (and even Kant) had by now passed their sell-by dates: the new 'masters of those who know' being increasingly Nietzsche, Heidegger (already the master for Rahner), Derrida and Foucault.

Thus the problems Ratzinger had to face when he was called by John Paul II to assume the post of Prefect of the Congregation for the Doctrine of the Faith were legion: among them that the sexual revolution of the 1960s had revealed a catastrophic failure in clerical education, 'updating' being casually taken to imply that the Protestants were right that it is unnecessary for a cleric to miss out on sexual activity (whether heterosexual or other). Accordingly, as we have noted, hundreds of priests and nuns abandoned their vows, the concept of clerical celibacy being widely called into question.

A second and related issue which had surfaced at Vatican I concerned the apparently competing claims of the 'magisterium' of the individual conscience (especially that of theologians still assumed to be clerical and therefore subject to episcopal or papal discipline) and the 'real' magisterium in Rome. As Ratzinger's prefecture in the Congregation morphed into his reign as Benedict XVI, and after his pontificate was succeeded by that of Francis, it became clear to intelligent Vatican-watchers that in ecclesial disputes there had arisen a new form of the implicit tension between morality and obedience. Had Catholic morality just become – even always really been – obedience (as claimed as early as Gregory VII)? But obedience to whom? Ultimately, of course, to the pope whose *de facto* 'spiritual' power and authority we have seen ever expanding – at least in theory and certainly in a hopeful practice – in the wake of Vatican I.

Already during the Council Ratzinger had begun to realize that present ecclesial problems were very different from those he had helped to resolve in his earlier theological career. Then the basic problem – whether or not widely recognized – was with too much authority, especially too much papal, as distinct from episcopal, authority. Now, by contrast, the pope's own authority was being repudiated by many Catholics: liberation theologians, 'progressives' like Küng and Schillebeeckx, ordinary folk in the pews who practised artificial contraception. Indeed ecclesial authority was now in crisis, and Ratzinger, the one-time 'poacher', was to find himself in the surely unwelcome though necessary role of 'gamekeeper'.

Ratzinger always insisted that his basic theological orientation had remained little changed; however, when appointed Prefect his job became

to prevent the Church from adapting itself heedlessly and untradition-
ally to the modern world – *inter alia*, from becoming democratic: or, in
theological language, congregationalist. The congregations might be
any set of individual believers (as in the 'We are Church' movement) or
more dangerously the national conferences of bishops now established
after the Council: the new 'Gallicans' whose programme, as Ratzinger
saw it, would entail an Anglicanization of the Church with different
doctrines taught in different areas of the world.

Ratzinger's principal battle while Prefect of the Congregation was
with the 'liberation theologians' – and clearly the issue of conscience
lay only slightly below the surface. Both sides thought that they were
following their consciences, though Ratzinger was clearly right that
the liberationists had imbibed much Marxism and tended to put the
kingdom of heaven within the parameters of the present world. For an
avowed 'Augustinian' like Ratzinger this was peculiarly hard to accept,
long-established teachings about the primacy of the worship of a
transcendent God and his Christ seeming at stake.

Not unrelated difficulties arose because the modern world had much
to say (not always wisely) about the role of women in society – and Paul
VI had made the ecclesial problems that arose from this more urgent.
During John Paul's visit to the United States in 1979, Paul's successor
was confronted after morning prayer at the Shrine of the Immaculate
Conception in Washington, DC, by an indignant Sr Teresa Kane,
president of the Leadership Conference of Women Religious. Speaking
on behalf of a number of nuns – certainly not of all – she insisted that
women should be 'included in all the ministries of the Church'.

John Paul evaded the immediate challenge, changing the subject to
express his vision of the vibrant love between women religious and
Christ their spouse. But the problem was not to be dismissed so easily,
since its underlying cause was the much-changed life prospects and
expectations of at least Western women, coupled with a deep suspicion
that many of the women's orders – whose membership was already in free
fall – had outgrown their usefulness and should be radically reformed
and in some cases amalgamated before they died out altogether.

At the heart of the disputes about the ordination of women – a matter
of particular urgency to both Ratzinger and John Paul – was that the
argument was less about a simple rejection of traditional teaching than
about its expansion; hence in this case problems of conscience might
seem inextricably linked with problems of doctrinal development –
hence of the authority – but whose? – to resolve them. More specifically,
on this question, as with others where a challenge to Church tradition
might seem to derive from a misapplication of Western 'worldly'

morality – especially of rights-theory – the 'woman-question' again seemed to demand a clarification of the power of the magisterium to compel clergy to choose whether to think and do what their conscience told them was wrong or to look for a new vocation.

Ratzinger as enforcer of traditional discipline now seemed to many to have turned out to be a new Ottaviani, relying on his own more specific clarification (as he saw it) of the concept of 'infallibility', especially that which might be attributed to the definitively taught doctrines of the ordinary and universal magisterium. Some began to talk about 'creeping infallibilism'; others, aware that the ordinary and universal magisterium of the Church had always been held definitive (though many had forgotten or did not 'understand' that), apparently concluded that 'infallibility' is the only way to avoid (or evade) the problem of conscience, while at the same time retaining ecclesial unity and uniformity.

As we have noted, on 15 October 1976, Ratzinger's predecessor as Prefect of the Congregation for the Doctrine of the Faith, Cardinal Seper, published *Inter Insigniores*, a document dealing for the first time with the problem of women's ordination. It tried to be irenic but concluded that the Church 'has never felt that priestly or episcopal ordination can be validly conferred on women'. But the problem did not go away and in 1983 a committee of American bishops began work on behalf of the American Bishops' Conference on a document (of which varying drafts were circulated) on women in the Church.

To that the Vatican had two main objections: first, that it implied that women's ordination was still on the bishops' table; their second objection concerned inclusive language in translation of the scriptures and the liturgy. Eventually Rome secured suppression of the American bishops' document, and in 1994 John Paul (defended vigorously by Ratzinger) issued the encyclic *Ordinatio Sacerdotalis* stating that the church had no authority whatever to ordain women to the priesthood. Inevitably there followed a strong reaction, though less to the (unwelcome) contents of the document than more tactically to its 'status' and to the force of its claim 'that this judgment [of the encyclical] is to be held definitively by all the church's faithful'. In the United States a nun, Sister Carmel McEnroy, one of some thousand who signed an appeal to the pope to allow debate to continue, was fired from her teaching post the next year.

Was this 'definitive' teaching infallible?[2] That question brought a long simmering concern as to the infallibility of Church teachings in general – the root of the dispute about *Humanae Vitae* – into the open.

---

2. For more detail of the whole debate see J.L. Allen Jr, *Pope Benedict XVI* (London: Continuum, 2005), pp. 179-88.

In 1995 Ratzinger answered a query (*dubium*) on the matter and after a somewhat cavalier account of the historical background of the problem he concluded that the pope's teaching 'requires definitive assent since it has been set forth infallibly [not specifically by papal authority alone but] by the ordinary and universal Magisterium': the pope had quite properly made a 'formal declaration to that effect'. Subsequently, John Paul affirmed Ratzinger's comments which seemed intended to clarify the by then customary distinction between teachings which derive from revelation and are to be believed (*credenda*) and those from church practice which are to be held (*tenenda*): a distinction which, according to some, nevertheless implies that the latter or some of them – presumably in accordance with 'legitimate' theories of doctrinal development – may be subject to change. But which ones?

Ratzinger's defence of John Paul's encyclical seemed to imply that the ban on women's ordination depended on revelation. But if so, only indirectly: his argument was based on the consideration that none of the Twelve were female, that in ancient Israel there were – remarkably – no priestesses, that only a male could be seen as acting *in persona Christi*, that the ban had always been observed, etc. These are all inferences, not quotations, from scripture (unlike, for example Jesus' words – soon too to be controverted – about the impossibility of remarriage in the lifetime of a spouse). Ratzinger, as we have seen, insisted that *Ordinatio Sacerdotalis* was not an *ex cathedra* teaching. Nevertheless, its being pronounced by a pope surely increased its likely acceptance and again speculation became rife among the *cognoscenti*. Some said that the pope and his Prefect were using the notion of the definitive infallibility of the ordinary magisterium to prevent *Ordinatio* from becoming a third example of 'strictly' *papal* infallibility: thus that it was not strictly infallible after all since only popes *ex cathedra* could pronounce infallibly. Others thought that Ratzinger was mistaken in (as they supposed) dissuading John Paul from appealing to papal infallibility, as this was desirable in this case. All in all chaos, not clarity, resulted.

There is little doubt that an unintended effect of Ratzinger's attempt to explain the relationship between what is infallible and what is definitively taught was to increase the debate not only about the *status* of the ban on the ordination of women but on the intelligibility of the concept of infallibility itself: a debate further muddied in that some argued that Ratzinger's defence of John Paul's encyclical was not and could not be itself infallible! For our immediate purposes details don't much matter; what mattered in practice was that Ratzinger (backed by John Paul) was able to use a now publicly pronounced account of the ordinary and definitive magisterium to license the silencing of dissidents: it was looking ever more plausible that in the Catholic Church, when push came to shove, not only morality but doctrine more broadly must ultimately be read as dependent on the will of the pope. Or to the 'Church' in communion with whatever pope was available to be in communion with! Recalling that already Pius IX was said to have declared 'I am the tradition', we might have to ask, 'Who is the "I" now?'

But if morality was ever more clearly looking like obedience, two problems arose: the first being (once again), 'What has happened to conscience?' – a question which (as we noted) received only scant attention at Vatican II; the second that in a morality where obedience is ultimately the test of goodness, will not those who obey settle for becoming ever more servile? Thus if Benedict and John Paul agree on some point of Church doctrine, they must be obeyed; if a later pope rejects their views – as would be fated to happen – the clergy must similarly reject them.[3] Hope of evading this conclusion must depend at least on a clarification of the notion of conscience itself – always, as we have noticed, a bit of a gap in Catholic theology!

The problem was made the more intractable when in 1998 John Paul produced a document – *Ad tuendam fidem* – which enshrined infallibility in canon law (under the headings of both 'divinely revealed' and 'definitively taught'). According to Ratzinger's commentary, a ban on women priests was added to a list of 'definitively taught' teachings which included such obvious candidates as the ban on euthanasia and the legitimacy of an ecumenical Council – but also, and provocatively, the invalidity of Anglican orders. Such 'definitively taught' teachings were not yet proclaimed infallible but – provided they could be shown to be logically entailed by the deposit of faith – candidates for such listing in the future. The extent of such proclamations might seem ill-defined.

The possibility of a proposed 'development of doctrine' on such matters was emphasized by an article by Archbishop Bertone, secretary of Ratzinger's Congregation, in the *Osservatore Romano* in December 1996, urging that three of John Paul's encyclicals (*Veritatis Splendor, Ordinatio Sacerdotalis* and *Evangelium Vitae*) should be regarded as infallible. It is easy to see why such a move was attractive; it would publicize a

---

3. There is an unfortunate analogy to this situation in English Tudor history. Queen Mary tried to enforce Catholicism not only in terms of what she believed to be its truth but as a creed which only traitors could reject. The next queen was similarly to define opponents of her very different religious teaching (that is, largely, Catholics) as traitors.

serious threat to dissenters to Catholic teaching on women's ordination, abortion, homosexuality and more generally on relativism; however, the risk of such a magnification of 'infallibility' beyond what was normally understood by the ordinary Catholic was that it would tend to trivialize the concept of infallibility itself.

That might seem too high a price to pay to control dissent which by this time might have seemed more or less satisfactorily under control. For what was in effect being proposed was that all utterances of the pope *ex cathedra*, of the college of bishops in Council and most extremely and implausibly all teachings of the ordinary and universal magisterium should be treated as virtually and potentially *revealed* truths, that is equated with the direct teachings of scripture. As we have noticed, the whole scenario was surely open to abuse in that what one pope might hold as 'infallible', or virtually infallible, might be cancelled out by another with very different views about Catholic truth and Catholic tradition.

Ratzinger, as Prefect of the CDF, had resorted to appeals to infallibility to enforce discipline on the clergy (the laity were harder to get at), in this restoring to the reformed Congregation something of the temper of the old Holy Office. It would turn out, however, that awe of such bodies – for reasons including those noted above – had declined, and not only among the laity, though the servility demanded by Pius X remained largely current among the remaining clergy, especially in its higher ranks. Yet servility – partly under the pretext of preserving institutional 'virginity' – must tend to be accompanied by deception: hence mental compartmentalization and, as a contemporary Kingsley might put it, a disregard 'for truth for its own sake' among Roman clergy. This would appear in the clear light of day in the next pontificate.

Already in John Paul's time the desire to preserve institutional pseudo-virginity was resulting in world-wide cover-ups of sexual abuse by clerics, usually of boys and young men: a widespread practice had developed, eventually to be revealed, of moving priest-abusers from one parish to another. One of the first senior clergy to be disgraced by this practice was Cardinal Law of Boston, archbishop of the home base of American Catholic 'liberalism'. It took a long time, however, for John Paul – either out of naivety or comparative unfamiliarity with the American Church– to realize how serious the problem had become, though eventually he felt obliged to act against Cardinal Law. The wider problem, however, was largely left for Ratzinger to face when he eventually became pope himself.

If the magisterium can overrule the conscience of its priests, at least at the pope's behest, what has happened to conscience? When

Montalembert, Döllinger and others in the nineteenth century (and such twentieth-century successors as Curran and Küng) appealed to their conscience, not only they but their opponents invoked the support of Aquinas on their behalf. Newman, responding to Döllinger, seems to have preferred to evade the issue, though, as we have seen, he developed his own, albeit puzzling account of conscience. Perhaps he should have preferred to look for support in Aquinas, usually regarded as the best starting-point for Catholic claims on the matter.

Aquinas discusses conscience in scattered sections of the *Summa Theologica* and elsewhere (*De Veritate* 17, ST I-II, q. 79, a.13 etc.). Yet though his position is disputed, to conclude that he holds unambiguously that conscience must be followed even if objectively erroneous (as argued, for example, by Johann Baptist Metz and other recent theologians[4] and rejected, as we noted, by Ratzinger) is an over-simplification. Aquinas holds that, even if we were bound to follow an erring conscience, our subsequent actions would not necessarily be such as to be excused; that would depend on whether we had defied prudence in earlier actions which had helped produce our conscience's malfunction. That might imply that in 'ecclesial' cases at least following one's conscience might be too risky.

So much for Aquinas; the more basic (rather than merely exegetical) problem is how could Catholics know – self-deception in the matter being all too easy – whether one's conscience is faulty? The answer seems to be – at least for those whose conscience tells them that a pope (or even a bishop) has proclaimed a moral (or a dogmatic) error – that they should ask said bishop or pope whether their conscience is right in supposing that he has made such a mistake. That circular procedure would again effectively reduce morality in an expandable range of instances to obedience.

Thus, at least in cases involving the infallible pope and by extension the infallible/definitive teaching of the ordinary and universal

---

4. For Metz's view see Rowland, *Ratzinger's Faith*, 40. A.D. Sertillanges in 1942 seems to have attributed a view of Peter Abelard to Aquinas, at least according to Ratzinger, in *Values in a Time of Upheaval* (San Francisco: Ignatius, 2006), p. 148. That mistake may lie behind recent differences over simple explanations of Aquinas's position. J. Lamont (referring to a now published lecture course (2015-18) of M.M. Labourdette) recently defended the traditional view that an erring conscience should not be followed in 'Conscience, Freedom, Rights: Idols of the Enlightenment Religion', *The Thomist* 73 (2009), pp. 169-239.

magisterium, any conscience which speaks out against the magisterium, papal or other, is erroneous. Hence on matters of doctrine the right and moral course would seem to be always to obey, though such a policy runs up against the historical realities that even papal utterances on faith and morals, though initially upheld, have regularly been criticized, sometimes condemned, sometimes annulled by later pontiffs and sometimes allowed to 'lapse' as though they had never been. To perpetuate confusion on such matters must, one hopes, be accounted neither a necessary mystification nor an adequate account of a Catholic conscience itself.

If in the last resort the Catholic must accept the authority of the magisterium, as Ratzinger in his capacity of Prefect of the CDF found it his duty to uphold, we must return to the effects this is likely to have – or to confirm – on the community of the faithful, more particularly when the views of one pope are contradicted by those of another. The by now more or less official answer to these questions seems to be made clear in recent history: it is safe to follow the current pope – and it is right to follow the conflicting views of sequential popes even if they are in contradiction with one another. So we get servility tempered with watching the papal wind: the unhappy result we can feel blowing through the contemporary Church.

That said, Ratzinger himself (as also John Paul) always insisted that the pope is no arbitrary monarch and must be restrained by traditional teaching; this at times Vatican I also had seemed to assert. But who is to point that out to an awe-protected pope, and what is to happen if he simply ignores his critics (as was fated to happen in due course)? Presumably nothing, at least immediately, since only he is competent to enforce the demands of the tradition on himself.

This is not an easily defensible position since talk of conscience becomes circular: obey conscience if it is correct, but we cannot know, except by reference to the obedience due to papal decrees, what is correct. Yet there is no doubt that, in insisting that popes are always bound by the traditions of the Church, Ratzinger and John Paul were in good faith, though to assume (as they seem to have done) that their successors would follow the same principles will look with hindsight to have been naïve. The Church in recent times has upheld Aquinas as her best philosophical and theological spokesman; perhaps, as I suggested earlier, more attention should be paid by leaders of the Church, as once it was, to the fact that, while Aquinas tells us what we ought to be in a world of theological abstraction, Augustine tells us what we are where we are – in which his judgement has been vindicated by thinkers as diverse as Niccolò Machiavelli, Thomas Hobbes and Sir Thomas More. As for 'lesser ranks' in the Church, some may recall the closing lines of that wise eighteenth-century Church historian, the author of *The Vicar of Bray*:

And in my faith and loyalty I never more will falter
And George my lawful king shall be – until the times do alter.

* * *

When elected pope, Joseph Ratzinger seemed to slough off the *Panzer-kardinal* image, appearing, not least in his remarkably successful visit to Great Britain, a gentle and even kindly figure, though lacking his predecessor's theatrical skills. Nevertheless, his willingness to confront reality was apparent in many of his decisions, not least about ecumenism, a theme which had been associated with 'progressives' (including in his early days himself) since the nineteenth century, and which had remained close to the heart (if not the head) of John Paul II.

In principle, Ratzinger longed for the union of the Churches, especially Catholic with Orthodox, but seems to have concluded that, while friendship between Western and Eastern Christianity is to be cultivated, the time for more specific advance is still far off. He had come to believe that for any possible reunification with the Orthodox Churches of the East, to include the patriarchate of Moscow, concessions must be made on both sides: the Orthodox would have to tolerate (though not to accept) the theological developments of the medieval and later West, while Rome should expect no more than that the Easterners acknowledge the 'primacy' of Rome in such terms as before the schism of 1054.

Yet in 1054 the doctrine of papal infallibility was virtually unheard of. True there had developed from antiquity a habit of holding the Roman see free of error, albeit to this the cases of popes Vigilius and Honorius gave the lie, but it was largely the later mistaken opinion of Aquinas (writing against 'the errors of the Greeks' and deceived by a selection of forged quotations) which gave Boniface VIII in his bull *Unam Sanctam* the cue to proclaim that to be subject to the Roman pontiff is necessary for salvation, the Roman pontiff being always right. It still remains, as we noted, true that infallibility (as currently understood) entails one of the more significant road-blocks in the way of any attempt, even such an irenic attempt as that of Ratzinger, to finesse the problem of the Great Schism.

Ratzinger's solution to puzzles about the relationship between the Western and Eastern Churches seems to imply that, although there are to be no 'Gallican-style' compromises in the West on doctrine (including the understanding of the papacy and of infallibility more generally), specific doctrinal divergences between East and West might be acceptable: that in a sense both parties are right! He seems to have paid too little attention to the fact that his position would also seem to imply that Western beliefs about the decisions of Councils organized as 'ecumenical' after 1054 – Councils which claimed to teach universal and infallible truths – are to be considered of uncertain validity, for such Councils cannot strictly be considered ecumenical since the Easterners – even without denying their authority in the West – might not merely neglect but (unofficially at least) reject their conclusions. (Admittedly this might prove useful in getting rid of embarrassing shifts in theological decisions of more recent popes and Councils: as about Judaism and more generally freedom of religion.)

Following Vatican II's decree on ecumenism, the rationale for much of Ratzinger's position is spelled out in the CDF document *Dominus Iesus* (2000): a document put together during his presidency of that body and which argues that Churches are legitimate so long as they have maintained the Apostolic Succession and avoid formally denying any theological doctrines developed (perhaps merely ignoring them) after 1054. In the West the Protestant and Anglican Churches were thus (as Vatican II had already pointed out) to be denoted not Churches but 'ecclesial communities': the phrase apparently originates with Cardinal König. The relationship of these communities can be understood in terms of an (unacknowledged) understanding of Aristotle's account of 'focal meaning': thus the views of the separated brethren can be understood with reference to the teachings of the model Catholic Church but the converse does not apply. It seems that Ratzinger recognized that his *Dominus Iesus* functioned in the eyes of many as 'an ecumenical train-wreck'. He himself judged it a necessary clarification.[5]

So much, unfortunately, for the Orthodox. The Lutherans were to be put on the back burner too, probably with less regret. Ratzinger had little time for the attempt of Lortz and his followers, whether historians or theologians, who admitted there was something wrong with Lutheranism, but were inclined to minimize Reformation disputes, seemingly considering that the real problem was that of the decadence of the late medieval Church. Yet this supposed decadence, however plausibly identified at the level of high-flown theology, is by no means obvious at the grass roots level of parish life: certainly not in England

---

5. So Rowland, *Ratzinger's Faith*, p. 98.

and perhaps not in Germany either. In Ratzinger's view the Catholic ecumenical 'revisionists' ignored the radical individualism of Luther's search for the certainty of individual salvation[6] – in total contradiction to the teaching handed down from New Testament times that the Church is a community and that the New Israel is the communion of saints with the Church its earthly manifestation.

Ratzinger was particularly hostile to what he saw as an attempt at cut-price ecumenism in the proposal of Karl Rahner and Heinrich Fries in 1982 that reunion between Catholics and Lutherans was possible on the basis of agreement that all that is essential is to be found in the scriptures and the Creeds – with little attention paid to how to reconcile the radically different ways in which these texts should be interpreted (or reinterpreted). As Ratzinger read it, the proposal implied that it does not matter if different 'churches' within the one revised Western Church have radically different (but still notionally 'Catholic') beliefs. Yet though he rightly disapproved of such possibilities, he was unable to prevent their constant recurrence in new guises, the most prominent, as we shall see, being that of 'Synodality'.

Apart from the apparent contempt for coherent theology and the individualistic mode of Luther's thinking (contributing to his actual dismissal of the Epistle of James from the scriptural canon), Ratzinger objected to the Lutheran banishment of love from a basic understanding of the faith that saves. Indeed banishing love from the foundations of Christian belief (perhaps by justifying its dismissal as a Hellenic intrusion on real Christianity), when combined with the aforementioned individualism, left Luther, in Ratzinger's view, with no possibly plausible theory of the Church: a reading only too justified by the fissiparous nature of succeeding Protestantisms.

Ratzinger also gave up on the Anglicans, reminding us that the non-validity of their orders was a definitive decision of the magisterium – and that non-validity, in his view, was only confirmed by their decision to admit women to their (schismatic) priesthood and episcopate. Hence, and contrary to the strong ecumenically flavoured advice of both his own bishops and those of the Anglicans, Ratzinger as Benedict XVI would establish the Ordinariate of Our Lady of Walsingham, which admitted Anglicans into a personal prelature, allowing them to keep

---

6. For individualism see P. Hacker, *The Ego in Faith: Martin Luther and the Origin of Anthropocentric Religion* (Chicago: University of Chicago Press, 1970). For Ratzinger's position see 'Luther and the Unity of the Churches', *Communio* 11 (1984), pp. 210-26.

many of their own liturgical traditions once these had been more or less purged of the Calvinist elements lurking therein.

Nevertheless, it is still worth remembering that relationships between Catholics and Anglicans are less grotesque than in Tudor times, for in the past Roman jurisdictional claims still extended into the secular sphere. A good example of what could happen as a result can be recognized in the aftermath of the excommunication of Elizabeth I. Doctrinally that excommunication merely pointed to a reality: the Queen had separated herself and her realm from Catholic truth; yet when doctrinal correction is connected with demands for political action by Catholics – threat of which, as we have seen, surfaced again during Vatican I – great care is required lest there arise serious difficulties for the Catholic sheep. In Elizabeth's time not only were Catholics reminded that the Queen was a schismatic and a heretic, but her subjects were invited to depose her (even, by implication, to have her 'eliminated', as some Jesuits seemed to hope). The pope might have been wiser if he had concentrated on doctrine and left his jurisdictional claims behind, for the result of his actions may indeed be compared with that produced by Humbert of Silva Candida (and backed by Pope Gregory VII) in 1054: that is, schism became permanent. If by the sixteenth century the papacy had learned nothing from its previous intemperance, we may appreciate that the loss of the papal states and the subsequent recasting of papal authority signals that, like it or not, this kind of mistake is less likely in the future – whatever sense of infallibility is accepted by Catholics.

*   *   *

As on ecumenism, so with interreligious dialogue; Ratzinger once elected pope was determined to use the power of his office to repel even those interreligious moves of his sainted predecessor which might seem to encourage, however unwittingly, 'indifferentism' between religions: another feature of modern thinking which he wanted the Church to repudiate unambiguously. As for John Paul's day at Assisi in 2006, for which all kinds of believers assembled to pray, the then still cardinal prefect declared that 'this is not the way to go': respect for other religions is one thing; any actions which might blur the unique saving role of Christ and His Church quite another.

Regarding another 'Abrahamic' religion Ratzinger as pope was notably and equally frank, telling Muslims at Regensburg that they need to look again at their faith's account of God's omnipotence which risks turning the deity (hence his followers) into an arbitrary and irrational (if merciful to the obedient) tyrant: which request most Muslim authorities had rejected since the twelfth century. One reaction to Ratzinger's challenge in the Islamic world was the commission of a few murders. Nevertheless, as we have argued, while clear that Muslim teaching of mere submission ('Islam') was no model for Christians, Ratzinger had left Catholics uncertain of the quality of obedience appropriate for themselves.

* * *

This is not the place to chronicle in detail other important actions and attitudes of Ratzinger when he held the papal office, not even his concern for a respectful and devout liturgy (with which the Orthodoxy would surely have sympathized), in which he primarily identified a beauty of holiness requiring to be purged of all alien forms of musical expression. Indeed, his hostility to musical desecrations of the soul was not restricted to liturgy; he had no time for sentimental ditties or pop-songs passing as hymns – even, presumably, if composed by American Jesuits. Any sort of 'Babe in the Manger, you're a game-changer' had to go, along with such French equivalents as 'Je chante au Dieu qui chante'. In Ratzinger's frank opinion much contemporary music – even at times in liturgical celebrations – points to the Antichrist rather than to Catholic piety; doubtless he had in mind the sexually violent, sometimes Nazi-flavored and even openly Satanic songs which pass muster in parts of popular Western culture. One of his first acts as pope was to cancel a Vatican pop-concert apparently proposed by his predecessor (supposedly to attract the youth), and replace it with a performance of Mozart's Coronation Mass by the Berlin Philharmonic.

Ratzinger's *Summorum Pontificum* reinstated the Tridentine liturgy as an 'extraordinary form' of the Mass: a decision which was to invoke the ire of his successor, as did his hostility to doctrinal authority being handed to bishops' conferences. That would lead to new forms of 'Gallicanism' (ever an ambition especially in Germany). Ratzinger also endorsed the new approach to sexuality, marriage and the human body developed by John Paul and attempted (once again) to correct the abuses of the historical-critical method in scripture studies which Catholic exegetes had learned from the more radical of their Protestant predecessors – just as the better Protestant exegetes were beginning to repent of them. His own three-volume book on Jesus, written as a 'private theologian', as he was at pains – rightly – to point out, can surely be seen (among its other merits) as a demonstration of the rational use of the new critical tools available to biblical exegetes.

In brief, Ratzinger as Pope Benedict had shown that considerations neither of ecumenism nor of interreligious dialogue nor of subservience to an alternative 'magisterium' of theological scholars and academics, nor of fear of the hostility of the modern world, would deter him from his assertion of a renewed version of orthodox tradition. To defend that tradition he had – after all – to re-emphasize the centrality of papal power, of papal infallibility, indeed of the 'infallible' character of the ordinary and universal teaching of the magisterium.

What Benedict (like John Paul) failed to recognize was that what one pope with enhanced power and an episcopate largely subservient or cowed might approve, another pope could reverse. He was to live long enough to see (if not, unfortunately, to admit) where he had been wrong. His death at the end of 2022 deprived him of the opportunity to acknowledge where things had gone wrong: how an attempt to control dissenting theologians and reassert tradition had contributed to the enhanced power of a successor pope to exercise a more unfettered authority; how one could not assume that tradition would necessarily inhibit any tendency for arbitrary, even heretical decisions to emanate from the Vatican; how the relationship between conscience and the magisterium still called for resolution; perhaps above all how the cowed servility of especially the higher clergy and the unthinking obedience of a naïve laity could lead the Church to a growing loss of moral and spiritual authority and integrity, hence to a chaos which – in human terms – might forbode its demise, at least in the West.

Chapter 11

Perón Meets Ignatius: The Choice Against Tradition

When the cardinals elected Bergoglio they did not know what a
Pandora's box they were opening; they did not know what a steely
character he was, they did not know that he was a Jesuit in very
deep ways; they did not know who they were electing.

Cardinal Murphy-O'Connor

And I am the Pope, I do not have to give reasons for any of my
decisions.

Pope Francis to Cardinal Müller

The first condition for doing theology is believing in it.

Yves Congar OP (1935)

The full explanation of Benedict's decision to resign remains mysterious:
the 'official' version, now backed by the authority of his secretary,
Archbishop Gaenswein, points to his unwillingness to be so worn out by
age or sickness as to be incapable of bearing the burden of necessary work
required of a holder of the papal office; for that would leave someone else
to manage the resulting chaos, as he had managed it in the latter days
of John Paul. Some, however, would add a reference to his supposed
inability to deal with what he denoted the 'filth' – largely homosexual –
in the Vatican (and more widely in the Church) and which had been
brought into the clear light of day when his butler, seemingly to let the

wider public know what was going on, stole incriminating papers from his desk.

Shortly before resigning Benedict had received a report he had commissioned (but which is still unpublished) from Cardinals Herranz, De Giorgi and Tomko on the rampant and blatant homosexuality flourishing among Vatican clergy. Perhaps the 'official' reason given for his decision to pass on the torch is largely correct, but no one doubts that unedifying 'insider' activity, both financial and homosexual, had increased dramatically in curial circles after Vatican II, arguably encouraged by John Paul's lack of interest in 'internal' Vatican business.

For present purposes what matters is that Benedict's resignation left his theological reconstruction of the Church unfinished and gave an opportunity to those among the hierarchy and their supporters (not least among the Jesuits) who wanted to undo much of the work not only of the now pope emeritus himself but of his predecessor John Paul. As we shall see, primary targets of the incoming pope's 'reforms' were John Paul's apostolic exhortation *Familiaris Consortio* (1981), his encyclicals *Evangelium Vitae* (1995) and *Veritatis Splendor* (1993) and Ratzinger's CDF document (endorsed by John Paul) on the theology of relations with other Christian Churches and other religions *Dominus Iesus* (2000): all, as we have emphasized, regarded by both John Paul and Ratzinger (before and after his election as Benedict XVI) as the flagship texts of the late twentieth-century papacy and certainly intended to clarify the future path for an apparently revitalized Church. All relate either to the Culture of Life, or to relativism in moral theology and indifferentism in religion.

But Francis's rejection of Benedict and what Benedict stands for is perhaps most easily understood if we look at his attitude to the Tridentine Latin Mass. In 2021 he issued *Traditionis Custodes* – an Apostolic Letter *motu proprio,* that is, without consultation and so by virtue of its character to be promulgated even if the reasons for it differ from those stated in its text – cancelling Benedict's attempt to quieten what he had seen as a potentially damaging liturgical dispute by ruling in *Summorum Pontificum* (2007) that the *Novus Ordo* of Paul VI is the 'Ordinary form' of the Mass but that the old Mass could be celebrated as an 'Extraordinary' alternative.

Though this seemed to resolve the problem in a way that more or less satisfied most of the disputants, Francis, in abrogating it, made it clear that (come what might) he wanted the 'extraordinary form' eventually to disappear. Yet one does not have to be an extremist devotee of the Old Mass – which carries with it reminders of the Church's struggle with Protestantism – to wonder why he should have wanted such a brutal and insensitive solution to a problem which had already been solved. His behaviour seems only explicable in terms of an inveterate hostility to traditional forms of Catholic expression (presumably viewed as dangerously out of keeping with the modern world, even though the Old Mass had (and has) considerable popularity among a fair number of practising and youthful Catholics).

*   *   *

The most active group of prelates who, after Benedict's retirement, looked for a very different sort of pope, became known as the successors and continuators of the 'St Gallen Mafia' (after the see of the diocesan bishop in Switzerland who had made such 'conspirators' welcome since Ratzinger's days as *Panzerkardinal*). When John Paul died in 2005 they had conspired – but failed – to prevent the election of Ratzinger as his successor; they preferred a 'liberal' (ideally Cardinal Martini SJ of Milan, though Jorge Bergoglio SJ of Buenos Aires was already regarded as a possible alternative); indeed by the time of Ratzinger's retirement Bergoglio was considered the best candidate in view of Martini's unwillingness to take on the papacy because of age and declining health. Though meetings at St Gallen had come to an end before the retirement of Benedict, members of the group were still lobbying (against John Paul's newly revised canon law regulations for conclaves) to secure Bergoglio's election. Among those involved were Cardinals Danneels of Brussels (known to have protected abusive clergy), Cardinal Kasper (to become Bergoglio's favourite theologian) and Westminster's Cormac Murphy-O'Connor ('blamed' by Bergoglio for getting him elected).[1]

Although Bergoglio – who in his earlier days had served as a bouncer at a nightclub – was well known – and in many places deeply distrusted and feared – in Latin America, and though he had impressed his fellow bishops at the synod of bishops debating the post-Council role of bishops in Rome in October 2001, he was hardly a familiar name in the wider

---

1. For biographical details about Bergoglio's career before and after his election to the papacy a helpful source is A. Colonna (aka Henry Sire), *The Dictator Pope: The Inside Story of the Francis Papacy* (Washington, DC: Regnery Publishing, 2018). For detailed accounts of various unorthodoxies promoted by Bergoglio as Pope Francis see J.R.T. Lamont and C. Pierantoni (eds), *Defending the Faith Against Pope Francis* (Ottawa: Acoura Press, 2021) and T. Rotondo, *Tradimento della sana dottrina attraverso 'Amoris Laetitia'* (http://www.tradimentodellasanadottrina.it).

Catholic world when the conclave which elected him was summoned. That required his supporters to engage in intensive lobbying to inform – alternatively to mislead – the assembled cardinals about the character of the man they were about to elect. They presumably omitted to emphasize that in earlier times even Kolvenbach, the General of his own Jesuit Order intended by John Paul to clean it up, had reported that Bergoglio was an unsuitable candidate for a bishopric. (The relevant document has now disappeared from Jesuit archives, but is said to have alluded to his deviousness and use of 'vulgar' language. The latter charge is now well substantiated, not least when in early 2023 the Holy Father, speaking in Spanish, apparently told seminarians in Barcelona to be wary of the 'f***ing careerists who f*** up people's lives'.)

The Bergoglio party in the conclave were presumably also able to discount reports from Argentina, which had damaged their candidate in the previous conclave, that he had cooperated with the military dictatorship: indeed was held complicit in the arrest and torture of two of his own priests. Better too that not much attention be paid to Bergoglio's evangelizing record while archbishop of Buenos Aires, since he had presided over a marked decline in the number of ordinations to the priesthood as well as a substantial drop in lay attendance at Mass.

Be that as it may, and despite it, Bergoglio's partisans had little difficulty in reassuring the cardinals assembled in conclave that they needed to look no further to find the next pope: slackness disastrous for the prospects of traditional Catholics and which – even had it produced a different result – must be recognized as grossly irresponsible. Some perhaps supposed that the Holy Spirit must get it right, albeit past history showed that to be a mistaken interpretation of a number of earlier conclaves. Others objected to uncanonical lobbying before the Conclave; still others would claim that proper procedures were not followed in the Conclave itself – such arguments deserving little credence in view of repeated irregularities in earlier times.

Like it or not, there is little reason to doubt that, however cavalierly addressed, the election of Jorge Bergoglio as Francis I was respectable as they come, and though his chosen name might have suggested an interest in animals and plants as well as humans, it gave little clue as to his ecclesial views – apart from apparently identifying him with that radical option for the poor to which his own Jesuit Society was by now firmly committed. Yet other features of more recent Jesuit behaviour, as noted earlier, were already suspect in the eyes of Paul VI, both John Pauls and Benedict, while time was to show whether even the option for the poor was always a matter of deeds rather than words.

Rather than identifying the principal characteristics of the coming papacy by his chosen name, a more helpful approach might derive from attention to Bergoglio's variable 'political' strategies as bishop in Argentina where he seemed to move easily between left and right, even between Catholic and ideologically anti-clerical. Elected pope, however, he was quick to establish his *progressive* credentials both within and without the Church, immediately abandoning much traditional etiquette and regalia in presenting himself to the public, choosing to live at the cardinals' guest house (Santa Marta) in the Vatican rather than in the traditional papal apartments (and failing even to keep the light on there at night, to the dismay of many Roman residents and visitors) and generally identifying himself as a 'pastoral' pope familiar with the 'smell of the sheep'. He also quickly made it apparent that he craved celebrity status and a conspicuous place on the world stage, to be earned not least by an expressed enthusiasm for the United Nations and other globalizing bodies, apparently hoping to achieve recognition by adapting the Church to the modern world rather than, as John Paul, by bringing that world to its moral senses. For Francis, despite earlier difficulties with the Society, was a Jesuit.

The Society of Jesus had been founded in 1540 as a papal Praetorian Guard (though betrayed and suppressed in 1773 by Clement XIV) and the bulwark of a Counter-Reformation which was to place massive emphasis against the Protestants on a previously more opaque understanding of papal authority. Although from their earliest days the Jesuits had determined to be close to power, whether ecclesiastical or civil – and in Catholic monarchies especially – Francis was the first member of the Society to be elected pope (in 2014), and thereby inherited massive and informed support from an organization which (as we have seen) John Paul had failed to recall from a prioritizing of social justice over dogmatic theology to its more traditional role as defender of orthodoxy – symbolized as he saw it by its special devotions to the Sacred Heart and the Holy See.

Despite the dubious orthodoxy of many in the Society and others in his immediate circle, Francis was expected – and promised – to sort out a variety of scandals in Rome and the wider Church which he had inherited from the neglect or incomplete successes of his predecessors: thus he would clean up the 'gay' morass in the Vatican and continue the purging of the Church world-wide of clerical abusers. Of these Benedict had defrocked some 800, including Fr Marcial Maciel, successful lecher, con-man and leader of the Legionnaires of Christ, who had deluded and manipulated John Paul – though Benedict had shrunk from calling to account those cardinals and bishops who had sheltered too many of their guilty clergy. Francis would put an end to the financial scandals involving massive theft of Church funds or their diversion to such improper ends as enhancing the living space of high-ranking clerics – not to speak of money-laundering on an industrial scale which his predecessors had long either neglected or failed to handle with the necessary determination and severity.

In fact, almost nothing was to be achieved by direct papal activity in any of these areas, though laypeople and a small number of cardinals and bishops kept pressure on the pope at least to go through the motions. Indeed Libero Milone, when appointed Vatican auditor-general, seemed on the point of at least identifying the financial morass: only to be unceremoniously removed from his post, a dismissal for which at the time of writing he is still trying to gain substantial financial compensation. Meanwhile Benedict's severity with clerical abusers has been moderated and notorious paedophiles or their protectors protected – not least if they happened to be cardinals such as Madariaga of Honduras or other South American friends of the boss.

Confronted with the rampant active homosexuality of the notorious Monsignor Rocca, Francis would pronounce the ominous 'Who am I to judge?', while Cardinal Pell, appointed as economic czar to oversee the cleaning up of financial abuses, was harassed and eventually compelled to face bogus charges of abusing altar boys in Australia many still believe were instigated from within the Vatican itself. From these, after long perversion of justice with accompanying mistreatment – and only by the integrity of one among the judges of the Appeal Court – he was finally wholly exonerated – but not offered his job back.[2] Eventually, in 2022, Francis shuffled the various Vatican departments and renamed some of them: thus the Congregation for the Doctrine of the Faith (CDF) – once the Holy Office – now became a Dicastery (DDF) while its powers and authority were further eroded to the advantage of the Dicastery for Evangelization and the Secretariat of State: this in line with the decreased interest in traditional doctrine in Francis's pontificate.

For the new pope, and those who had promoted him, had other fish to fry, nor could better be expected on financial and sexual problems if one looked back to Bergoglio's time as archbishop of Buenos Aires

---

2. See BBC, *George Pell: Court quashes cardinal's sexual abuse conviction*, https://www.bbc.co.uk/news/world-australia-52183157. This case was separate from the Royal Commission into Child Sexual Abuse, which investigated Pell's management of abuse claims while Archbishop of Melbourne, but did not accuse Pell of abuse himself.

and before. Then too paedophile priests had been protected and victims at times insulted, moneys had disappeared and in some cases been transferred to the Vatican for no apparent reason other than perhaps to build up a favourable image for the cardinal (and hopefully soon pope) in Rome.

Books have appeared by John Lamont and Claudio Pierantoni, by Henry Sire and by Don Tullio Rotondo documenting such matters in great detail They also emphasize what is more immediately important for our present enquiry, that the new pope quickly revealed an intent to undo much of the reform (or, as he would have said, the merciless rigour) of John Paul and Benedict: not only in his approach to theoretical questions of moral theology, but also in direct and public policy. Thus in 2016 we were to see John Paul's Academy for Life cleared of its original members and handed over to a largely new group headed by Archbishop Paglia, former chaplain of the Sant' Egidio community – he who when a diocesan bishop had authorized the production of a homoerotic fresco in his cathedral depicting himself (among others) 'in the raw' for the delectation of some at least of his parishioners.

Other papal appointees were to include advocates of euthanasia and abortion – Bergoglio gave an Orwellian justification in November 2022 of the appointment of one of these, Marianna Mazzucato, an atheist pro-abortionist, as 'giving a little humanity to it [i.e. to the Academy for Life]' – while elsewhere praise and recognition were showered – and continue to be showered – on such as Emma Bonino, pro-abortion politician and self-declaring doctor-abortionist herself – yet 'a hidden great' according to Pope Francis – and Jeffrey Sachs, as henchman of George Soros a highly paid subverter of Catholic moral traditions. Paglia, head of the Academy for Life was also put in charge of the John Paul II Institute for Marriage and Family at the Lateran University (significantly unrepresented in the synods on the family which Bergoglio had arranged and which will demand further discussion). Under Paglia's direction the number of students in the Academy sank dramatically

As we have already implied, the active practice of homosexuality, traditionally deviant, was now to be (if ambiguously) encouraged. Fr James Martin SJ has already cropped up in our story, and in January 2022 Francis wrote an approving letter to Sr Jeannine Gramick, co-founder with the by then deceased Fr Robert Nugent of the New Ways Ministry whose support of homosexuals had already drawn down condemnation both from the CDF and from the American bishops, who had determined that it could not be called a Catholic organization. There is no need further to chronicle all this since the facts are in the public domain.

What is important is to ask why Jorge Bergoglio, now pope, so easily got away with it – with for years very little protest among those higher clergy who (like the pope himself) have always been supposed guardians and teachers of true Catholic and traditional belief.

That said, there were protests, however limited and ineffectual, against the Bergoglio régime, and we must look at these, as also at the techniques the new pope consistently has used to enforce his will – thereby exhibiting no mean capacity to manipulate that respect of the faithful for the papacy which it has been the purpose of this essay to show growing ever more exaggeratedly since the days of Pius IX. For it is clear that like Pius (and his successors) Francis knows that he can count on a continuing deference to the Holy See and to the person of the pope himself: that the clergy and an uncritical laity have come to assume the high moral quality and honesty which they expect of the successor of Peter and so are unwilling to admit that any pope falls far short of such excellence. At best they may grant that he has made mistakes. Only very recently have they begun to ask, however hesitantly, 'Is the pope a Catholic?': question unheard of for centuries.

It is also to be noted that the succession of more or less worthy (and increasingly canonized) popes of the twentieth century has encouraged such a mentality, if unwittingly. We no longer suppose we must discount such moral monsters as Alexander VI (Borgia) or Julius II (De La Rovere), and given our recent comparative good fortune in our popes, we are tempted to bend over backwards so far as to reach the floor with our heads to pretend that what we see with our eyes and hear with our ears cannot really be the story. ('After all, he is the pope' as Cardinal Di Nardo reportedly put it.) Of course, the papal court, of which we shall have more to say later – not to speak of hagiographical biographers – has done its best to encourage such blindness, accusing critics of the pope of being disloyal, rigorist, aridly intellectual, out of touch with the modern world. These 'rigorists', however, have at least normally avoided the vulgar abuse which their hot-tempered master is liable to launch at his 'enemies'. His preferred term for these is 'backwardists' (English for his newly minted Italian 'indietristi'), which ironically might alternatively signify those who wish to return to a more orthodox Catholicism!

Henry VIII said of Bishop Fisher that he would cut off his head with the cardinal's hat on it. Execution having gone out of use in most of Western society, Pope Francis merely bawled – with reference to cardinals who queried his ways – that he 'would have their red hats'. In practice, of course, he backed off punishing quite so drastically; Cardinals Müller and Burke kept their hats while being brusquely dismissed from their posts at the Congregation for the Doctrine of the Faith and the Roman Signatura respectively; even Cardinal Becciu retained his, though not its privileges, when Francis judged that he was no longer of use. To explain papal rages away to the more distant and ignorant public, the courtiers can resort to the lie, standard in autocratic circles, that it was not the pope who was furious: it was the people around him. Henry VIII would have appreciated that too.

Perhaps it remains unclear what Francis hopes to achieve (apart, that is, from wielding the power of his office and being recognized as a celebrity): some suppose that he views the Catholic Church as a kind of spiritually flavoured NGO whose doctrines need to be regularly adjusted in the prevailing secular wind. That might imply – like some of his sidelinings (at best) of the teachings of Jesus (as about the remarriage of a spouse while his or her original partner is still alive or his talk of reconciliation without repentance) – that he is not a Christian, except in the sense that he supposes Jesus a prophet and a good man (perhaps like Muhammad or the Buddha). However, if that were the case, we would have to explain (perhaps citing the need for ambiguity to which we shall later attend) his seemingly more or less sincere devotions, also his reiteration that (as traditional Catholic moralists also put it) abortion is a 'dreadful crime'.

Ambiguity apart, however, we also need to explain Francis's apparent deference to the Chinese Communist Party as in his withdrawal of backing for the 'underground' Chinese Catholic Church and in his deafening silence about the persecution (to put it mildly) of Uighurs or the establishment of a virtual dictatorship in Hong Kong.[3] Perhaps this is envisaged as a desirable return to the (appeasing and largely futile) *Ostpolitik* of Paul VI and Cardinal Casaroli, though recalling Francis's frequent willingness to speak up for selected others he judges oppressed, his enemies have speculated that he is in receipt of Chinese money, like those he much favours in the World Health Organization. Indeed, for some years now some of his opponents in Rome have even concluded he is being blackmailed – potentially over homosexuality, which would explain his response to Monsignor Rocca's identification as a practising homosexual, 'who am I to judge?'

Whatever the truth about his overall motivation, what has become clear is that Francis wants to abandon large parts of Catholic theological

---

3. For a grim summary of the details of Francis's complacency see B. Rogers, 'Soiled Hearts and Bloodied Fingers', *Catholic Herald* 6631 (December 2022), pp. 32-33.

tradition (of which he seems to know little and care less). Part of the explanation of his troubling contradictions is presumably that he judges that too much traditional Catholicism would go down badly in the secular world in which he values a celebrity status. His choice, therefore, is between power and authority on the one hand and a consistency of doctrine on the other, and he has chosen against doctrine, leaving a question of how far the subservient followers in the pew and in the hierarchy will tamely toe the novel lines.

Francis advances 'pastoral' change as needed – one suspects in the hope that new practice will consign older beliefs to be eventually forgotten. Yet though his document *Amoris Laetitia*, for example, is advertised as 'pastoral', he seems to encourage Catholics to treat it as though it enjoyed much higher magisterial status, thus leaving less room for criticism by concerned theologians. We have already identified the longstanding likelihood that at some point such a policy would be adopted – indeed it had been advocated under the rubric of orthopraxy as early as the 1930s. But the question remains as to how might it be achieved without bringing the Church and its moral authority into such wide-ranging contempt as to stir even the episcopate – bureaucratic and servile as the pope knows it to be – into effective protest.

Unless his frequent resort to ambiguity is merely an interiorized reflex, Francis apparently recognizes that, although he can normally rely on passive acceptance by most Catholics of whatever he does as pope, he will arouse widespread fury – and that beyond the 'usual suspects' – if he simply says (for example) that artificial contraception is fine, that abortion is a right,[4] that euthanasia is licit in certain circumstances, that we must keep up with 'the science' as regards experiments with embryos, etc. – or that there is nothing idolatrous in Catholic devotion to the Andean fertility goddess Pachamama who still at times, it seems, accepts human sacrifices.[5]

While it is uncertain, that is, how much change in Catholic moral practice (with Catholic doctrine presumably following) is required, a direct assault on tradition should on the whole be avoided. Here,

---

4. Though at the end of November 2022 he edged closer to that position by declaring that he would not comment on whether the unborn child is a person, while his recent preaching that Catholics are wrong to oppose the decriminalization of homosexual acts suggests that here too Francis is progressing toward a more direct opposition to traditional Catholic teaching.
5. See the copious news coverage from 2019 and since, for example https:// insidethevatican.com/news/newsflash/letter-59-2019-in-plain-sight.

as Henry Sire has pointed out, we need to take Francis's Argentinian background into account, as exemplified in the tactics of the former Argentinian dictator Juan Perón: not that there is reason to suppose that Bergoglio has ever been a Perónist or consistently anything else.

Perón's political effectiveness depended in no small measure on seemingly agreeing with all sides in any dispute and more generally being willing to shift his programme as circumstances might demand. That, as Bergoglio discovered both in Buenos Aires and now in Rome, is the way to go. For example, as we have noted, we find both references, echoing *Gaudium et Spes*, to the 'dreadful crime' of abortion (sometimes with the added suggestion that Catholics should not make too much of it), and simultaneously a flow of kind words and invitations to prominent and blatant abortionists, especially those among them in high office who boast of their Catholic faith: thus Francis will compliment President Biden, whose policies include abortion up to birth and the massive funding of that 'dreadful crime' both inside and outside the United States, as a good Catholic.

Such calculated ambiguity has proved very effective. Francis's more conservative remarks can delude the naïvely faithful that he preaches Catholic truth while in practice his praise of those who defy or despise it both helps confirm his celebrity status with the liberal media and strengthens his claim to a seat at the top table in international politics – whatever those politics happen to be. Indeed that this papal tactic has been remarkably successful is revealed by the complete failure of both high-ranking clerics and ordinary-thinking Catholics to restrain his moves towards indifferentism in theology: note again the idolatrous worship of the South American fertility goddess at the Vatican (now complemented by the pope's participation in pagan rituals in Canada) and the 'indifferentism' apparent in a joint religious declaration in Abu Dhabi with Muslim leaders from Al-Azhar. In the latter case Francis might claim to be following the policy of John Paul with his prayer meetings at Assisi – though to a degree far beyond anything which John Paul in his most 'ecumenical' moments might have thought acceptable.

In any case ambiguity is a dangerously potent tool – and not only in its shorter term effects, as those who use it regularly can hardly be unaware. Although it may seem to leave the field open, it may also be intended to secure subversive changes in the future: this on 'Hegelian' princi-ples. If we call traditional Catholic teaching on sexuality and marriage the thesis (T), and call desired changes to that teaching the antithesis (A), putting the thesis and antithesis together, we get a synthesis (S). In matters of moral doctrine this is a distinctively subversive procedure, since if the antithesis (A) is in radical contradiction to the thesis (T), then the synthesis (S) will itself not only be faulty but will become the basis for further ill-founded deductions.

*   *   *

How much support in the hierarchy can Francis realistically claim to enjoy? Let us chronicle a few of the attempts of those few in the Church who have been concerned that he is pushing to its limits Pius IX's dictum that 'I am the tradition' – tradition being understood not as what I am 'ontologically' but what I want. '[After all,] I am the pope'. We record in each case the pope's non-response and the comparative silence which followed it.

First then a little background to an important part of the story? In October 2013 Francis announced that he had decided to hold two synods on the family: an 'extraordinary' synod in 2014 and an 'ordinary' synod in 2015. It soon became clear that his intent was to prepare the ground for official support for the views of Cardinal Kasper (of the 'St Gallen Mafia') that a more 'contemporary' attitude to marital breakdown should be adopted, and in particular that under certain circumstances those who remarry while a first spouse is living should yet be allowed to receive communion: this appearing to be in direct contradiction to the words of Jesus in scripture, so implying that Jesus' teaching is out of date.

Details of how the synods were rigged so as to give the impression that Kasper's view obtained more support than it did have been chronicled by Edward Pentin (*The Rigging of a Vatican Synod*) and by Henry Sire (*The Dictator Pope*). Pentin draws attention to (among other oddities) the attempt of Cardinal Baldisseri during the 2015 synod to prevent its members obtaining copies of a book, projected by Cardinal Burke (who had recently been unceremoniously removed by the pope from his position as President of the Roman Signatura and excluded from the synods) and edited at his request by Robert Dodaro OSA. The book, entitled *Remaining in the Truth of Christ*, defended traditional teachings, but Dodaro was carpeted by the General of his Order and told first that the pope was furious with him, then later (and, as we noted, characteristically) that the anger came from those *around* the pope. Such manoeuvring, however, did not entirely escape protest.

Already on 12 October 2015, the Italian journalist Sandro Magister had revealed that thirteen cardinals had written to the pope indicating that they were displeased with what was happening at the synod: they included Cardinal Müller, Prefect of the Congregation for the Doctrine of the Faith, Cardinal Pell, Prefect of the Secretariat for the Economy, and Cardinal Sarah, Prefect of the Congregation for Divine Worship: all appointees of Pope Francis himself. Their intervention was resented, this being the occasion of which it is reported that a furious pope declared he would have their red hats (so Sire, *The Dictator Pope*, p. 113). Publicly, the pope complained that his views had been subjected to subversive misrepresentations deriving from an 'hermeneutic of conspiracy' which was 'spiritually unhelpful'. Thus was the intervention of the cardinals trashed.

With the final draft of the synod completed – seven out of the ten draftees being progressives; the names of the little-known Archbishop Dew of Wellington and the Jesuit General Adolfo Nicolas are worth noting[6] – Francis got what he wanted: the chance to use the rigged synod to propose a summary of its contents in his post-synodal apostolical exhortation *Amoris Laetitia* (translated by scoffers as 'Plaisir d'Amour'). This was published in March 2016 and became the first Bergoglian document to be challenged in a more formal manner, this time by four (plus two undeclared) cardinals not signatories to the protest delivered during the synod itself. The four were Cardinals Brandmüller, Burke, Caffarra and Meissner.

Their prime objection was that the document was ambiguous (as was only to be expected), and that some bishops, notably in Malta and Buenos Aires, had explained it – their explanation then being apparently endorsed by Francis himself – in a sense which (especially paragraph 305 and note 351) contradicts the plain teaching of scripture by allowing the divorced and remarried 'in certain cases' and 'after discernment' to recover full access to the sacraments without confession or profession of intent to change their ways. Characteristically Francis made no reply directly either to the four cardinals or to other clerics who claimed that *Amoris Laetitia* must be interpreted in line with previous tradition. One of these, Archbishop Chaput of Philadelphia, was conspicuously to be denied his expected promotion to the status of cardinal.

---

6. Dew is often identified as the bishop who, according to papal spokesman and convicted plagiarist Fr Thomas Rosica, urged the Church to stop condemning sins: no new phenomenon among laxists. Lamont ('Conscience, Freedom, Rights', p. 186) pointed out that an earlier commentator of the same stripe, 'A.D' for Antonin Diana, was hailed as Agnus Dei since he 'took away the sins of the world'. As for Rosica, despite his international fame as a plagiarist he is now returning to public life as a spiritual leader and authority on the scriptures, most recently backed by the Canadian Jesuits.

The confusion about how *Amoris Laetitia* should be explained revealed a deeper unreality in that the conservative position in such debates often depends on the 'logical' claim that it is impossible for a papal document to contradict its predecessors: a claim intelligible only in a world of fantasy but which enables us to understand better something of that wider Catholic mentality significantly affecting debate between progressives and conservatives.

The dissenting cardinals, 'with all due respect', requested the pope to clarify: (1) whether it is licit to admit the divorced and remarried to Holy Communion; (2) whether the Church still teaches that there are objective moral norms; (3) whether those who disobey the Commandments are still to be considered as living in objective sin; (4) whether circumstances or intentions can transform an act intrinsically evil into an act 'subjectively' good; and (5) whether the Church still teaches that conscience cannot legitimate exceptions to absolute moral norms (this being more or less the view of Aquinas).

The action of the cardinals should remind us of the words of St Paul when he tells us (Galatians 2:11-14) that he opposed Peter to his face because he stood condemned: a passage well explained by Cardinal Müller[7] who notes that, because Peter had baptized Gentiles and then refused table fellowship with them he was guilty of 'hypocrisy', of 'talking out of two sides of his mouth'. 'Peter had departed from the truth of the Gospel', notes Müller, 'not on the level of the confession of faith but because of an hypocrisy which has dangerous consequences': he had thereby 'sowed doubts'. Müller (p. 157) cites a letter of Cyprian, the influential third-century bishop of Carthage, who observes on the same scriptural incident that 'He [Peter] did not say that he held the primacy, and that newcomers and late arrivals must obey him ... Instead, he took his [Paul's] reasonable advice to heart and joyfully agreed with the correct view that Paul put forward.'

The queries (or *dubia*) of the four cardinals were submitted to the Congregation for the Doctrine of the Faith, and received no reply – presumably on Francis's instructions. Henry Sire has pointed to a significant later interchange on the matter between Archbishop Bruno Forte, the secretary of the synod, and Pope Francis himself.[8] Francis,

---

7. G. Müller, *The Pope: His Mission and Task* (Washington, DC: CUA Press, 2017), p. 156.

8. Sire, *Dictator Pope*, p. 133. Cf. C. Chrétien, 'Archbishop Told me we Must Avoid Speaking "Plainly" on Communion for Remarried', *LifeSiteNews*, 9 May 2016.

according to Forte, told him that 'If we speak explicitly about Communion for the divorced and remarried, you don't know what a terrible mess we will make. So we won't speak plainly; do it in a way that the premises are there, then I will draw the conclusions.' On this Forte commented 'Typical of a Jesuit'.

The concerned cardinals did not yet give up. After vainly seeking an audience with the pope, they went public, bringing the dispute to the attention of more than the small group of Vatican insiders: thus whatever his intentions, the result of Francis's non-action was a serious and visibly public division among the leaders of the Church. The 'divisiveness' got worse, with Francis showing no wish to accommodate his critics. As he is reported to have put it himself,[9] whether in truth or irony, 'It is not impossible I will go down in history as the one who split the Catholic Church': triumph indeed for one sitting in the Chair of Unity, and a clear example of his misuse of papal authority. Of course, one cannot deny that, historically, divisiveness has often competed with the generation of unity as a feature of papal activities, not least in the case of the great schism with the Orthodox in 1054.

Papal vindictiveness, however, was not yet sated. We have already noted that in 2016 both the Academy for Life and the John Paul Institute for Marriage and the Family had been diverted from their original purpose. In the same year three priests who worked for the Congregation for the Doctrine of the Faith with special attention to cases of clerical abuse were unceremoniously removed from their posts, stirring Müller to action in defence of his subordinates. Although in his book on the papacy (already presumably written but not yet published in German) Müller had spoken with great warmth of Pope Francis, indeed telling his readers how close the new pope's views were to those of his predecessor, the 'worm had now turned' and Müller demanded to know why priests in whom he had full confidence had been dismissed. He was told that popes do not have to give reasons for their actions – and the following year found his expected term of office truncated.

Though the *dubia* of the four cardinals went unanswered, they failed to proceed to an appropriate 'Filial Correction': a task therefore left for others, and duly, on 29 June 2016, a letter signed by a group of clergy and laity was sent to Cardinal Sodano, Dean of the College of Cardinals, urging that the pope retract errors in the interpretation of *Amoris Laetitia* in a 'definitive and final' manner. Again no answer was forthcoming,

---

9. According to R. de Mattei, 'Papa Francesco quattro anni dopo', *Corrispondenza Romana* (March 2017).

though attacks on 'pharisees' and 'rigorists' were stepped up, strikingly by the Jesuits in *La Civiltà Cattolica*, now edited by Antonio Spadaro SJ and an organ (as we have noted) normally regarded as closely associated with papal views, as previously at Vatican I.

Later still (on 11 August 2017) appeared a 'Filial Correction' concerning the 'propagation of heresies', now signed by 40 clergy and laity. More challengingly, in Easter Week, 2019, nineteen clergy and laity (including the present author) signed an Open Letter (later endorsed by some 50 others) to the bishops inviting them to face the reality of a possibly heretical pope: 'heretical' because, for example, defying or finessing the recorded words of Jesus, about marriage and other moral teachings in scripture, must imply some diminution or rejection of the divinity of Christ.

This was too far for some of Francis's more cautious critics who duly retreated from facing the facts by advancing formal and bureaucratic considerations as to how such charges and investigations should properly be prosecuted.[10] Presumably the writers of the Letter thought it the business of the College of Cardinals (the descendant representatives of those Roman clergy in ancient times who acted against their bishop Honorius I) to debate and consider appropriate action in the present crisis. The predictable papal silence followed. Moreover, the intervention prompted attempts and threats to harm signatories. Whether or not the pope had any involvement, one cannot help but recall 'Who will rid me of this troublesome priest?'

By attending not only to papal words but also to papal actions, the Open Letter raised wider questions than those about *Amoris Laetitia* and other official papal utterances: friendly attitudes to abortionists, to clergy-abuse protectors, etc. – the intent being to show that if Francis's words about the kind of changes he wishes to make in the Church may remain ambiguous, there can be no ambiguity defence in the case of his actions: *facta non verba* will reveal what is projected. Thus there could be no doubt about the making a Dutch parliamentarian and active promotor of abortion in her own country a papal dame, nor about the praise as a 'hidden great' of pro-abortionist and herself performer of abortions, Emma Bonino. Of course, the Open Letter, like its predecessors, had no effect on papal activity, nor, one presumes, did most of signatories expect that it would; the aim was not to convert but to put

---

10. For a reply to such criticisms see J.M. Rist (interviewed by Edward Pentin), https://www.ncregister.com/news/professor-john-rist-why-i-signed-the -papal-heresy-open-letter.

down a marker. Indeed, unfriendly critics of the signatories might make the case that it prodded Francis, perhaps fearing an early demise, to step up his attempts to 'reform' the Church. Nor was it the last attempt to seek redress for apparent papal unorthodoxies, but nor were its successors any more effective.

At this point we need to consider how Francis – so often challenged – is still highly regarded by the great majority of the faithful. Henry Sire in his book evinced an unwarranted optimism when he implied (as have other well-informed persons since) that Francis's papacy would 'implode'. For there are features of the democratic world and the contemporary Church – the latter, as I have argued, in part due to the effect of infallibility both in theory and in reality since Vatican I – which make the present ecclesial situation substantially different, and more unpredictable, than in the days of Pius IX. We must consider both the power and temptations of contemporary media, then the present form of the papal court. By taking in the relevance of these aspects of contemporary life, we shall better understand why Francis still supposes he can proceed by ignoring his critics – except when he abuses them.

*   *   *

First then the media, including the 'social' media, for those who control them will have a very different view of what should be done to accommodate 'the signs of the times' than would have been approved by Pope John XXIII and his successors. We cannot expect the media, nor even the Catholic media, to have a clear idea about the respective weight of an encyclical, an apostolic exhortation or a few papal words thrown out during an interview on an aircraft. Nor have most popes gone out of their way – as did Benedict when writing about the life of Jesus – to distinguish their views as private theologians from those of the successor of Peter with authority to clarify the received rule of faith: nor can we assume they will always want to make that distinction, since they can, as they know, shelter under that infallibility of the ordinary and universal magisterium also and recklessly invoked by Benedict in the cause of 'right-thinking' papal activity: a magisterium, that is, which, to all intents and purposes, the pope controls.

There is a further feature of contemporary reporting from which a 'liberal' pope can profit: the big news agencies, such as AP and Reuters, though well aware, for example, of the financial malpractices in the Vatican, seem to find it inconvenient to draw to the attention of the wider media the apparent sins of a liberal pope while in the past having being less unwilling to expose the mistakes, real or trumped up, of his more conservative (read 'reactionary') predecessors. The deafening silence of the mainstream press about the Milone case is a good example of this phenomenon.

It must be allowed that those who at Vatican I drew up their account and interpretation of infallibility, or of papal power more generally, could not have foreseen how developments in the media, both secular and religious, would affect its reception. In particular, two features of modern media should be noted: the appetite for novelty and the facility to spread a message across the globe in seconds. In the eleventh century, the decrees of Pope Gregory VII took weeks or months to reach outlying parts of the Catholic world, and in some cases hardly did so at all; thus we find his call for priestly celibacy barely reached the shores of Iceland, whereas it now takes a couple of clicks for the latest gaffe of an airport celebrity to go viral. Yet speed is no guarantee of accuracy – not even in the reporting of gaffes.

Catholicism, especially if it looks (or can be made to look) reactionary, is hot copy, and in a world which has come to assume that a celebrity pope can answer questions at any time more or less authoritatively, it is likely that he will be tempted – or happily accept – to tell journalists what they want to hear – or want to filter. Their reporting will, in turn, encourage people, including many of the faithful, to make their judgements as to what the Church is doing largely on the basis of reported papal activity and pronouncements. Some journalists are reasonably friendly to the Catholic Church as she presently operates and presently believes; others manifestly are not and see in the present reliance on papal utterances which they can publish with or without context – thus inviting 'clarification' – a golden opportunity for mischief, as for influencing – usually for the worse – popular beliefs (including those of Catholics).

Apart from risks inherent in 'off the cuff' papal pronouncement in the present climate, it is clear that the more the central government in Rome is pushed into saying and doing, the less bishops will act as they should and the more they will evade their responsibilities and take recourse in 'just obeying orders': more especially if they can find justification for inaction – as well as a means to protect themselves from popular hostility – under the pretext of a bishops' conference. A good example is the ill-informed decision of the French and Italian bishops to oblige the pope by mistranslating – and arguably misinterpreting – a section of the Lord's Prayer.[11]

---

11. Coverage of this ongoing issue includes https://www.thetablet.co.uk/news /11763/-lead-us-not-into-temptation-falls-out-of-lord-s-prayer.

Such servility to higher authority within the Church will promote a similar mentality in dealing with secular authorities, though Catholics (and especially bishops) have need of moral courage in a hostile age. In any case, our contemporary media, by their close attention to papal performances, guarantee that the papacy becomes more and more regarded as the real instantiation of the Catholic Church as a whole – which may provide the incumbent with enhanced fame or at least notoriety. We have already noted Francis's musing on the effects of his own works. Likewise, Augustine long ago recorded of Nero that glory was not enough for him; notoriety was just as good, or even better – and what could be more notorious than to be known for causing a schism?

The question of servility needs further attention, appearing as it does in the wider Church, but first we need to attend to a second important feature of the contemporary scene: namely that despite denials by complacent theologians, the Vatican is still run as an early modern court, complete with courtiers whose attitudes depend largely on the regard or disregard of their master. Although courts exist in other political and even commercial jurisdictions, the Vatican's situation as an *ecclesiastical* court is unique – albeit abuses associated with secular, authoritarian courts can also be recognized there – since in the case of the Vatican, the risks are less political or social than spiritual. This model of the Roman Curia (the meaning of the word is court) situates the pope as head of an autocratic régime, whether reactionary or liberal – and neither variety is appropriate, since the pope is not the Church, nor the Church's Master, but first of its servants (*servus servorum Dei*). Nor is he to be identified with that Church which is known as the Body of Christ.

All courts, royal and ecclesiastical, prove secretive and given to financial misdemeanours. Everything curial – and not least the power of courtiers ever struggling for position and influence – depends on the monarch. The corollary is that the monarch (barring a revolution) can do no wrong: if mistakes are made and heads must roll, they will be those of courtiers who 'misled' their master or got in his way, not of the master himself, who can deploy the high repute of his office to conceal inadequacies of his personal performance: his status, whether civil or ecclesiastical, thus will resemble that of a 'superstar' or demigod. By contrast, the Apostle to the Gentiles was at pains to point out that he and Barnabas were mere men (Acts 14:15).

As for the courtiers, their dependency might seem too dangerous, potentially too humiliating to be worth accepting, but such is the price one must pay to climb greasy poles, and history records how many are prepared to pay it. Popes, bishops and theologians regularly deprecate ecclesiastical careerism; yet 'scarlet fever' remains rife, generating aggressive competition even flavoured with blackmail, with the smearing or other intimidation of opponents portrayed as guilty of moral delinquency – when, it may be, telling the truth about the delinquencies of others.

Over the ages, criticism of the Roman Curia (or 'court') has been a regular feature of Catholic life. Few would refer to its activities (least of all during the present pontificate), as did von Balthasar in 1974 – I quote from the English version of 1986[12] – in terms of 'the usefulness of the Roman curia, particularly as hard-working an organization as the present one'. On the contrary, many would argue that it has always tended to be corrupt and now is unusually so. For its character depends on its master.

There are no devotional nor doctrinal reasons why the successor of Peter should be surrounded by a court; other models might guarantee more continuity in the presentation of Catholic doctrine and the organization of the Church's mission while dispensing with dependent flatterers who hardly discourage those outside the charmed circle from aping their mentality. All government may be government by élites, but there is no reason to treat élites as *ipso facto* virtuous, nor to refrain from criticizing the abuses they may regularly entrain and protect. Court flattery is bad for the flatterers and for the flattered – and encourages the development of a personality cult. The present problem of such 'celebrity' (which Benedict tried to moderate) goes back at least to John Paul II, whose thespian skills encouraged it. Even so, and as we have seen, he recognized in his 1995 encyclical *Ut Unum Sint* that the role of the see of Peter should be re-examined.

Though the context of that encyclical was largely relations with the Orthodox, the question of the nature of the primacy, if taken up, could hardly not be extended further – and surely, if seriously undertaken, to a re-examination of the effects of the current version of a 'papolatry' which goes back at least to Vatican I. John Paul recognized that he must try 'to find a way of exercising the primacy which, while in no way renouncing what is essential to its mission, is nevertheless open to a new situation'. How that might be achieved is the hard question we shall examine further in our next and final chapter. Some indeed might think that the present mode of appointing bishops, in leaving most of the decision-making to the pope or his nuncios, tends to support a 'business model' of the Church, with the pope as CEO and the bishops, his nominees, as

---

12. H. Urs von Balthasar, *The Office of Peter and the Structure of the Church* (San Francisco: Ignatius Press, 1986), p. 41.

middle managers: a situation encouraging them simply to obey orders and keep their mouths shut when their 'conscience' might be troubling them. Such orders, as we have seen, will have a very different character when Francis follows John Paul and Benedict.

*   *   *

Throughout this book we have noticed how frequently, and especially in the nineteenth century, the Jesuits have been closely associated with the reigning pope: such as the role of Kleutgen, first at a key moment in Vatican I then in designing both Leo XIII's decree on a renewal of Thomism and prescribing the variety of Thomism on offer. We noticed the power of the Jesuits of *La Civiltà Cattolica*, being almost to a man devoted ultramontanists, during the proceedings of Vatican I itself. We also noticed that, though Jesuit ideas have changed, Jesuit power is still at work, now encouraging and supporting a new vision both of the role of the Jesuit pope himself and of the social justice and ecological programme which, in company with the great and the good of the secular world to whom Jesuits have so often managed to be close, the pope must pursue if he is to maintain his position as international and globalizing celebrity.

Although certain features of the modern Society of Jesus – such as the requirement to take an oath of loyalty to the General – remain unchanged, the immediate ambitions of the Society have shifted radically. As we noted, that shift did not escape the notice of recent popes, not least John Paul II who tried to redirect the energies of the diminishing numbers of the Society, but, as we also noticed, did not follow up his anxieties; rather he allowed the Jesuits to drift back into their re-established programme whereby an exaggerated notion of the 'Church of the Poor' points to helping human beings less to prepare their souls for the after-life than (even exclusively) to acquiring greater prosperity in the hard times of the present age.

Pope Francis is a Jesuit, trained in recent Jesuit practice, as are many of his most ardent supporters (again as represented by *La Civiltà Cattolica*, *America* and other Society publications, not least in the United States, where homosexuality, both within and beyond the Church has been promoted, as by Father James Martin SJ). In sum, Pope Francis combines the 'training' of an Argentinian politician with the tendency to moral laxity which opponents of the Society have attributed to it for many centuries. Jesuits are expected to show an absolute obedience not only to their General, but also to the pope: hence if the pope tends to orthodoxy, to remain orthodox, but if he tends to novel positions he will find many of his Jesuit colleagues happy to be at his side. The General of the Jesuits most responsible for the immanentist and secularizing turn of the Society in recent years, Pedro Arrupe, came first to wider notice when, newly appointed (as we observed), he addressed the Vatican Council on absolute loyalty to the pope and the papal office. As we noticed, when Francis was selecting the committee to draft the final summary of his Synods on the family – itself to become the basis for *Amoris Laetitia* – the only non-episcopal member was the General of the Jesuits, Adolfo Nicolas. Indeed, as Francis's pontificate has developed, the pope has found in his fellow Jesuits a reliable source for unquestioned loyalty to his revisionist policies. By late 2022 the list of much promoted members of the Society is impressive and informative.[13]

Obedience viewed as Society-loyalty is only part of the wider problem we have been trying to describe. We need finally to ask ourselves why so many – following the lead of the Maltese (and indeed Argentinian) bishops who had applauded the traditional vision of the Church affirmed and invigorated by John Paul and Benedict – so quickly changed their tune when confronted with a very different bishop of Rome. Jesuits perhaps might be expected to swing in accordance with the policies of their superiors – that being the nature of absolute obedience; as an old anti-absolutist put it, 'absolute power corrupts absolutely' – but the more fundamental and widespread problem of what amounts to a reduction of moral theology to mere obedience to the will of the bishop of Rome calls for a very different, wider and more disturbing explanation (or explanations).

Ancient Greek philosophers assumed there to be two basic enemies of the good life: pleasure and pain. The man 'foursquare without reproach', though no puritan, will be master of both. Plato depicts Socrates in the *Symposium* as master of pleasure and in the *Phaedo* as master of pain. To put it bluntly, in the Church, and especially among the clergy, there are many who either seek the pleasurable rewards (or so they suppose them) of careerism – to which in the last analysis the pope holds the key – or fear the pain of defenestration for which purpose the pope is best able to open the window. Few in the know would deny that under the present papacy the Vatican is a place of fear. 'Let them hate so long as they fear' (*oderint dum metuant*): the old motto adopted by Caligula fits the control which Pope Francis exercises over his subordinates.

---

13. The following link gives relevant information: http://magister.blogautore .espresso.repubblica.it/2022/10/31/francis's-team-in-command-of-the -church-all-jesuits/.

Thus for misguided tolerance of the present papacy the clergy are primarily to blame, too easily accepting the comforting but mindless view that the core of morality for them is obedience to the pope; but the laity (or too many of them) must also bear considerable responsibility. Just as a bishop, brought up on exaggerated but opaque accounts of infallibility, must feel uncomfortable when obliged to tell the pope that he is in theological error, so a layperson – used to thinking that popes have come and gone but most of them have done their job reasonably well – must normally assume things will so continue.

In the short term, they may have little incentive to think otherwise, if for them it is hardly possible to suppose that a pope should be seriously mistaken or misguided, let alone to believe that one of the effects of Vatican I's incomplete, indeed opaque, rendering of the concept of infallibility – taken advantage of as it is by the all-encompassing media – can have anything to do with any current crisis in the Church. Yet if things are to improve, the laity need to pay attention to what is happening at the higher levels of their Church – and realize that they and their children will pay the price for serious ongoing mismanagement.

Yet one further sad reality which hinders such needed surveillance is that too few even among Francis' critics, let alone in the wider Catholic community, have more than the most general ideas about theology or Church history: they may know that abortion, for example, is a 'dreadful crime' but are unaware that it has been unanimously condemned for the best part of two thousand years in recognizably Catholic communities: that is, that it is no novel (or ephemeral) target of such as John Paul and Benedict. Yet if the Church no longer knows what the tradition has taught for millennia, how can it be aware of what is happening when that teaching is chipped away? Thus does ignorance help Pope Francis escape notice in 'modernizing' Church thinking, while many Catholic universities fail the Church in this same regard. Most incoming students at such institutions 'know' *that* they are Catholics when they arrive; if by the time they leave their 'Catholic' institution they do not know *why* they are Catholics the institution has failed in one of its primary tasks.

Some have noticed that, even when saying the Mass in the form prescribed by Paul VI's *Novus Ordo*, Francis' attitude to traditional pieties can look dismissive. Henry Sire, citing Lucrecia Rego de Planas's *Letter to Pope Francis*, notes that at key points in the Mass Francis never genuflects to the tabernacle nor even to the consecrated Host: a ritual act prescribed in the rubrics.[14] Appositely he cites a pungent epigram

---

14. Sire, *Dictator Pope*, p. 191 and n. 31.

by Lorenzo Strecchetti which sums up the pope's apparently laid-back attitude to traditions of divine worship along with his deference to the Civil Power whose encouragement and support he craves:

> *Sono Francesco, papa ed argentino:*
> *Non all' Ostia, ma al secolo mi inchino.*

Perhaps one may render this in inferior form in English as:

> *I'm Francis the Argentine Pope.*
> *With Christ and his truth I can't cope.*
> *When the altar I tend,*
> *my knees fail to bend,*
> *but this age and its gods are my hope.*

The Jesuit from Argentina has successfully (one might hope temporarily) subverted some of the basic beliefs of the Catholic Church, starting with moral theology; yet moral deviations point to more fundamental heterodoxies. He has done so through the exercise of the very powers which John Paul II and Benedict XVI had used to uphold tradition. That suggests that less ambivalent weapons to promote the Faith in good faith must be sought by those concerned with the Church's well-being.. For since Francis has demonstrated that the power of the papacy, soft or hard, can be used against Catholic orthodoxy, the nature and understanding of that power needs to be reconsidered and repaired: this not merely, as John Paul already suggested, to encourage improvements in the relationship of Catholicism and Orthodoxy, but to maintain the very credibility of the Catholic Church as an alternative to a 'world' longing to see its demise. As for Francis himself, rather as some in 'pasquinade' asked of Pope Urban VIII whether by chance he was Catholic, so, as we noted, have some now begun to wonder whether – though in some sense infallible – Jorge Bergoglio is problematic in the same way.

If so, 'perhaps we should be told'. For if Francis is in no meaningful sense Catholic, his ambiguous attitude to abortion,[15] clergy sexual abuse

---

15. A recent development (December 2022) suggests that even the ambiguity is being sloughed off and Francis is revealing himself as quite unconcerned about the 'grave sin' of abortion. While earlier, as we noted, he has honoured those who commit and encourage it, now, by his diktat laicizing Fr Frank Pavone, long-time leader of 'Priests for Life' in the United States, the pope has taken a further step: prominent anti-abortion priests are

(normally of young males) and anal intercourse more generally, is far more intelligible. One could even compare his 'smell of the sheep' to the 'filth' which haunted Benedict XVI's later days in office. That said, perversities of an individual, even of an individual pope, are not the primary and basic problem in the contemporary Church. That, as I have constantly suggested, resides in the attitude of large sections of the wider Catholic community, especially of senior members of the clerical hierarchy. It is impossible to believe that many of these are unaware (even somewhat uneasy) about what has been happening in Rome and in the wider Church for the last 50 years: including their own servility and the servility their example encourages in others.

*　　*　　*

As explained by John Wheeler-Bennett, historian of the 'German Army in Politics', when Colonel Claus von Stauffenberg concluded in 1944 that now if ever the Nazi régime must be overthrown from within, he realized that the success of his plot depended on his eliminating the Führer at the outset. If that were not achieved, then the terror that Hitler had installed, coupled with the misguided loyalty to him of the Officer Corps in particular, as represented by their oath of allegiance, would effectively stymie any attempt to overthrow the régime. In which case the Army, once the pride of the German nation, would face its nemesis in a humiliation deriving from its subservience to evil.

The situation in the Catholic Church is unfortunately analogous. Large swathes of its members, not least those at the top of the hierarchy, in fear of their master and paralysed by the belief that speaking the truth, far from clearing the air, would merely reveal that the Bride of Christ has lost her virginity, have chosen to 'go along', in the notorious language of the Nixon presidency. You must remain silent, they conclude, if not actually collaborate in evil: hence a loss of moral integrity in prominent parts of the Catholic Church. What effect must that loss eventually have on the larger group of believers? Primarily, it will erode the necessary confidence that the bishops and other Church leaders are to be trusted. That lack of trust would be more than the long established, even populist,

---

now threatened with having to read in the newspapers that they have been laicized; this is a direct challenge not only to the pro-life movement in the Catholic Church but to the moral integrity of the clergy more generally. If protests against it are as ineffective as those against earlier activities of Pope Francis, my thesis in the present work will sadly be given enhanced plausibility.

cynicism often met in Italy when you hear that truth and the Vatican are unlikely bedfellows. More fundamentally, it would derive from a genuine distortion of established authority which must be recognized as deeply corrosive.

Optimists in the Church might argue, with some plausibility, that the pontificate of Francis has, in the longer term, been an eye-opener, hence very beneficial. We now know that a ecclesial structure and mentality that allowed for the apparent strengthening of traditional Catholicism under John Paul II and Benedict XVI could be put to very different purpose with comparative ease. Indeed by late 2022 the problem has at last being recognized by a small number of bishops and cardinals, perhaps the most outspoken now being Cardinal Müller who, as a former head of the Congregation for the Defence of the Faith, has perhaps the strongest obligation, however unwelcome, to call for honesty – though as yet there are no significant calls for the pope to stand down or be dismissed. However, if those who are beginning to understand what is happening fail to stop the rot, whether in the present papacy or the next, there is little doubt that the Catholic Church (in the first instance in the West, once its intellectual powerhouse) will disintegrate as (like the ancient Israelites) she goes 'whoring after false gods'.

Chapter 12

Modest Conclusions, Less Modest Suggestions

It is the task and the mission of the pope and the bishops in unity with him, like Peter long ago as the visible head of his Church together with the apostles, to confront the chief priests of the Zeitgeist and the rulers of the earth as witnesses to the truth and as advocates of freedom.

Cardinal Müller

Peter does not depend on our lies and flatteries. It is precisely those who blindly and uncritically defend every decision of the pope that make the greatest contribution to undermining the authority of the Holy See.

Melchior Cano OP

Get thee behind me, Satan.

Mark 8:33

Since Pius IX there have been ten more popes, of whom four (Pius X, John XXIII, Paul VI and John Paul II) have been canonized, Pius IX himself only (so far) attaining to beatification. If we exclude the reigning pontiff and look at the popes of Vatican II and subsequently, the number is three saints out of five – out of four if we discount Benedict XVI whose future ecclesial status remains uncertain: a proliferation unparalleled since canonization became a formal process rather than the result of popular acclamation or regal manipulation. As for John Paul I, the only recent pope (apart from Benedict) so far passed over, his beatification is now completed, opening the way to possible canonization in due course; popes, it seems, now must be acknowledged saints.

Blessed Pius IX got what he wanted but not in the form that he foresaw: that is, the pope (supported by his still centralized Curia) has remained increasingly in charge, able to bend the Church to his will to a degree hitherto unprecedented, but the effect has been less to confirm the tradition than to confirm the pope – of whatever 'ideologically' theological stripe – *as* the tradition, in accordance with the reported words of the forefather of this trend. There has thus emerged a risk that the word 'tradition' has lost much of its original sense. Perhaps we have indeed reached the world of those 'instant traditions' which the writer recalls as a feature of his schooldays.

A traditional view of papal authority – and not limited to the world after Vatican I – was expressed fairly recently by Cardinal Müller as follows:[1] 'All the orthodox teachers of the faith have been firmly convinced that the *cathedra Petri* has remained free of every error and always will remain free of error...' But the truth or falsity of this claim will depend on how 'error' is understood and what is referred to by the *'cathedra Petri'*. If it suggests that Peter himself never made – indeed for a time insisted on – a *de facto* doctrinal error, and even after the Resurrection, it is false. If it tells us that no pope has been in doctrinal error, it is false (the star but not unique example being Honorius I, condemned posthumously by an ecumenical Council as a heretic after rejection by his own clergy). Such 'economy with the *actualité*' is not only false; it encourages a compartmentalizing self-delusion among those who could 'know' it to be false yet deny its falsity, bringing the likelihood of their spreading delusion among others too ignorant wilfully to compartmentalize their minds.

Yet if it asserts that little has been declared infallible by a pope in virtue of his Vatican I-approved authority, that is true but uninformative. Our problem in the present discussion has been less with 'official' accounts of infallibility, whether of the pope or of the bishops in communion with the pope, or the Church in communion with the Roman see or the 'ordinary and universal magisterium'; it has been rather with how, from the highest-ranking clerics to the 'humblest' members of the laity, we the faithful interpret 'infallibility' and 'ordinary and universal magisterium' and accordingly how we behave.

That problem has reached centre-stage since – and substantially because of – Vatican I, since to accept *Pastor Aeternus* and the pope's

---

1. Müller, *The Pope*, p. 214.

infallibility gives little direction as to how that infallibility is to be understood. It has been suggested, for example, that a papal declaration of an infallible truth is merely the recognition by the pope in a formal proclamation of what has hitherto been an unarticulated consensus; yet this interpretation surely fails to represent the intention of the bishops assembled at Vatican I. Indeed, if their very declaration of the infallibility of the Roman bishop had always been the unacknowledged view of the Church, why did it arouse such fierce disputes when the ultramontanes fought to get it defined?

It would be wholly out of keeping to judge the Church by any democratic model: there is, and has always been, an inequality of power and authority among its members. Nor is the basic problem, as we have seen, to be located in the use of the concepts 'left' and 'right', or even 'progressives' and traditionalists or 'conservatives'. No one will dispute that such divisions will always exist to some degree in the Church. Rather what we are concerned with is how disputes between 'progressives' and 'conservatives' have been resolved – especially since Vatican I. Our argument is that they have been resolved – in whatever direction and with whatever degree of sincerity or respect for the traditions of the Church – by decision of the reigning pontiff, and that this mode of resolution has been caused in no small measure by the uncertainties and ambiguities surrounding not only the infallibility of the pope himself but by the very concept of infallibility when highlighted in its papal manifestation.

The ideal of Pius IX seems to have been that the pope should rule paternalistically, and Leo XIII would follow in that same direction: I styled him the 'top-down pastor', but a good case can be made that he always intended his reforms to be legitimate reaffirmations or extensions of traditional Catholic tenets. Thus, the Thomism of *Aeterni Patris* was proposed in the hope – however misguided – of restoring the Thomism of Thomas himself as against the varying different versions flourishing in the nineteenth century and later. Similarly, Leo's innovations in regard to the Church's social teaching aimed to develop what was to be found, at least in embryo, in his predecessors. Despite some errors in formulation, his proclamation of rights was to be a corollary of very traditional Catholic ideas about human dignity. For this he was much praised.

However, serious underlying difficulties with 'paternalism' came to the surface at Vatican II. Certainly the views of many of the 'progressive' *periti* and of some of the bishops were well known before the Council began – though were often viewed critically by the disciplinary organs of the Church. But when the Council got under way, as we observed, it was by no means clear what it was supposed to do – or rather what Pope John wanted it to do, not least because he seemed at times to send out contradictory signals. Somehow – but how? – it was to 'come to terms' with the modern world. But the progressives and the bishops (largely French- and German-speaking) who supported reform only showed their hands when Pope John gave the appropriate signals. The conservatives (more expectedly) followed the same track: we noted that on one significant occasion the emphatically conservative Cardinal Siri was happy to say that only the pope (Paul VI) could have saved the situation.

What, therefore, I am arguing is less that popes now simply set the agenda in all its details, though Pius IX may have hoped for that sort of outcome, but that the desires and ambitions of the various factions within the Church are only fulfilled when the pope is willing to fulfil them. His role, that is, is not necessarily – though possibly – that of originator or denier of change (or more traditionally as arbitrator and final authority of change) but rather as the power to enable change (whatever it might be) to happen. To a degree this is still his traditional role, but the Second Vatican Council had hardly closed when the ecclesial world (reflecting disputes in the contemporary world) changed dramatically, demanding a new orientation of the pope's authority: the change being that the 'progressives' split into more or less conservative interpreters of what the often ambiguous documents of the Council actually taught. Hence arose the problem of which 'hermeneutic' should be applied to them: a hermeneutic of continuity or a hermeneutic of radical change entailing the abandonment of much that conservatives (and neo-conservatives) regarded as basic doctrine. Some popes proceeded to follow the former path (if with variations of emphasis); one chose the latter.

Thus for a while paternalism still seemed to work, though many were dissatisfied, for example, with the changes in the liturgy foreseen to a degree by the Council and approved when worked out in post-conciliar detail by Paul VI and his radical advisers, especially Cardinal Lercaro and Archbishop Bugnini. But the clearest sign that things might come seriously unstuck, and papal control of the agenda falter, was given by Paul VI's *Humanae Vitae*, to Paul's surprise rejected at least *in pectore* by numbers of bishops and in practice by huge numbers of the laity, yielding indeed a crisis of paternalism. For how could the pope re-establish control of the ecclesial agenda – even when urged to do so by former 'radicals' already discerning an approaching crisis and now confronting it – when that agenda was driven not least by pressures from outside the Church and therefore beyond ecclesiastical control?

Popes John Paul II and Benedict XVI took one route: they would restore the ancient doctrine though modernizing it so far as could be permitted without any change in essentials, and clamp down (this with varying degrees of success) on dissidents. It seemed to work: there were only minor revolts, though much hostility, especially to the activities of Ratzinger while Prefect of the Congregation for the Doctrine of the Faith. For we recall that seeing, as he and as John Paul believed, that basic principles were at stake, he did not hesitate to take firm action against those dissidents, not least among Latin American (and other) Jesuits, who remained in the Church.

At no time in Ratzinger's theological career did his 'teenage radical-ism' extend (like that of a more-than-teenage Hans Küng and others) to challenging the ultimately absolute and indeed still theoretically extendable power of the pope and his infallibility or virtual infallibility taught by Vatican I. Hence, as we have seen, 'creeping infallibility', now more clearly presented as doctrine 'definitively taught', with increas-ingly obvious problems of conscience and corresponding resort to double-think.

Doubtless when Ratzinger (as Pope Benedict) resigned, he assumed that the policies he and his predecessor had worked on for decades would be continued. That is, he followed something of the line we saw in the quotation from Cardinal Müller cited near the beginning of this final chapter: the point being that the chair of Peter, in some ambiguously open sense, does not make mistakes: which assumption is the theoretical core of ecclesial paternalism. When something quite unexpected occurred in an outright attack on traditions, now assumed to be at best out-of-date, there emerged a real risk of traditional paternalism turning into dictatorship. If Pio Nono's dictum 'I am the tradition' is understood in a radical sense, the untrammelled authority of the pope simply prevails, with traditional doctrine discarded at will.

The difference between paternalism and dictatorship, whether in a secular or an ecclesial context, is marked by differing attitudes to the rule of law or of some equivalent, and in the Church the equivalent is the centuries-old tradition. Nevertheless, in one respect paternalism and dictatorship draw closer: that is, in the attitude of the governed. Under a paternalist system, so long as it remains widely acceptable, the habit of obedience is justified by the assumed good for which the paternal ruler stands. But even under paternalism it is easy to slide from obeying the ruler because he does the right thing into obeying him because you acquire the habit of believing that he must do the right thing, and in the latter condition the governed become infantilized. There is plenty of evidence that this has been the situation in the Church, certainly in recent times. Important to recognize the difference between saying 'I follow the teaching of the Catholic Church because I believe it is morally correct', and 'I accept this teaching simply because the Catholic Church says it is morally correct' (even though if I allowed myself to think about it I might have my doubts). The follower of the latter practice runs considerable risk of 'losing his or her moral compass' and integrity.

Any engrained habit of thinking that all things will go well because the pope is in charge runs into difficulties when we transfer allegiance from one pope to another. Thus (as happened at the conclave which elected Pope Francis) many were too inclined to assume that the established procedures would work more or less satisfactorily and that the teaching of the new pope would be more or less traditional. We now know that that cannot be assumed, and it has been universally admitted that many of the electors knew very little (as even a partisan of Bergoglio, Cormac-Murphy O'Connor, noted) of the character and history of the man they were about to elect. Such irresponsibility can only be explained by a widespread belief (and presumably not only among cardinals) that they in conclave would (and could only) do the right thing. That is, that those 'in the know' about what the Holy Spirit wants will be acting for the good of the Church, even if this involves misleading their colleagues in the conclave or encouraging them to persist in ignorance.

So can we recognize what paternalism may lead to: an assumption that all will be well and that we do not need to keep an eye on those 'fathers' who lead us – an opportunity for a pope apt to abandon tradition to presume on that respect due to his office and built up in happier days. To that we must add the age-old problem of the fear of reprisals if clergy challenge decisions made by their superiors, whether or not their motives are a concern for the well-being of the Church as a whole. We have seen plenty of that sort of behaviour in the papacy of Francis I – as might testify Cardinals Burke, Sarah, Müller, Archbishop Chaput. Some have been passed over for an expected – and deserved – cardinal's hat; others, though well informed, simply ignored: such too has been the fate of Cardinal Zen, a man with much experience of the dictatorship of the Communist Party of China. Nor has papal contempt been limited to cardinals and archbishops; it has at times been brought to bear also on rank-and-file clergy. A dictator-pope – as such no *servus servorum Dei*, but rather operating on the principle of 'let them hate so long as they fear' – can make their lives very uncomfortable, especially if their immediate religious superiors behave like the dictator's bureaucrats. After a few have been punished, *pour encourager les autres*, the rest – or most of them – will keep their heads down.

Contempt for tradition at the top, a sheepish passivity among the rank and file, whether clerical or lay, irresponsible behaviour during a conclave to elect a pope: these were probably not the consequences hoped for by Pius IX when he encouraged the promulgation of his own infallibility. But if that is so, history has proved him wrong. While no one should claim that the 'inopportune' infallibility of Vatican I is the sole cause of present discontents in the Roman Catholic Church, it has been my aim to show that it has contributed substantially to a situation where the pope *is* the tradition, and not in the sense that he knows it and tries to develop it, but in the sense that he replaces it on some Hegelian ground that old traditions have by now passed their sell-by date. To put it in other terms, I have argued that the 'culture' of the Church – and especially though far from exclusively of the clergy – has become deeply flawed.

The Catholic Church must have some significant hierarchical structure; yet the present version has failed and could fail again. There is no point in repeating, with von Balthasar,[2] that the pope is 'obligated to follow Scripture and Tradition' if he manifestly declines to do so. There is nothing in present structures to prevent a future paternalist evolving (again) into a dictator, especially if he wants to be on good terms with secularists – even with atheists or pagans – of the age. Indeed secularizing policies would not be readily acceptable in the Church if pursued paternalistically: among the rank and file there is arguably still too much respect for scripture and tradition to permit that. Only dictatorial methods will do the trick – and sorcerer's apprentices will duly appear from time to time. Yet a ray of hope in our present situation is that it is 'conservatives', not 'progressives', who are having to wonder where the structures of authority and the mentality which these structures promote within the Church need reform. Not that we should forget that over the centuries there have been conservative heresies too; that is inevitable if the *development* of Catholic doctrine is taken as a given and understood. In a 'fallen' world some, on some occasions, will be left behind.

Nor should we forget, as I have tried to show, that the infallibility of the pope speaking *ex cathedra* is not the basic problem, merely the most visible: the tip of a perilous iceberg. The concept of infallibility itself may run into difficulties when we consider changes in apparently 'infallible' teachings of the ordinary magisterium – such as presented in Conciliar documents. That will be apparent to a careful reader not

---

2. Balthasar, *Office of Peter*, p. 219.

governed by a desperate concern to deny historical fact – unless, that is, some concept of *degrees* of 'infallibility' be more openly acknowledged, more clearly developed. The sense of that requirement will demand further explication if top-down despotism and lower-rank servility is not to continue.

*   *   *

There is no doubt that the pope is needed as a symbol and source of that unity which infallibility is in the last resort intended to guarantee; the alternatives are the endless subdivisions of Protestantism or the nationalist Churches of Orthodoxy as presently constituted, and where the authority of the Orthodox patriarch is frequently and unreasonably countered, not least because of the Caesaropapist power of Moscow, the 'Third Rome'. That being so, a model must be constructed whereby the pope is clearly recognizable as the focus of doctrinal unity but which will simultaneously provide a structure for his activities such as can inhibit the kind of abuse of office which – combined with and encouraging the passivity of too many Catholics – has threatened the Church since papal infallibility was defined at Vatican I and has now seriously infected it.

The required model must therefore be robust enough to establish unambiguous limits to what a pope – under pain of being declared heterodox, hence dismissed – can proclaim and promote, whether through the ordinary or the extraordinary magisterium, let alone through arbitrary pronouncements – as also to identify the limits of his jurisdiction. Without such checks, we can be sure that the abuse of office we have seen under Francis I will be repeated, gradually moving 'tradition' further away from what has been the Catholic tradition, including on essentials: as has happened in other Christian denominations – and to illustrate the seriousness of that phenomenon I record a conversation with an Anglican bishop as we walked many years ago across the campus of the University of Toronto: a conversation to be noted by all those who want to follow a papally approved 'synodal path' which invites doctrinal variations within the Western Catholic 'patriarchate'.

For the effect (if not the aim) of such a synodal path must be to silence opposition, even from Rome itself, to groups who want less Catholic dogma, especially (in the first instance) on moral issues. Thus the Roman centre would devolve its teaching authority, while hopefully left unchallenged to perform on the international secular stage: at the United Nations, at Davos and at similar locales. Divide (the doctrine) while ruling and representing (the corporation).

Here, then, is the conversation:

> Bishop: What is all this fuss about bishop X being unorthodox?
> JMR: Well, I myself have heard him say things which are quite alien to all mainline varieties of Christianity.
> Bishop: What do you mean?
> JMR: Well, does he believe in the Resurrection of the body?
> Bishop (apparently deciding I was from another planet): Well, of course he doesn't.[3]

Even the 'ultramontane' Bellarmine, often cited by upholders of papal autocracy, was well aware that if a pope preached heresy he should be removed from his position before he could further damage the reputation of the Holy See and of the Church more widely. That said, no wedge must be driven between an abstract conception of an infallible papacy or 'Roman See' and the arguably infallible decisions of any particular pope. The Church (as Newman knew) cannot find its centre of unity in an abstraction, but only in a flesh and blood individual.

* * *

It might seem wholly improper, even cowardly, to lay down such a challenge as is summarized in this chapter to current ecclesial arrangements without offering any hint of concrete proposals for reform. I will therefore close with a few suggestions – none of them entirely novel and none of them individually adequate – in light of the past 170 years of papal and broader Catholic history. In making these suggestions I would hope to avoid any anachronistic reference to the nature of the authority of the bishop of Rome in earlier epochs.[4] For as with our understanding of

---

3. For a succinct analysis of recent theological chaos in the Anglican communion see A. Nichols, *The Panther and the Hind* (Edinburgh: T&T Clark, 1993), esp. pp. 160-72.

4. There are countless examples of papal hagiographers reading the early history of the Roman see in terms such as neither earlier Roman clergy nor their contemporaries would have recognized. A particularly misleading case is to refer to Clement, a first-century spokesman of the Roman Churches, as 'pope' (so e.g. Balthasar, *Office of Peter*, p. 244). This sort of inaccuracy, also widely apparent in the tourist shops and church buildings of Rome, has no place in a historical study. For my view of the early

doctrine itself, our understanding of the proper role of the Roman bishop has developed over the centuries.

Hence, and with due hesitancy, I would suggest that:

1. Since before the Great Schism of 1054 the Roman bishop had little say in the appointment of local bishops, the Church should revert to a modified and improved version of the centuries old (and patristic) practice of electing them locally. The modification would be that the pope should have the specifically defined power in the 'Western' Church to veto local proposals, at least in the first instance, if he judges the intended candidate out of order on the truths of Revelation itself or on substantive and well-established moral teachings, especially (in the modern world) those intended to protect marriage and humanize sexuality. He should in such cases supply reasons for his rejection. Hence to be ruled out is anything approaching the following declaration (cited by Tillard[5]): 'The right to institute bishops belongs properly and by nature to the Roman pontiff.' Historically, that claim is generally false, and where such a 'right' has prevailed it has often generated inadequate appointments, not least where a pope prefers bishops primarily loyal only to himself – forgetting that loyalties to doctrine may change while loyalty to Rome persists.

2. The election of the bishop of Rome (hence of the 'pope') should be returned in part to a revised group of 'Roman clergy'. It would seem desirable, for example, if the 'College' of electors consisted of some 60 members, one quarter of whom would be from the clergy of the diocese of Rome (to represent their new bishop's immediate role in the city itself), while another quarter should be drawn from the curial cardinals, especially heads of dicasteries, the remaining 50 per cent from cardinals or other archbishops from the 'outside' Church, all selected by lot (as in Acts where 'the lot fell on Matthias'). Such a 'College' should also be the decisive Court of Appeal if serious objection is made to the pope's own theological orthodoxy, thus acting as 'successor' to the Roman clergy who condemned Honorius.

---

development of the see of Rome see J.M. Rist, *What is Truth?* (Cambridge: Cambridge University Press, 2008), pp. 201-32.

5. Tillard, *Bishop of Rome*, p. 182.

3. The aim of these proposals would be to encourage local bishops to represent their local interests and to be aware of local concerns while ensuring that Church teaching remains identical – without risk of arbitrary change – throughout the Catholic world. For, as we noted, there is now a serious threat of the 'Anglicanization' of doctrine; it is not difficult to imagine how what is taught as Catholic in Germany might come to differ, especially in moral import, from what would be preached in Poland, let alone what would be regarded as clearly Catholic in Nigeria.

4. Since the term 'infallibility' was absent in the ancient church and rather little employed until the nineteenth century, misuse of its implications should be strictly curtailed. It should be understood primarily as indicating that the Church and the pope must always cling to basic Catholic dogma. A number of recent popes have set a good precedent by stating at the outset of their pontificates that they have no intention of pronouncing 'infallible' teaching solely on their own initiative. But that is not enough: Catholics should no longer be 'encouraged' to accept uncritically any 'creeping infallibility' applied to non-dogmatic teachings either of the pope or of the ordinary and universal magisterium. As we have noted, some of these teachings (for good reason) have turned out to be non-infallible and non-retainable.

5. In view of the manifest changes in at least some apparently authoritative teachings, it is clear that a hierarchy of non-dogmatic truths must be recognized; some decisions of the ordinary and universal magisterium (as well as of the pope) will be more 'infallible' than others. Since all such decisions are propositional (and thus existentially incomplete), they form a hierarchy of completeness. Just as many propositional truths may contain errors of detail, while remaining more or less accurate, so it is – or should be – with decrees of the papal and ordinary magisterium. We have already noticed that Vatican II moved in this direction, not only proclaiming itself a 'pastoral' Council but differentiating between the force of its own decrees. As Cardinal Brandmüller put it,[6] 'The Council documents have binding force in widely varying degrees.

---

6. W. Brandmüller, *Light and Shadows: Church History among Faith, Fact and Legend* (San Francisco: Ignatius Press, 2009), p. 224.

This was ... something quite new in conciliar history'. In other words, some of the hierarchy of propositional truths set out by the Council, as I argue is desirable, can claim to be 'more infallible' – better 'inerrant' – than others.

That admitted, the necessity of any consequent denial of historical reality in the Church can be avoided while at any particular time defined teachings can be judged, as with the best scientific hypotheses, as to be believed until an improved version of their basic truth is recognized. We may thus identify (as some have suggested) a trajectory of teaching over time where errors will eventually be spotted, the trajectory being recognized (temporarily and for however long) to have swerved – rather like an Epicurean atom – off course. That trajectory – and the hierarchy of truths it implies – needs to be more clearly identified. Vatican II's *Unitatis Redintegratio* 11 pointed in that direction.

6. The Church can no longer afford to tolerate either the pointless persistence ('Only God knows what the Augustinians are for', as you may hear in Rome) or the consistently over-weening pretensions of a number of uncontrolled religious formations, especially the Jesuits and those women's orders roughly grouped under the Leadership Conference of Women Religious (LCWR) which attempt to blend Catholicism (or post-Catholicism) with the most uncritical and man-hating versions of feminism, hence offering no sane route to success in solving the 'woman problem' as we have seen it developing for reasons both good and bad (or is it sometimes the 'man problem'?) in the Church.

The impudence of such groups must no longer remain unchecked (as Cardinal Pell noted shortly before his death of the Jesuits), nor can any renewed 'Gallicanism' (now deriving from an excessive desire to conform to the passing fashions of the secular world) be tolerated in national hierarchies: not least in Germany where the claim to pursue a local 'synodal path' is reinforced by a belief developed over the last 200 years that they and they alone are the Church's intellectual élite. To support such oversight, no significant canonical status should be granted to bishops' conferences (which are to be seen as merely pragmatic tools), lest, as I have argued, they provide individual bishops with an opportunity to avoid taking that personal responsibility in and for their own dioceses which their consecration demands of them.

* * *

I would argue that these proposals, taken together, would enable the pope – no longer the prisoner (or master) of some faction – to remain a symbol and protector of doctrinal orthodoxy while diminishing the likelihood that in the exercise of his office he become a focus of division. They would also encourage a more honest appraisal of Church history and a greater readiness to admit errors in theory or practice rather than attempt to cover them up: an attitude which, as in recent matters of clerical child-abuse, is bound eventually to come to public notice, hence a source of even greater damage to Catholicism. Not only is honesty morally desirable but it will be practically more helpful in preserving the reputation of the Church and its 'officials'.

We should also, from the ecumenical point of view, recall that before the Great Schism popes were prepared to tolerate from the Eastern Churches variations not only in matters of jurisdiction, but also in matters not of actual doctrine but of doctrinal *development*. Thus, in 808, in the dispute between Greeks and Latins over the *filioque* clause in the Nicene Creed, Pope Leo III was himself convinced of the correctitude of the addition but did not want to impose it outside his own patriarchate; perhaps it has to be recognized (with Benedict XVI) that the Western and Eastern Churches – while both in some sense acknowledge papal 'primacy' – will develop doctrines at different speeds.[7] To encourage this, the pope's title of 'Patriarch of the West' should be restored. It would be helpful too, if on taking office, he took an oath to act in accordance with scripture and tradition; something like this existed before the 'Conciliar period' of ecclesiastical history and should be revived.

A final beneficial effect of my proposed changes would be to promote that 'freedom of the Christian man' (in patristic Greek *parrhesia*) emphasized by the Desert Fathers and rightly preached by at least some sixteenth-century reformers: an attitude opposite to the servility and bad faith frequently to be found among contemporary clergy and (as by osmosis) among the laity. At Luke 10:16, Christ told Peter that he who hears you hears me. In saying that, He was surely well aware that whatever Peter said (and did) would not necessarily be what He would wish, evidence to the contrary being readily available to Him. Luke's text

---

7. For further discussion of this example see Tillard, *Roman Bishop*, p. 163.

should be read as implying that Peter (and presumably his legitimate successors) would never fail in their deepest conviction about his Messiahship, divinity and Resurrection, on which, as St Paul preached, our whole faith depends.

*   *   *

Infallibility, I would therefore argue, should be understood to mean that the Church, through its official magisterium – its bishops, popes and councils – will be infallibly led to all truth – eventually. The magisterium will make mistakes, as did Peter himself, but it will be subject to correction, as Augustine noted in the text I cited at the beginning of the present study. That said, at any particular time present teachings should be accepted as truth as far as we know it, but subject to correction if shown to be based on unavoidable ignorance or theological contradiction.

To engage in the search for such correction is part of the task of the theologian, the other part being to teach accurately what has come to be known over time and until the present, without intruding as certain truths possible corrections which every theologian has a duty to discuss with his colleagues, indeed with any member of the Church who shows himself or herself equipped to engage in theological debate, it being understood that such people do not constitute a rival 'magisterium'. Indeed, the term 'magisterium' itself, as we have implied, has been a source of unnecessary confusion and excessive clericalism.[8] It needs to be viewed in line with our revised account of an *eventually* complete inerrancy guaranteed by the Holy Spirit. We should recall that among the Orthodox the infallibility even of councils, let alone of individuals, has never been insisted on – a view again endorsed by Augustine as cited in my preface to the present work; hence any restriction of infallibility-talk in the West would be ecumenically helpful, although by itself not leading to inter-communion.

Ecumenism apart, what is certain is that the Church can do without further double-think about infallibility and inerrancy. God, we are taught, will lead us to all truth, yet – and leaving aside the *depositum fidei* – we do not know what degree of truth we have thus far obtained. Our best approach would therefore be to give up debating whether even papal or conciliar utterances are necessarily perfectly formed; rather to try to understand how some 'infallible' teachings of the ordinary

---

8. For something of the history of the term see Congar, *Eglise et papauté*, pp. 283-315.

magisterium have been abandoned: as the denial of religious freedom taught by Lateran IV and the faultily corrected attitude to Judaism developed in the mid-thirteenth century – not to speak of the absolute ban on usury still insisted upon as late as 1745 in Benedict XIV's encyclical *Vix Pervenit*: a document published in blatant denial of long practice, not least that of popes. For all such past errors and confusions, albeit still too often denied to be such, can be shown to depend on ignorance of fact or incomplete theology.

As I already noted, the term 'magisterium' is of comparatively recent provenance, becoming central only in the nineteenth century. It implies a distinction not only between the officially licensed teachers (i.e. an identifiable group of clergy) and the officially passive learners, but more specifically between a group of often ill-informed office-holders and that subset of the 'passives' who for centuries have studied truth in the hope of finding and teaching it, however provisionally, in the Church. That these have not been restricted to clergy has enabled this married layman here to conclude an essay which otherwise he could not even have embarked on. Yet that same layman regrets that he felt the necessity of writing it, not only because he expects it to be ignored (if not, more hopefully, blackguarded), but because no obligation to construct it should have arisen.

Very Select Bibliography

Alberigo, G., 'Transition to a New Age', in G Alberigo and J.A. Komonchak, *History of Vatican II*, vol. 5 (Maryknoll, NY: Orbis; Leuven; Peeters, 1996-2006)

Allen, J.L. Jr, *Pope Benedict XVI* (London: Continuum, 2005)

Aubert, R., *Le Pontificat de Pie IX (1846-1878)* (Paris: Bloud & Gay, 1952)

Aubert, R., 'Aspects divers du néo-thomisme sous le pontificat de Léon XIII' in G. Rossini (ed.), *Aspetti della cultura cattolica nell'età di Leone XIII* (Rome: Gregorianum, 1961), pp. 133-227

Balthasar, H. von, *The Office of Peter and the Structure of the Church* (San Francisco: Ignatius Press, 1986)

Balthasar, H. von., 'The Fathers, the Scholastics and Ourselves', *Communio* 24 (1997), pp. 347-96

Boersma, H., *Nouvelle Théologie and Sacred Ontology* (Oxford: Oxford University Press, 2009)

Bonino, S.-T., *Saint Thomas au XXe siècle, Actes du colloque du Centenaire de la Revue Thomiste* (Paris: Centre National de Livre-Saint Paul, 1994)

Bouillard, H., *Conversion et grace chez S. Thomas d'Aquin* (Paris: Aubier, 1947)

Brandmüller, W., *Light and Shadows, Church History among Faith, Fact and Legend* (San Francisco: Ignatius Press, 2009)

Brezik, V.B. (ed.), *One Hundred Years of Thomism: Aeterni Patris and Afterwards* (Houston, TX: Center for Thomistic Studies 1981).

Butler, C., *The Vatican Council 1869-1870* (London: Longmans, Green & Co, 1930)

Carlen, C., *Papal Pronouncements: A Guide, 1740-1978* (Ann Arbor: Pierian Press, 1990)

Carlen, C. (ed.), *The Papal Encyclicals*, 5 vols (Wilmington, DE: McGrath, 1981)

Chadwick, O., *A History of the Popes, 1830-1914* (Oxford: Oxford University Press, 1998)

Chantraine, G., *Le cardinal Henri de Lubac: l'homme et l'oeuvre* (Paris: Lethielleux 1983)

Chenu, M.-D., *Une école de théologie: Le Saulchoir* (Paris: Etiolles, 1937)

Chenu, M.-D., *Un concile pour notre temps* (Paris: Cerf, 1961)

Congar, Y., 'The Historical Development of Authority in the Church: Points for christian Reflection', in J.M. Todd (ed.), *Problems of Authority* (London: Darton, Longman & Todd, 1962), pp. 119-55

Congar, Y., *Eglise et papauté* (Paris: Cerf, 1994)

Congar, Y., *The Meaning of Tradition* (San Francisco: Ignatius, 2004)

Congar, Y., *My Journal of the Council* (Collegeville, MN, Liturgical Press, 2012)

Conzemius, V., 'Der Verfasser der "Römischen Brief vom Konzil" des "Quirinus"', *FS Hans Forster: Freiburger Geschichtsblatter* 52 (1963-64) pp. 229-56

Conzemius, V., 'Lord Acton at the First Vatican Council', *Journal of Ecclesiastical History* 20 (1969), pp. 267-94

Coppa, F.J., *The Life and Pontificate of Pope Pius XII: Between History and Controversy* (Washington, DC: CUA Press, 2013)

Costigan, R.F., *The Consensus of the Church and Papal Infallibility: A Study in the Background of Vatican I* (Washington, DC: CUA Press, 2005)

Coulson, J., *Newman and the Common Tradition* (Oxford: Oxford University Press, 1970)

Cubitt, G., *The Jesuit Myth: Conspiracy and Politics in Nineteenth Century France* (Oxford: Oxford University Press, 1993)

Daniélou, J., 'Les orientations présentes de la pensée religieuse', *Etudes* 249 (1946), pp. 5-21

De Lubac, H., *Entretiens autour de Vatican II* (Paris: Aubier Mantaigne 1985)

De Lubac, H., 'A Theologian Speaks', in *30 Giorni*, July 1985

De Lubac, H., *The Drama of Atheist Humanism* (San Francisco: Ignatius Press 1995)

De' Mattei, R., *The Second Vatican Council* (Fitzwilliam, NH: Loreto Publications, 2012)

Dipippo, G., 'Paul VI did Not Exist: A "Nostalgic" Response to George Weigel', in P.A .Kwasniewski (ed.), *Sixty Years After* (New York: Angelico Press, 2022), pp. 47-58

Dodaro, R. (ed.), *Remaining in the Truth of Christ* (San Francisco: Ignatius, 2014)

Duffy, E., *The Papacy: Myth and Reality*, Michael Richards Memorial Lecture (London: Catholics for a Changing Church, 1997), pp. 1-16

Duffy, E., 'Luther through Catholic Eyes', in *A People's Tragedy* (London: Bloomsbury, 2020), pp. 125-42

Dulles, A., 'Newman on Infallibility', *Theological Studies* 51 (1990), pp. 434-49

Dupré, L., *The Enlightenment and the Intellectual Foundations of Modern Culture* (New Haven: Yale University Press, 2004)

Feingold, F., *The Natural Desire to See God According to St. Thomas Aquinas and his Interpreters* (Notre Dame, IN: Ave Maria, Sapientia Press, 2010)

Fields, S.M., 'Ressourcement and the Retrieval of Thomism for the Contemporary World', in G. Flynn and P.D. Murray (eds), *Ressourcement: A Movement for Renewal in Twentieth-Century Catholic Theology* (New York: Oxford University Press, 2012), pp. 355-71

Fields, S.M., 'The Reception of Aquinas in Twentieth-Century Transcendental Thomism', in M. Levering and M. Plested (eds), *The Oxford Handbook of the Reception of Aquinas* (Oxford: Oxford University Press, 2021), pp. 408-22

Flynn, G. and Murray P.D. (ed.), *Ressourcement: A Movement for Renewal in Twentieth-Century Catholic Theology* (New York: Oxford University Press, 2012)

Fouilloux, E., 'Une "école de Fourvière"?', *Gregorianum* 83 (2002), pp. 451–59

Fouilloux, E. and B. Hours, *Les Jesuites à Lyon, XVIème-XXème siècle* (Lyons; ENS, 2005)

Gallagher, C.R., 'The Perils of Perception: British Catholics and Papal Neutrality, 1914-1923', in J. Corkery and T. Worcester (eds), *The Papacy since 1850* (Cambridge: Cambridge University Press, 2010), pp. 162-81

Garrigou-Lagrange, R., 'La nouvelle théologie, où va-t-elle', *Angelicum* 23 (1946), pp. 126-45

Grave, S.A., *Conscience in Newman's Thought* (Oxford: Oxford University Press, 1989)

Gray, Janette, *M.-D. Chenu and Le Saulchoir* (Oxford: Oxford University Press, 2011)

Gross, M., '*Kulturkampf* and Unification: German Liberalism and the War Against the Jesuits', *Central European History* 30 (1997), pp. 545-66

Grumett, D., *De Lubac: A Guide for the Perplexed* (London: T&T Clark, 2007)

Grumett, D., *Henri de Lubac and the Shaping of Modern Theology* (San Francisco: Ignatius Press, 2020)

Hacker, P., *The Ego in Faith: Martin Luther and the Origins of Anthropocentric Religion*, (Chicago: University of Chicago Press, 1970)

Hamer, J, 'Histoire du texte de la declaration', in J. Hamer and Y. Congar (eds), *La liberté religieuse* (Paris: Cerf, 1967)

Harrison, B., 'Reading *Dignitatis Humanae* within a Hermeneutic of Continuity', in T. Crean (ed.), *Dignitatis Humanae Colloquium* (Norcia: Dialogos Institute, 2017), pp. 45-55

Hillebert, J., *T&T Companion to Henri de Lubac* (London: T&T Clark, 2011)

Himes, M.J., *Ongoing Incarnation: Johann Adam Möhler and the Beginning of Modern Ecclesiology* (New York: Crossroad, 1997)

Horst, H.U., 'Kardinalerzbischof Filippo Maria Guidi OP und das 1 Vatikanischen Konzil', *Archivum Fratrum Praedicatorum* 49 (1979), pp. 429-511.

Howard, T. A., *The Pope and the Professor: Pius IX, Ignaz von Döllinger, and the Quandary of the Modern Age* (Oxford: Oxford University Press, 2017)

Hünermann, P., 'The Final Weeks of the Council', in G Alberigo and J.A. Komonchak, *History of Vatican II* (Maryknoll, NY: Orbis; Leuven; Peeters, 1996-2006), vol. 5, pp. 408-19.

Joannes, V., *The Bitter Pill: Worldwide Reaction to the Encyclical Humanae Vitae* (Philadelphia: Pilgrim Press, 1970)

Joy, J.P., *Disputed Questions on Papal Infallibility* (Lincoln, NE: Os Justi Press, 2022)

Kaplan, G., *The Catholic Recovery of Historical Revelation* (New York:, Crossroad, 2006)

Kasper, W., *Die Lehre von der Tradition in der Römischen Schule* (Cologne: Habilitationsschrift, 1962)

Kasper, W., *Faith and the Future* (London: Burns & Oates, 1985)

Keely, C.B., 'Limits to Papal Power: Vatican Inaction After Humanae Vitae', *Population and Development Review* 20 (1994), supplement: *The New Politics of Population: Conflict and Consensus in Family Planning.*

Kerr, F., *After Aquinas: Versions of Thomism* (Oxford: Blackwell, 2002)

Kerr, F., 'Yves Congar: From Suspicion to Acclamation', *Louvain Studies* 229 (2004), pp. 273-87

Kerr, F., *Twentieth Century Catholic Theology* (Malden, MA: Blackwell, 2007)

Ker, I., *John Henry Newman: A Biography* (Oxford: Oxford University Press, 1988)

King, P., *The International Impact of the Lateran Agreements* (New York: St Martin's Press, 1981)

Komonchak, J.A., 'The Struggle for the Council during the Preparation of Vatican II (1960-1962)', in G. Alberigo and J.A. Komonchak, *History of Vatican II* (Maryknoll, NY: Orbis; Leuven: Peeters, 1995), vol. 1, pp. 350-56

Kwasniewski, P., *The Road from Hyperpapalism to Catholicism: Rethinking the Papacy in a Time of Ecclesial Disintegration* (Waterloo, ON: Arouca Press, 2022)

Kwasniewski, P. (ed.), *Sixty Years on: Catholic Writers Assess the Legacy of Vatican II* (New York: Angelico Press, 2022)

Lamont, J.R.T., 'Conscience, Freedom, Rights: Idols of the Enlightenment Religion', *The Thomist* 73 (2009), pp. 169-239

Lamont, J.R.T. and C. Pierantoni (eds), *Defending the Faith Against Pope Francis* (Ottawa: Acoura Press, 2021)

Lehner, U.L., 'Johann Nikolaus von Hontheim's *Febronius*: A Censored Bishop and his Ecclesiology', *Church History and Religious Culture* 82 (2008), pp. 205-33

Levering, M., *The Abuse of Conscience: A Century of Catholic Moral Theology* (Grand Rapids, MI: Eerdmans, 2021)

Loisy, A., *My Duel with the Vatican,* tr. Richard Boynton (New York: E.P. Dutton, 1924)

MacIntyre, A., *Three Rival Versions of Moral Enquiry* (London: Duckworth, 1980)

Martina, G., *Pio IX,* 3 vols (Rome: Gregoriana, 1970-90)

McClory, R., *Power and the Papacy: The People and Politics behind the Doctrine of Papal Infallibility* (Liguori, MO: Triumph Press, 1997)

McElrath, D., J.C. Holland, Sue Katzman and W. White (ed.), *Lord Acton: The Decisive Decade 1864-1874* (Louvain: University Press, 1970)

McGovern, J.J., *The Life and Work of Pope Leo XIII* (Chicago: Allied Printing, 1903)

McPartlan, P., '*Ressourcement,* Vatican II, and Eucharistic Ecclesiology', in G. Flynn and P.D. Murray, *Ressourcement: A Movement for Renewal in*

Twentieth-Century Catholic Theology (New York: Oxford University Press, 2012), pp. 392-404

McPartlan, P., 'The eucharist, the church and evangelization: the influence of Henri de Lubac', *Communio* 23 (1996), pp. 776-85

McPartlan, P., *The Eucharist Makes the Church: Henri de Lubac and John Zizioulas* (Fairfax, VA: Eastern Christian Publications, 2005)

Mettepenningen, J., *Nouvelle Théologie – New Theology: Inheritor of Modernism, Precursor of Vatican II* (London: T&T Clark, 2010)

Müller, G., 'Die Immaculata Conceptio im Urteil der mitteleuropäischen Bischöfe', *Katholische Dogmatik* 14 (1968), pp. 46-70

Müller, G., *The Pope: His Mission and Task* (Washington, DC: CUA Press, 2017)

Newman, J.H., *Letters and Diaries* (Oxford: Oxford University Press, 1961-1977)

Nichols, A., *Yves Congar* (Wilton, CT: Morehouse-Barlow, 1989)

Nichols, A., *The Panther and the Hind* (Edinburgh: T&T Clark, 1993)

Nichols, A., 'Thomism and the Nouvelle Théologie', *The Thomist* 64 (2000), pp. 1-19

Nichols, A., *The Thought of Benedict XVI: An Introduction to the Theology of Joseph Ratzinger* (London: Burns & Oates, 2007)

Nichols, A., *Conciliar Octet* (San Francisco: Ignatius, 2019)

Noonan, J.A., *Contraception* (Cambridge, MA: Harvard University Press. 1965)

O'Gara, M., *Triumph in Defeat: Infallibility, Vatican I and the French Minority Bishops* (Washington, DC: CUA Press, 1988)

O'Malley, J.W., *Vatican I: The Council and the Making of the Ultramontane Church* (Cambridge, MA: Belknap Press of Harvard University, 2019)

Pentin, E., *The Rigging of a Vatican Synod* (San Francisco: Ignatius, 2015)

Philips, G. (ed.), *Le service théologique dans l'Eglise: Mélanges offerts au Père Congar* (Paris: Cerf, 1974)

Pink, T., 'Dignitatis Humanae: Continuity after Leo XIII', in T. Crean (ed.), *Dignjtatis Humanae Colloquium* (Norcia: Dialogos Institute, 2017), pp. 105-145.

Potworowski, C., *Contemplation and Incarnation: The Theology of Marie-Dominique Chenu* (Montréal and Kingston: McGill-Queen's University Press, 2001)

Printy, M., *Enlightenment and the Creation of German Catholicism* (Cambridge: Cambridge University Press, 2009)

Prudlo, D.S., *Certain Sainthood: Canonization and the Origins of Papal Infallibility in the Medieval Church* (Ithaca, NY: Cornell University Press, 2015)

Ratzinger J., *Theological Highlights of Vatican II* (New York: Paulist Press, 1966)

Ratzinger, J., *Die letzte Sitzungsperiode des Konzils* (Cologne: Bachem, 1966)

Ratzinger, J., 'The Dignity of the Human Person', in H. Vorgrimler (ed.), *Commentary on the Documents of Vatican II*, vol. 5 (New York: Herder & Herder, 1966), pp. 115-63

Ratzinger, J., 'Luther and the Unity of the Churches', *Communio* 11 (1984), pp. 210-26

Ratzinger, J., *The Ratzinger Report* (San Francisco: Ignatius, 1985)

Ratzinger, J., *Values in a Time of Upheaval* (San Francisco: Ignatius, 2006)

Reid, A., *The Organic Liturgy of the Litany,* 2nd edition (San Francisco: Ignatius, 2005)

Rist, J.M., *Augustine: Ancient Thought Baptized* (Cambridge: Cambridge University Press, 1994)

Rist, J.M., *What is Truth? From the Academy to the Vatican* (Cambridge: Cambridge University Press, 2008)

Rocca, G., 'Thomas Aquinas on Papal Authority', *Angelicum* 62 (1986), pp. 472-84

Rogers, B., 'Soiled Hearts and Bloodied Fingers', *Catholic Herald* 6631 (December 2022), pp. 32-33

Rotondo, T., *Tradimento della sana dottrina attraverso 'Amoris Laetitia'*, http://www.tradimentodellasanadottrina.it

Rowland, T., *Culture and the Thomist Tradition: After Vatican II* (London/New York: Routledge, 2003)

Rowland, T., *Ratzinger's Faith: The Theology of Pope Benedict XVI* (Oxford: Oxford University Press, 2008).

Schatz, K., *Papal Primacy from its Origins to the Present,* tr. J.A. Otto and L.M. Maloney (Collegeville, MN: Liturgical Press, 1996)

Schatz, K., *Vaticanum I,* 3 vols (Paderborn: Ferdinand Schöningh, 1982-94)

Schmitz, K.L., 'Postmodernism and the Catholic Tradition', *American Catholic Philosophical Quarterly* 73 (1969), pp. 223-53

Simmonds, G., 'Jansenism versus Papal Absolutism', in J. Corkery and T. Worcester (eds), *The Papacy since 1500: From Italian Prince to Universal Pastor* (Cambridge: Cambridge University Press, 2010), pp. 90-106

Sweeney, G., 'The Forgotten Council', in A. Hastings (ed.), *Bishops and Writers* (Wheathampstead: Anthony Clarke, 1977)

Tagle, L.A.G., 'The "Black Week" of Vatican II', in G. Alberigo and J.A. Komonchak, *History of Vatican II* (Maryknoll, NY: Orbis; Leuven; Peeters, 1996-2006), vol. 4, pp. 388-452

Talmon, J.A., *The Rise of Totalitarian Democracy* (Boston: Beacon Press, 1952)

Thils, G., *L'infaillibilité pontificale: Sources, conditions, limites* (Gembloux: Duculot, 1969)

Tierney, B., *The Origins of Papal Infallibility 1150-1350* (Leiden: Brill, 1972)

Tillard, J.M.R., *The Bishop of Rome* (London: SPCK, 1983)

Valuet, B., '*Dignitatis humanae:* – Contrary to Tradition?', in T. Crean, (ed.), *Dignitatis Humanae Colloquium* (Norcia: Dialogos Institute, 2017), pp. 147-69

Viaene, V. (ed.), *The Papacy and the New World Order; Vatican Diplomacy, Catholic Opinion and International Politics at the Time of Leo XIII* (Leuven: Leuven University Press, 2005)

Voderholzer, R., *Meet Henri de Lubac: His Life and Work,* tr. M.J. Miller (San Francisco: Ignatius Press, 2008)

Weigel, G., *Witness to Hope: The Biography of Pope John Paul II* (New York: Harper Collins, 1999)

Weigel, G., *The End and the Beginning* (New York: Doubleday, 2010)

Weigel, G., *To Sanctify the World: The Vital Legacy of Vatican II* (New York: Basic Books, 2022)

Wilde, M., *Vatican II: A Sociological Analysis of Religious Change* (Princeton: Princeton University Press, 2007)

Wolf, H., *The Nuns of Sant'Ambrogio. The True Story of a Convent in Scandal* (New York: Alfred A. Knopf, 2015).

Worcester, T., 'Jesuits Today', in T. Worcester (ed.) *The Cambridge Companion to the Jesuits* (Cambridge: Cambridge University Press, 2008), pp. 319-27

Index

abortion vii, 125, 143, 147, 187
absolute impartiality 62, 64, 65, 76
Abu Dhabi declaration 187
Abuse, *see* clerical abusers
academic freedom 15-16
Academy for Life 146, 183
Acton, Lord 15, 27, 32
aggiornamento 88, 162
Alfrink, Cardinal B.J. 95
ambiguity 185-187
Anglican orders 46, 167
Anglicanism 46, 51, 75, 152, 173, 213
anti-modernist oath, 60
Aquinas, T. 33, 36, 48, 49, 52, 59, 67, 69,
   72,74, 93, 109, 168, 170
Arbués, P. de 21-22
Arnauld, A. 6
Arrupe, P. 7n9, 74, 111, 156-157
Assumption of Mary 3, 23, 77-78
Augustine, Augustinianism vii, 49, 52,
   53, 58, 68, 73, 75, 122-123, 145

bad faith ix, 63
Balthasar, H.U. von 68, 134-135, 161, 209
Bea, Cardinal A. 84, 111, 113, 195
Bellarmine, Cardinal R. 5, 18, 36, 212
Benedict XVI, Pope 129, 160-176, *see also*
   Ratzinger, J.
Bergoglio, J *see* Francis, Pope
Bertone, Cardinal T. 167
biblical criticism 8, 52-54, 57, 83-84,
   110, 175
'Black Week' 103
Blondel, M. 57, 72, 77
Boncompagni, U. 44

Bonino, E. 183
Bossuet, Bishop J.-B. 7
Bouillard, H. 82
Bouyer, L. 69
Brandmüller, Cardinal W. 189
Bugnini, Archbishop A. 109
Buonaiuti, E. 57, 59, 66
Burke, Cardinal L. 184, 189, 20

Caffarra, Cardinal C. 189
Cajetan, Cardinal T. 67, 91
canon law 57, 62, 167
Cappellani, B. 8, *see also* Gregory XVI,
   Pope
Casaroli, Cardinal A. 133, 186
Catechism of the Catholic Church 142
Catherine of Siena 2
Catholic Universities 1, 141-142
Chalcedon, Council of 2, 24, 31, 47
Chaput, Archbishop C. 189, 208
Charlier, L. 81
Chenu, M.D. 69, 70, 72, 73, 81, 94, 95
Christocentric theology 79, 85, 194
Civiltà Cattolica 15, 23, 25, 28, 29, 35, 88,
   157, 192, 197
Clement of Rome 7
clerical abusers 168
Clifford, Bishop W. 32, 36
Communio 134, 137
communism 63, 64, 66, 68, 135-136, 144
Communist Party of China 185, 208
Compendium of Social Teaching of the
   Church 12
Concilium 134
Concordats 68

You may also be interested in:

Gift to the Church and World

Fifty Years of Joseph Ratzinger's
Introduction to Christianity

Edited by John C. Cavadini and Donald Wallenfang

Few books in theology have faced the twentieth century with all its horrors and yet revoiced the redemptive Christian antidote as convincingly as Joseph Ratzinger's 1968 masterpiece, *Introduction to Christianity*. In *Gift to the Church and World*, John Cavadini and Donald Wallenfang present papers from the conference held at the University of Notre Dame to celebrate the fiftieth anniversary of this classic book's publication and, through it, Ratzinger's lasting influence on the world of Christian theology. Bishops, priests, and lay men and women set their hands to 'the trowel of tribute,' honoring the legacy of Joseph Ratzinger and the pivotal role he has played in the recent history of the Catholic Church.

Covering Ratzinger's work on fundamental theology, philosophical theology, dogmatic theology, spiritual theology, and pedagogy, the essays gathered here shed new light on Ratzinger's theological genius. Throughout, the authors return to his compelling expression of the divine call to reawaken to our true identity as beloved children of God. Altogether, readers will deepen their appreciation and understanding of the theological contributions of Joseph Ratzinger, and his continued relevance to mission and evangelisation today.

> *'This book identifies a classic that has never received the notice it's due. '* – **Scott Hahn,** St Paul Center of Biblical Theology

John C. Cavadini is the McGrath-Cavadini Director of the Institute for Church Life and Professor of Theology at the University of Notre Dame. **Donald Wallenfang**, OCDS, Emmanuel Mary of the Cross, is Professor of Theology and Philosophy at Sacred Heart Major Seminary in Detroit.

Published 2023

Paperback ISBN: 978 0 227 17882 9
PDF ISBN: 978 0 227 17883 6

You may also be interested in:

Sino-Vatican Relations

From Denunciation to Dialogue

by Ambrose Mong

For those interested in Christianity in China, the state-church relationship, and the present Communist regime and its attitude towards religion, *Sino-Vatican Relations* offers a wealth of information and insights. This work traces the tortuous history of the relationship between the Chinese government and the Roman Catholic Church, from denunciation of Communism by the Church, to seeking dialogue by recent pontiffs such as John Paul II, Benedict XVI and Francis.

Besides examining the religious policy of China since 1949 and how the Chinese government deals with religious revivals, this work also traces the history of the church regarding the appointment of bishops in Europe from its early days to modern times. Monarchies in Europe have always been involved in the appointment of bishops. Thus, the recent agreement between Pope Francis and the Chinese authorities regarding the appointment of bishops has historical precedents. The overall aim of this work is to help readers to get the right information needed to have a well-informed opinion on the complex matter of the Sino-Vatican Relations, particularly on the agreement signed by Pope Francis with Beijing in 2018.

'Well informed and well documented, Ambrose Mong's book offers a critical but objective evaluation of the Communist and Catholic positions.' – **Jeroom Heyndricks,** Catholic University, Leuven

Ambrose Mong, PhD, is assistant parish priest at St Andrew's Church, Hong Kong, part-time lecturer and research associate at The Chinese University of Hong Kong. His publications with James Clarke and Co Ltd include *A Tale of Two Theologians: Treatment of Third World Theologies* (2017) and *A Better World is Possible: An Exploration of Eastern and Western Utopian Visions (2018).*

Published 2019

Hardback ISBN: 978 0 227 17702 0
Paperback ISBN: 978 0 227 17701 3
PDF ISBN: 978 0 227 90700 9
ePub ISBN: 978 0 227 90701 6